Breakthroughs in College Reading

Breakthroughs in College Reading

The Promises and Tensions of Disciplinary Reading Apprenticeships

Edited by

Nelson Graff, Nika Hogan, and Rebecca Kersnar

ROWMAN & LITTLEFIELD
Lanham • Boulder • New York • London

Published by Rowman & Littlefield
An imprint of The Rowman & Littlefield Publishing Group, Inc.
4501 Forbes Boulevard, Suite 200, Lanham, Maryland 20706
www.rowman.com

86-90 Paul Street, London EC2A 4NE

Copyright © 2024 by Nelson Graff, Nika Hogan, and Rebecca Kersnar

All rights reserved. No part of this book may be reproduced in any form or by any electronic or mechanical means, including information storage and retrieval systems, without written permission from the publisher, except by a reviewer who may quote passages in a review.

British Library Cataloguing in Publication Information available

Library of Congress Cataloging-in-Publication Data

Names: Graff, Nelson, editor. | Hogan, Nika, editor. | Kersnar, Rebecca, editor.
Title: Breakthroughs in college reading : the promises and tensions of disciplinary reading apprenticeships / edited by Nelson Graff, Nika Hogan, and Rebecca Kersnar.
Description: Lanham, Maryland : Rowman & Littlefield, 2024. | Includes bibliographical references and index.
Identifiers: LCCN 2024014747 (print) | LCCN 2024014748 (ebook) | ISBN 9781538198162 (cloth) | ISBN 9781538198179 (paperback) | ISBN 9781538198186 (epub)
Subjects: LCSH: College reading improvement programs. | Reading (Higher education) | Language arts (Higher)—Correlation with content subjects
Classification: LCC LB2395.3 .B74 2024 (print) | LCC LB2395.3 (ebook) | DDC 418/.4—dc23/eng/20240516
LC record available at https://lccn.loc.gov/2024014747
LC ebook record available at https://lccn.loc.gov/2024014748

This book is dedicated to the many courageous educators and students who surface their thinking in metacognitive conversation, sharing their histories, uncertainties, and discoveries as they negotiate disciplinary understanding and identity. We admire you all for taking this brave, empowering journey together.

Contents

Preface — xv

Acknowledgments — xvii

Introduction: Making Visible Disciplinary Learning: Faculty Crossing Thresholds to Support College Reading — 1
Nelson Graff, Nika Hogan, and Rebecca Kersnar

In this introduction, we review the scholarship on threshold concepts and college reading, introduce readers to the Reading Apprenticeship (RA) framework, and describe the threshold concepts we found in a survey of RA practitioners' breakthroughs in teaching reading. We found three candidate threshold concepts: reading is a problem-solving process; students must be entrusted with the work of making sense of text; and reading is social and personal. We also discuss a tension underlying all of these thresholds between apprenticing students to become like us and welcoming their differences to change the academy.

PART I: WHAT IS READING APPRENTICESHIP? — 15

Chapter 1: Making It Real: Reading Apprenticeship in College — 16
Nika Hogan

Nika Hogan, professor of English at Pasadena City College and the Reading Apprenticeship college coordinator for WestEd, provides an overview of how the Reading Apprenticeship framework has been utilized in higher education settings. Beginning with an explanation of the framework and a brief history of the college level work, Hogan also describes how the Reading Apprenticeship framework works in classroom and professional learning settings and begins to establish why the approach supports instructors to persist with the risky and difficult project of changing their teaching practices.

Chapter 2: The College STEM Reading Apprenticeship Classroom — 27
Theresa Martin

Theresa Martin, professor of biology at College of San Mateo, shares insights gleaned from her observation of seven community college and university STEM instructors who had participated in a California statewide community of practice focused on incorporating the tenets of the Reading Apprenticeship framework into their teaching practices. She investigates how practitioners use scaffolded work around texts to create active, student-centered construction of understanding in unique STEM disciplines and describes what a "college STEM Reading Apprenticeship classroom" looks like in practice.

Chapter 3: Exponential, Not Linear: Designing for the Four Dimensions in Noncredit ESL   36
Tiffany Ingle

Tiffany Ingle, professor of noncredit English as a second language (ESL) at Glendale Community College, elaborates on the way she designs the first five weeks of instruction to build the personal, social, cognitive, and knowledge building dimensions of the course, and at the same time build students' capacity to take a deep dive into language learning.

Chapter 4: Peer Educators as Reading Apprenticeship Practitioners   42
Crystal Kiekel

Crystal Kiekel directs the Center for Academic Success at Pierce College. Describing peer education in its most common forms, Kiekel connects the practice of peer education with the Reading Apprenticeship framework. For each of the four dimensions of the RA framework, Kiekel describes its application in the learning center context and provides activities that can be used by peer educators to engage that dimension of learning.

PART II: EQUITY MATTERS: TENSIONS OF ACADEMIC APPRENTICESHIP   49

Chapter 5: Consciously Apprenticing Students   51
Lauren Servais

Lauren Servais, now dean of Humanities at College of Marin following a long career of teaching English at Santa Rosa Junior College, reflects in this chapter on the nature of "apprenticeship" in learning and formal schooling. Considering her own varied experiences as a multilingual woman of color coming to hold the "standard bearer" position of first year composition teacher, Servais develops an idea of "conscious apprenticeship" as a way to provide access to higher education but reinforce students' agency.

Chapter 6: Culturally Responsive Teaching and Reading Apprenticeship: A Conversation   58
Yhashika Lee, Salina Lopez, and Ibrahim Shelton

These three part-time faculty at California State University, Monterey Bay (CSUMB) in a variety of departments lead professional learning on the campus related to culturally responsive teaching. In this conversation, they discuss how their work with the two frameworks (CRT and RA) intersect and the tensions they navigate while using both frameworks in their teaching and professional development.

PART III: READING IS A PROBLEM-SOLVING PROCESS   67

Chapter 7: Reading Historically through Metacognitive Logs   71
Christopher Padgett

Padgett, professor of history at American River College in Sacramento, CA, argues that the critical skill of historical thinking, so crucial and yet so unfamiliar to many students, is scaffolded and supported by metacognitive conversation. This chapter details how he helps students develop as historical thinkers, chiefly through the use of double and triple column notetakers and careful assessment/self-assessment of that work.

Chapter 8: Not a White Rabbit—Reflection on Metacognitive Conversations and TAPPS — 83
Corin Slown

Slown, professor of biology and chemistry at CSUMB, considers the affordances of metacognition with disciplinary reading and the student and teacher moves that amplify metacognition in this reflection on student problem solving with biology and chemistry texts. She argues that metacognition is key to students' taking control of their learning and describes assignments that she uses to foster both individual metacognition and conversations about strategies.

Chapter 9: Reading into Information Literacy — 87
Ryne Leuzinger

In this chapter, Leuzinger, a research and instructional librarian at CSUMB, reflects on his journey to seeing instruction in reading as an essential part of his practice as a librarian and information literacy instructor at CSUMB. He describes his initial exposure to Reading Apprenticeship, discussions with other librarians about teaching reading, and the value he's found in the practice of metacognition with students.

Chapter 10: Equitable and Metacognitive Approaches to Library Sessions — 90
Anamika Megwalu

Megwalu, interim associate dean of student & faculty engagement and a research librarian at San José State University, provides a broad framing of the nature of information literacy sessions provided by librarians, describing the challenge of such sessions and explaining how the metacognitive approaches of Reading Apprenticeship can support making such sessions both more effective and more equitable. After contextualizing her sessions with the Association of College Research Libraries (ACRL) framework, she provides two lesson plans that illustrate the role that metacognition can play in sessions that address particular needs for information literacy instruction faculty may identify.

PART IV: STUDENTS MUST BE ENTRUSTED WITH THE WORK OF MAKING SENSE OF TEXTS — 97

Chapter 11: Permission to Take Risk — 102
Shelagh Rose

Shelagh Rose, professor of English and ESL at Pasadena City College, describes the way she leverages Reading Apprenticeship routines to support the students in her high-intermediate transfer-level ESL Reading and Writing classes to engage in the "risky business" of reading in English.

Chapter 12: Reading in Calculus: Why, What, and How 106
Alison Lynch

Lynch, a tenure-track professor of Mathematics at CSUMB, argues in this chapter for the importance of reading in calculus, sharing how she arrived at her decision to teach reading, the benefits of doing so, and some strategies she uses in her class.

Chapter 13: Thinking Matters: Universal Design for Learning and Reading Apprenticeship in Math 110
Kristen Purdum and Nika Hogan

The authors of this chapter, Nika Hogan and Kris Purdum, identify productive intersections between Reading Apprenticeship and Universal Design for Learning and describe the way they are operationalized in a Statistics course that Kris designed specifically to be supportive for learners requiring accommodations for learning differences documented through the colleges Disabled Students Programs and Services (DSPS) office.

Chapter 14: The Role of the Productive Struggle in Authentic Learning: Why Student Learning Insights Matter as Much as Student Learning Outcomes 119
Shirley Kahlert

Kahlert, an English professor at Merced College and UC Merced, explores the value of text sets for engaging students in the productive struggle that leads to empowered learning. She describes what makes texts difficult and explains how text sets can mitigate that difficulty, illustrating by describing student engagement with a particular text set focused on metacognition.

Chapter 15: Introducing Perusall to Support Reading Apprenticeship in Upper-Division Mathematics Courses in an Online Modality 125
Peri Shereen and Jeffrey Wand

Shereen and Wand, both tenure-track faculty in the department of Mathematics and Statistics at CSUMB, consider the evolution of their approach to upper division math student text reflection in the pandemic by unpacking their use of student social annotation with Perusall. They provide a model for eliciting substantive math text annotations and reflect on the features in Perusall that support thoughtful, lengthy exchanges and allow a helpful window into the collective student reading experience.

Chapter 16: Snapshots of First-Year College Reading 130
Nanda Warren

Warren, a lecturer in Communication Across the Disciplines at CSUMB, explores what it means to lead authentic conversations with students about academic texts in a first-year college composition course, and what it looks like when students take on the work. She provides three snapshots of classroom experiences, revealing successes and struggles, and then considers takeaways for supporting student power and transformation.

PART V: READING IS SOCIAL AND PERSONAL — 135

Chapter 17: Feel-the-Text: A Metacognitive Reading Strategy Where Readers Make Emotions Visible — 142
Sue Lee

Because students sometimes struggle to engage intellectually with texts in predictable ways, Lee, an English professor at Kwantlen Polytechnic University in Canada, has developed an activity she calls "feel the text" that takes advantage of students' emotional responses when they read to facilitate that engagement. Her innovation combines tools from Social Emotional Learning and Reading Apprenticeship to teach annotation, and she details the process in this chapter.

Chapter 18: Using the Reading Apprenticeship Framework to Change College-Level Math Instruction — 149
Christie Knighton

Knighton, Education and ELCAP (English Language, Career, and Academic Prep) faculty member at Highline College in Washington, argues that although culture change is difficult, perhaps more so in a discipline such as mathematics, it can be scaffolded and supported with particular instructional approaches and moves. She describes a successful program in which the contextualized, team teaching/I-BEST model, infused with Reading Apprenticeship, provided supports for changing instruction in math.

Chapter 19: The Early Bird Special — 153
Caren Kongshaug

Student retention is always an issue, especially for faculty teaching in community colleges or the lower division of four-year colleges. Kongshaug, a College Readiness instructor in the Transitional Studies program at Bellingham Technical College in Washington, suggests that one way to reduce the number of students disappearing from her Adult Ed/GED class is to implement routines and experiences in the first few weeks of the semester that build community and confidence. In this chapter, she describes the nature of that "early bird special" and how she enacts those routines and experiences.

Chapter 20: Building Semester-Long Groups to Support the Social Dimension of Learning and Problem Solving in the Large Biology Classroom — 157
Erin Stanfield

In this chapter, Stanfield, a lecturer in biology and chemistry and applied environmental science at CSUMB, shares her approach to engaged learning with disciplinary reading in large, lower division STEM classes, as she considers how best to offer students community and structure for taking on scientific ways of being and real world problem solving with challenging STEM texts. She explores group structure, work routines, strategies for unpacking complex texts, and key challenges in considering how to incorporate reading, metacognitive conversation, and roles in Complex Instruction, a cooperative engagement approach.

Chapter 21: Restorative Pedagogy in Online Courses: Capitalizing on Relationships through Reading Apprenticeship Routines — 164
Andréa Pantoja Garvey

Panoja Garvey, a professor of psychology at American River College, argues that the Reading Apprenticeship practice of "making the invisible visible" (and explicitly spoken about) has to do not just with cognitive and knowledge building moves, but often about emotional or cultural undercurrents that are impacting students' and teachers' bandwidth for intellectual labor. She describes assignments that address different aspects of invisible undercurrents that can be addressed productively by putting them on the table for discussion or revision in various ways.

Chapter 22: Readers Wanna Read: Developing Self-Regulated Readers in the Online Classroom — 174
Julie Gamberg

Drawing on the focus in writing studies on helping students become *self-regulated revisers* of their writing, Gamberg, an English professor at Glendale Community College, describes a sequence of instruction in an asynchronous online writing class that led to students improving as self-regulated revisers of their *reading*. She describes the video modeling she did, strategies for peer review of reading, and her own feedback on reading and metacognition.

Chapter 23: Social Annotation as a Transdisciplinary Strategy for Engaging Diverse Learners — 180
Jonelle Strickland

Strickland, who teaches in both the Criminal Justice department at California State University, Long Beach and the English department at Santiago Canyon College, describes her use of social annotation with the text *Four Hundred Souls* to develop students' reading strategy development with a topical text. She explains how she teaches students to use social annotation and the low(er) tech way she does social annotation that doesn't depend on specialized software.

Chapter 24: The We and the Me: The Social and Personal Dimensions — 186
Lora Bagwell

Through anecdotes from her classroom, Bagwell, an English and college success professor and now assistant dean of English at Pelissippi State Community College in Tennessee, describes the strategies she uses to make the most of the fact that reading is always both a social and personal activity. She describes the way that she supports students to embrace engaged reading through an emphasis on "Intelligent Practice" (Success comes from Effort, Good Strategies, and Help from Others) and repeated attention to growth mindset.

Chapter 25: It's Time to Eighty-Six the Old Menu — 192
Aimee Beckstrom Escalante

A lecturer in liberal studies at CSUMB, Escalante reflects on how reading can make students feel like insiders and outsiders and how she uses RA routines and other strategies to help students build insider identities in her class. Escalante focuses specifically on how observations of her classes revealed inequities particularly for Latinx males, and how she revised her curriculum and activities to address those inequities.

Afterword   197

> We revisit the notion of reciprocal apprenticeship—in which faculty learn from students as they are introducing students to the problem-solving strategies of their disciplines. We review how the stories and strategies in the collection negotiate the tensions of reading apprenticeship and close with suggestions for continuing this work.

References   199

Index   211

About the Authors   219

Preface

As is so often the case, the roots of this project lie in a single question. It was Nelson who voiced it, back in 2016, as he and Rebecca chatted with Nika at a Reading Apprenticeship seminar.

"Where are all the college stories?"

There was amazing work going on, fueled by tremendous energy. When Nelson started as director of communication across the disciplines at CSU, Monterey Bay, he already had *Reading for Understanding* in his hand, having used the approach for years in his work as a professor of teacher education. The director of the Teaching, Learning and Assessment Center (TLA) at the time, Dan Shapiro, introduced Nelson to Rebecca, who had just started working on a Reading Apprenticeship project for TLA. Rebecca had attended one of the statewide workshops supported by the California Community Colleges' Success Network (3CSN) community of practice that Nika was leading and came away inspired. Nika and Dan knew each other from that network as well. With these and many more happy coincidences and connections, a years-long collaboration—at 3CSN conferences, over email and Zoom, through WestEd courses—rooted in designing powerful learning spaces for students and other educators was born. In the intervening years, CSUMB has become a leader among California State University campuses in implementing Reading Apprenticeship across the curriculum, with the Mathematics and Statistics department even adopting the approach formally for first-year classes.

But still, the question remained: How is all of the wonderful work college faculty across the disciplines have been doing being recorded and shared? How can other college faculty learn from that work to improve their own teaching? This book is our answer to that question.

As Nika has been at the center of college work on Reading Apprenticeship, she has been privy to the amazing work done by Reading Apprenticeship practitioners across disciplines, institutions, and states. The authors represented in this collection are those practitioners. While many are scholars in their own disciplines, few are scholars of reading in the disciplines or postsecondary literacy. Thus, this is a book first and foremost by and for teachers. One of the advantages of the Reading Apprenticeship community is that it has provided opportunities for practitioners to engage with a tough topic that is often evaded in college: What do we do with reading? These chapters are some answers to that question.

As editors, we have tried to contextualize the practices described here in terms of threshold concept theory and research in higher education and academic literacy. We believe that the project of using reading to learn across the academy requires more than the adoption of a set of routines or activities. It requires a change of mindset of the kind that threshold concept theory describes. We must see reading and our students differently in order to make the most of their educations.

HOW TO USE THIS BOOK

We have provided an annotated table of contents that summarizes each of the chapters briefly. We encourage you to skim through to find chapters first in disciplines or domains related to those you teach or lead. These more familiar settings may offer the initial hints for new ways to approach reading and learning in your classes. As these chapters evoke new questions or ideas for you, we encourage you to broaden your lens—read chapters in unrelated disciplines, read the introduction and the introductions to the parts based on our tentative threshold concepts, read more about the Reading Apprenticeship framework and the tensions of academic apprenticeship. We do not intend for this book to be a linear journey for readers. Encountering and crossing thresholds in understanding is messy; it involves misunderstanding, tentative understandings, oscillation, epiphany, and extension. We hope you find opportunities for all of those experiences in the amazing work of the committed educators who write in these pages. And we hope you build from these ideas in your own teaching and learning.

Acknowledgments

We dedicated this book to all of the courageous teachers and students who enter into the messy and liminal space of making sense of text together. And for creating a model that supports teachers and students to make metacognitive conversations with texts part of the way they now "do school," we must first acknowledge Ruth Schoenbach and Cynthia Greenleaf. Their invention, the Reading Apprenticeship framework, is brilliant, but the most genius aspect of Ruth and Cyndy's creation has been the inquiry-based and collaborative nature of their project over 30 years and counting. Teachers learn, teachers try things, teachers innovate, teachers teach other teachers, teachers and researchers evaluate their work and distill new questions, and the cycle continues. It doesn't end because humans keep changing, as do our literacy practices. It is impossible to quantify how many lives and careers have been improved by Ruth and Cyndy's work and their generative, capacity-building approach to professional learning. We honor you and we thank you! We also thank the talented WestEd staff carrying on Ruth and Cyndy's legacy, and especially those who have directly contributed to the college-level work on Reading Apprenticeship: Sukhraj Bassi, Jane Braunger, Will Brown, Linda Friedrich, Emma Fujii, Margot Kenaston, Diane Lee, Kate Meissert, Misty Sailors, and Mary Stump.

As executive director of the California Community Colleges' Success Network (3CSN), Deborah Harrington had the wild idea to create a statewide community of practice based in Reading Apprenticeship. This investment accelerated the growth of college-level Reading Apprenticeship implementation and created an enormous network of faculty across disciplines and contexts looking for ways to support students with their reading. We owe so much to Deborah's vision and leadership, and to the hard work and deep expertise of the 3CSN coordinators over the years who helped to develop and lead the Reading Apprenticeship Project: Ann Foster, Jeanne Costello, Lauren Servais, Sarah Sullivan, and Devon Werble.

It has been our privilege to work with so many brilliant educators as we explored the possibilities of Reading Apprenticeship on our campuses and in our classrooms. Although we couldn't possibly name them all, we do want to thank a few coconspirators in particular. For taking the state of Washington by storm and showing us how it is done, we thank the indomitable Michele Lesmeister, as well as Caren Kongshaug and Christie Knighton. For their early leadership, creativity, and energy in building the college network, we thank Kim Costino, Cindy Hicks, Shawn Frederking, Walter Masuda, and Trish Schade. For helping to develop models for Reading Apprenticeship embedded into first-year-experience seminars and programs, we thank Myriam Altounji, Lora Bagwell, Cecile Davis-Anderson, Laura Garofoli, Tiffany Ingle, Shelagh Rose, and Carrie Starbird. For their valuable thought partnership in developing resources for Reading Apprenticeship–infused writing courses, we thank Erik Armstrong, Jennifer Escobar, Nicole Glick, Kyle Hull, Kelan Koning, Carla Maroudas,

Natasha Oehlman, Scott Sandler, Kate Sullivan, and Nanda Warren. And for their work in exploring and defining what Reading Apprenticeship can look like in college STEM contexts, we thank Richard Abdelkerim, Kelly Burke, Elizabeth Cannis, Lilit Haroyan, Theresa Martin, Erica Seubert, Corin Slown, and Linda Zarzana.

At CSUMB, we have been fortunate to benefit from the unwavering support of former Center for Teaching, Learning, and Assessment (TLA) director Dan Shapiro and current TLA director Vivian Waldrup-Patterson. At the California State University Chancellor's Office, Emily Magruder has been a booster for statewide professional development and supported bringing the Reading Apprenticeship framework to the CSU. Thank you for your partnership in supporting disciplinary reading engagement across our campus and beyond.

Finally, we deeply and sincerely thank our loved ones for putting up with our devotion to this project: Dave Reichard, Kevin Jepson, and Kim and Marco Costino.

Introduction

Making Visible Disciplinary Learning: Faculty Crossing Thresholds to Support College Reading

Nelson Graff, Nika Hogan, and Rebecca Kersnar

If the educational disruptions of 2020 highlighted anything about higher education, it's that we must do a better job of helping students learn from texts. Across the disciplines, although faculty have long complained that students do not do the assigned reading, remote learning and the concomitant increased need for students to learn through reading have inspired faculty at all levels and in all disciplines to think hard about how we help students learn how to learn. In addition, a recent meta-analysis of studies of the associations between reading comprehension assessments such as the ACT, the SAT, and others found a correlation between scores on those tests and college grades (Clinton-Lisell et al., 2022). If instructors accept, as the National Academies of Sciences and Engineering put it in *How People Learn II*, that "purposefully teaching the language and practices specific to particular disciplines, such as science, history, and mathematics, is critical to helping students develop deep understanding in these subjects" (2018, p. 161), we must do better at embedding that instruction in our work with students and helping them access those languages and practices through text.

This collection shines a light on the beliefs and practices of community college and university instructors who have transformed their instruction to focus on disciplinary literacy through deep and long-term study of the Reading Apprenticeship framework. Reading Apprenticeship (Schoenbach et al., 2012) is an instructional framework focusing on supporting students' work with disciplinary texts. Specifically, the framework focuses on four dimensions of classroom life—social, personal, cognitive, and knowledge-building—in order to facilitate students' engagement with texts. The central procedure in Reading Apprenticeship classrooms is *metacognitive conversation*, sharing and discussing the problem-solving strategies that readers use to make sense of text. Those conversations generally move from sharing personal histories of reading to surfacing the approaches students currently use to read, then learning new strategies from all of the readers in the room. Often, this involves the creation of a shared reading-strategies list, teacher modeling, and shared student practice. The Reading Apprenticeship framework shares much with the work of the Project Zero team at Harvard University (Ritchhart et al., 2011; Ritchhart & Church, 2020) and the project on decoding the disciplines (Pace & Middendorf, 2004) in that all three approaches emphasize making visible the invisible components of thinking and problem solving. Chapter 1 explains the framework in more depth and outlines the history of a network of college instructors engaged in Reading Apprenticeship professional learning to prepare readers to engage with the practices described in the chapters that follow.

Building on a prior exploration of threshold concepts instructors confront when first attempting to incorporate literacy instruction into their teaching (Graff et al., 2022), we asked experienced Reading Apprenticeship practitioners to reflect upon their breakthroughs in transitioning to an instructional approach that encourages students to grapple with disciplinary texts—surfacing their insights, struggles, and confusions through metacognitive conversations—as a means of engaging with core concepts and content. In this chapter, we present the themes that emerged and consider what appear to be threshold concepts at the heart of teaching reading and using reading to teach disciplinary content. In the chapters that follow, practitioners elucidate what that transformed teaching looks like in practice and explore these conceptual thresholds for teachers and students in more depth.

We begin this chapter with a focused review of research on threshold concepts to ground our project in that body of work, following that with an overview of the research on disciplinary and college reading. We describe the methods we used in this project to develop our tentative threshold concepts and then spend some time describing what we see as a "metaconcept" that joins the concepts we inferred and the concepts themselves.

THRESHOLD CONCEPTS

Examining the teaching of reading through the lens of threshold concept theory offers opportunities to make invisible ideas about teaching and learning visible to faculty. In this section, we review some of the scholarship on threshold concept theory with an eye toward how the theory helps us think about becoming more effective teachers of and with reading.

One of those insights is the idea that crossing the threshold involves a change in perspective and ontology (Land et al., 2014). In the case of reading instruction, when faculty in all disciplines cross these thresholds of understanding about teaching reading, they begin to see themselves differently—as reading teachers in their disciplines rather than as teachers of disciplinary content who assign reading in order for students to absorb that content. They also begin to see reading differently, not as a basic skill but as a disciplinary practice central to learning in their disciplines. Just as writing in the disciplines involves inhabiting "ways of knowing and doing" (Carter, 2007) in those disciplines, reading in the disciplines involves internalizing problem-solving strategies for making sense of text and the world according to the values and practices of those disciplines.

Broadly, threshold concept theory proposes that there are certain concepts that form the boundaries of disciplinary thinking and action. As learners approach those concepts, they enter a liminal state, attempting to cross the threshold from disciplinary outsider to disciplinary insider. Meyer and Land (2005) characterize threshold concepts as *transformative, troublesome, bounded, integrative,* and probably *irreversible,* leaving uncertain how many of those characteristics a concept needs to possess in order to be a true threshold concept. In a critique of threshold concept theory, Adler-Kassner and Wardle (2020) suggest that a focus on boundedness, for instance, may inhibit the application of threshold concepts to interdisciplinary work. As they further suggest, because threshold concepts named at any time represent what is accepted in the field at that time, they are always "threshold concepts for now" and should not be treated as fixed and permanent.

Despite those critiques, there does seem to be value in explicitly stating shared understandings of the disciplines, particularly those that challenge newcomers to the disciplines. Naming those concepts helps us, as faculty and faculty development professionals, to mindfully construct encounters with those concepts that may help learners cross those thresholds. For that reason, we want to pay particular attention to a few constructions of liminality. First, we examine how Land and colleagues (2014) describe liminality within the framework of threshold concept theory, elaborating what is happening for learners as they encounter thresholds using a visual metaphor of a tunnel and the vocabulary of semantics (signifier, signified, sign). In particular, they describe learning a concept as matching the correct signifier (a word or image that gives meaning) with the correct signified (the mental concept evoked in the mind). The liminal state is one in which the signifier remains the same but the signified transitions from old to new, representing a move from imitative to transformed understanding.

Their semantic analysis of the transition from pre-liminal to post-liminal mirrors in important ways an analysis done by Smagorinsky and colleagues (2003) using a Vygotskian framework to study new teachers' concept development. Their study provides a helpful way to understand what it means for a threshold concept to be "troublesome" and how to understand liminality as faculty approach and engage with the threshold concept. Focusing on new teacher talk and practice around *constructivism* (the idea that we actively construct knowledge through learning experiences in relation to our prior knowledge), they illustrate the slipperiness that characterizes understanding while moving toward and across the threshold. New teachers, for instance, may understand group work as an important part of constructivist pedagogy but fail to recognize the ways that group work must be structured in order to enable collaboration and shared construction of new knowledge. This variation highlights a particular interest to our project: the idea that a complete understanding connects *theory* to *practice*, and the development of that understanding is "mediated by activity in cultural practice" (2003, p. 1404). It is in the *practice* and *implications* of threshold concepts of teaching reading that we see the most interesting developments among our survey respondents. As Smagorinsky and colleagues describe, "This understanding goes well beyond simple categorizing, requiring instead the ability to understand and act within networks of social relationships" (p. 1405). What are classrooms and disciplines but "networks of social relationships"?

RESEARCH ON COLLEGE READING

Research on college reading has established that learners must actively construct new knowledge in order to learn effectively. For instance, according to Bransford and colleagues (1999), students must (1) have their prior knowledge engaged, (2) understand and organize knowledge in the context of a conceptual framework, and (3) take a metacognitive approach to their own learning. In their updated and expanded *How People Learn II* (2018), NAS draws on the research of James Gee to explicitly call out the role of academic literacy in deep learning. Gee (2004) describes the importance of "academic varieties of English" and the specialized languages of the disciplines to develop the discourses of those disciplines. One of the key ways that students encounter and internalize that academic language is through reading. In this review, we consider what scholarship suggests about different kinds of reading—specifically disciplinary reading and digital reading—what researchers have discovered about teaching reading at the college level, and what research reveals about college students' reading difficulties. We close by considering what those findings suggest not only for students' understanding of reading but faculty understanding of reading.

Disciplinary Reading

As the Writing in the Disciplines movement has established for writing, reading is not a basic skill, learned once and applied readily across disciplines and contexts. Nor are the strategies taught in first-year composition sufficient to prepare students for the reading and writing they will do in disciplinary classes. Rather, reading is a profoundly disciplinary activity, instantiating the epistemologies and everyday practices of disciplinary thinking in meaning-making activities (Fang & Chapman, 2020; Moje, 2015; Shanahan & Shanahan, 2008). This move toward reading across the curriculum and in the disciplines echoes transitions in writing instruction to focus on writing across the curriculum and in the disciplines, an echo surfaced by some scholars. Horning (2013) edited a special issue of *Across the Disciplines* that addresses this idea explicitly and argues that "because of the need for connection, faculty must help students read in context, not only within their courses, but also within their disciplines, to make connections to materials and ideas beyond the classroom" (Horning et al., 2017, p. 14). It also echoes the work of the Decoding the Disciplines Project (Pace & Middendorf, 2004).

Some research attempts to understand *how* reading differs across disciplines. For example, Goldman and colleagues (2016) describe a framework for helping faculty and students conceptualize disciplinary differences in reading, consisting of

> clusters [of types of knowledge] for each discipline into five higher-order categories of what we called disciplinary core constructs: (a) epistemology; (b) inquiry practices/strategies of reasoning; (c) overarching concepts, themes, and frameworks; (d) forms of information representation/types of texts; and (e) discourse and language structures. (p. 224)

Such a model resonates with the work of Abbot and Nantz (2017). Researching reading in an interdisciplinary class they taught, Abbot and Nantz (2017) find that the ways that students read and the ways the texts were organized differed significantly between the history and economics texts they assigned. This aligns with research on disciplinary reading at the secondary level, with researchers critiquing simplistic models of literacy instruction (e.g., Fang & Chapman, 2020; Moje, 2015; Shanahan & Shanahan, 2008) and proposing more nuanced disciplinary literacy instruction.

Davies (2017), too, argues for teaching reading processes in science classes in high school and college, suggesting that many of the problems with content knowledge identified by faculty are really the result of weak reading skills. She suggests that faculty focus on productive (and disciplinary) ways of prereading, reading, and revised reading and models this technique by describing such activities for popular science books and articles, textbooks, and professional science articles. Pearlman (2013) similarly argues for disciplinary modeling of literacy practices as a solution to patchwriting and students' failure to deeply understand the disciplinary texts they are reading.

Digital Reading

Disciplinary reading, like all reading, occurs in a context. With recent efforts to address the affordability of college focusing significantly on reducing the cost of course texts, many institutions and faculty are moving to use Open Educational Resources (OERs). These electronic textbooks raise important questions about reading online—whether it is (or can be) as effective as reading in print. While research specifically on e-textbook use suggests positive outcomes for students (e.g., Hurley and Fekrazad, 2020), broader questions about digital reading may apply for reading other texts, including scholarly articles online. In *How We Read Now*, Baron (2021) summarizes research on reading online, claiming that while the evidence is not conclusive, it is probably better to read in print for comprehension and deep reading. Similarly, Wolf (2018) describes the neuroscience of reading and warns that the ways we read online may be reshaping our brains in ways that diminish our ability to do the deep reading necessary for disciplinary inquiry. And Miller (2016) outlines various dimensions of "reader-writer relationship"—writer, audience, publication, distribution, information, and mastery—to illustrate the ways in which digital reading differs from reading on paper (p. 154), an illustration echoed by Yancey and colleagues (2017).

These studies suggest that there is at least the potential for diminished comprehension in digital reading, though Miller (2016) in particular emphasizes that digital reading differs from print reading, not that it is inferior. Jeong and Gweon (2021), however, find in a direct comparison that readers demonstrate similar ability to understand and similar reading speed across media (print versus computer versus tablet). Their subjects reported (and eye fixation data confirmed) that digital reading took greater effort. Thus, it appears that the weaknesses attributed to digital reading relate more to the *behaviors* associated with reading on screen rather than the medium itself—distracted reading, skimming, searching rather than deep reading. Such a conclusion is consistent with other research on digital reading that sounds a more positive note (Downs, 2021; Rodrigue, 2017a, 2017b). When Rodrigue asked students to think aloud with their on-screen readings, she notes that they apply reading strategies associated with comprehension, such as "making a personal connection to the text; stating an opinion, disagreeing and agreeing; discussing themselves and their experiences in relation to the text; and commenting" (p. 7). Rodrigue also finds that print-based skills such as genre awareness can help students negotiate digital texts (2017b). Along slightly different lines, Downs (2021) claims that concerns about digital reading are "inaccurate or hyperbolic" (p. 206) and argues that what readers need to read effectively online and to counter "fake news" is meta-awareness of the "nature [of web texts] and of the reading act itself" (p. 218). Downs describes reading web texts in terms of "quantum textuality," highlighting the ways in which the instability and multimodal nature of web texts call for different skills than we use in print-based reading.

Both the concerns about digital reading and arguments for the potential of digital reading highlight the need for helping students develop metacognition as they are reading, a central focus of the Reading Apprenticeship approach.

Teaching Reading

To support the complex process of disciplinary reading, one strand of college reading research addresses approaches to reading instruction, with specific approaches such as mindful reading (Carillo, 2015), deep reading (Sullivan et al., 2017), antiracist reading (Inoue, 2020), and reading like a writer (Bunn, 2013). All of these approaches treat reflection and metacognition as central to the reading process, whether it relates to how students read differently in different contexts for mindful reading (Carillo, 2015) or the "habits of language and judgment [that] help a reader read a text" (Inoue, 2020, p. 1) in antiracist reading. Odom (2013) focuses on the connection between reading and writing, finding that assigning writing based on the readings did not necessarily help students read better. She did find, however, that some assignments helped. In particular, she notes "The material they draw on from their course readings needs to fulfill a particular role in terms of their thinking and writing, making their interaction with the text far more genuine and purposeful than many reading assignments may appear to be" (p. 11). She describes, for instance, a "memo to self" assignment that asks students to apply their readings to understand and improve their activities in life. This focus on the need to treat reading as serving a particular purpose in context is similar to work in disciplinary literacy at the secondary level that suggests teachers must assign student reading to be purposeful and to require that students *use* the text-based learning they acquire through reading (Greenleaf & Valencia, 2017). And Abbot and Nantz (2017) describe various techniques—such as mapping arguments and using other strategies for visually interpreting texts—that would have been helpful to encourage their students and support them in their reading.

Focusing on transfer from first-year writing classes, Lockhart and Soliday (2016) demonstrate that it was students' knowledge about and strategic approaches to reading that transferred. Specifically, they "detail four key patterns that emerged from analyzing and coding student responses: connecting reading and writing (a) to become more active and focused readers, (b) to advance critical reading practices, (c) to promote higher-order thinking, and (d) to become more rhetorically aware and effective readers and writers" (p. 28). Thus, as in the research on digital reading, research on reading pedagogy emphasizes the need to develop students' metacognition.

College Students' Reading Struggles

Despite this research on teaching reading, reviewing research on college students' reading abilities, Carillo and Horning (2021) paint a bleak picture, claiming that "no matter how critical reading skills are measured, half or more of the students currently in college classrooms lack the ability to analyze, synthesize, evaluate and make ethical use of what they read" (p. 3). They ponder whether such a finding helps to explain why roughly half of students who enter college leave without degrees. Reading scores and college grades across disciplines and academic level have been found to correlate (Clinton-Lisell et al., 2022), and studies tracing college students' weak reading skills are widespread. For instance, using findings from other studies and the Citation Project (a body of research unified around examining students' use of source texts in their writing), Jamieson (2013) argues that typical sophomore college students lack important skills needed to read critically for the purpose of academic research. She argues that the lack of summary and successful paraphrase in students' source-based writing suggests weakness in their comprehension of the texts they read. Like Jamieson, Young and Potter (2012) begin with questions about students' difficulties with academic reading and find evidence of difficulty with "the purpose and expectations of academic discourse," with academic vocabulary, and with more complex engagement with academic sources beyond summarizing (p. 17). While they study students in their first- and second-year writing classes, they argue that attention to academic reading in first-year composition by itself will be insufficient to help students develop the skills they need to succeed in college. They instead suggest an approach to reading across the curriculum in both first-year composition and disciplinary instruction that emphasizes practice engaging with literary texts, connection of those texts with student experiences, and examination of the "material and cultural forces" in which those texts participate (p. 19).

Other researchers have similarly highlighted the need to address students' weak reading skills in college contexts. Manarin and colleagues (2015) studied reading logs produced by their students in four different general education areas to examine what they call "critical reading." They define critical reading in terms of both academic and social engagement purposes and examine it in terms of a hierarchy of four key abilities—comprehension, analysis, interpretation, and evaluation—with evaluation being the most advanced of the skills. They conclude that "students are comprehending the texts they read" (p. 116) but that they may not need to read critically in order to succeed in their classes, despite faculty intentions otherwise. Such a finding echoes research in secondary schools that suggests that students are not called on in most of their classes to develop critical reading abilities (Greenleaf & Valencia, 2017; New Teacher Project, 2018). The New Teacher Project (2018) makes the case that students overwhelmingly successfully complete assignments and engage in activities that are not at grade level and do not fully engage and/or stretch their abilities. Similarly, Greenleaf and Valencia (2017) found that students lack the "opportunity to use texts for purposeful learning in the subject areas, and thereby to gain needed dispositions, strategies, and skills" (p. 235), a lack of opportunity supported by faculty who do not address whatever readings are assigned with meaningful activities or accountability (Carillo & Horning, 2021).

Whether in high school or college, students and faculty strike "a bargain" that exempts students from challenge and eases the discomfort of faculty. It can be uncomfortable for faculty to watch students struggle; they guide them through the struggle if they require grade-level engagement with complex texts (Erickson et al., 2006; Windschitl, 2019). In this context, difficult text(s) are frequently read aloud to students, digested, and presented in more "bite-size" PowerPoint slides and/or lecture notes, replaced or supplemented with video, and/or rendered optional by assessments that don't require independent reading, sense-making, and knowledge construction. Students are frequently not entrusted to read, understand, and react to texts even when they are supposedly engaging in argumentation or project-based assignments. Even in subject area, classrooms focused intensively on disciplinary literacy tasks, "best-case scenario" classrooms by many standards, Greenleaf and Valencia (2017) found that "teachers would knit together and reinterpret, translate, and elaborate on students' contributions, adding new information as they orchestrated these 'discussions.' Seeking to engage students in discussion, through their talk, teachers nevertheless did the work themselves of reading and interpreting and knowledge building for students" (pp. 239–240).

College Students with Learning Differences

One population of students that has garnered special interest from researchers investigating reading challenges in college is students with learning differences (LD; usually described as disabilities in the research). These include students with dyslexia (Andreassen et al., 2017; Pedersen et al., 2016), autism (Accardo & Finnegan, 2019; Hua et al., 2012; Knight & Sartini, 2015; Sartini et al., 2018); learning disabilities (Ruban et al., 2003; Trainin & Swanson, 2005), and what researchers have described as a history of reading difficulties (Bergey et al., 2017; Chevalier et al., 2017; Deacon et al., 2012).

Some of the researchers suggest that because learning disabilities may be underreported at the college level, investigating students who self-report early difficulties in learning to read (history of reading difficulties or HRD) is a good proxy for investigating specific learning differences (Bergey et al., 2017; Chevalier et al., 2017; Deacon et al., 2012). For instance, Deacon, Cook, & Parrila (2012) found similar profiles of reading practices and strategy use among students with HRD and those with dyslexia, and both groups of students differed from those without a history of reading difficulties (NRD). Chevalier and colleagues (2017) also found a correlation between metacognitive strategy use and grade point average (GPA); students with HRD who reported using metacognitive reading strategies had better GPAs than those who did not.

Across disabilities categories, in fact, researchers found the use of particular reading strategies predictive of greater academic success. For instance, Ruban and colleagues (2003) drew the conclusion that "learning strategies made a larger positive difference in the academic achievement of students with LD than in students without LD after controlling for other variables" (p. 281), as did Trainin and Swanson (2005). In their review of 23 articles reporting interventions to support reading comprehension among students with autism, Knight and Sartini (2015) found two practices that they rated as evidence-based: "response prompting strategies and visual supports" (p. 1224). The former involves explicit prompting for the use of strategies in making sense of text.

These results are consistent with a broader move in K–16 education toward Universal Design for Learning (UDL) to plan for the full range of students' participation *before* instruction rather than adapting afterward. While UDL may be best known for its focus on multiple means of engagement, representation, and action and expression, another key focus of UDL is on developing "expert learners," helping students develop the metacognition and self-regulation to practice productive learning behaviors such as goal setting and choosing appropriate problem-solving strategies for their purpose and context.

Implications for Instruction

While this is hardly a comprehensive review of literature on reading instruction and reading challenges, a few points of commonality should be clear:

1. Researchers agree that reading is a complex problem-solving task that is context dependent;
2. Approaches to reading instruction with the greatest success involve helping students understand the problem-solving nature of reading and become self-regulating learners; and
3. Metacognition is a key element in providing students that guidance.

These points of commonality suggest a break from the norms of "doing school" (Windschitl, 2019) and a transformation in practice. They require faculty to allow students to grapple with texts and engage in productive dialogue about those texts as a core element of their learning. It may be that the existing scholarship on teaching reading has not made it into the hands of working instructors. Yet the necessary transformation in practice may require deeper transformations of understanding and attitudes. While the field of Composition Studies has taken up threshold concept theory in the study of writing—note for instance, *Naming What We Know* and the follow-up, *Reconsidering What We Know*—it has done so less in the study of college reading. Two exceptions are Gogan's (2017) focus on reading as transformation as a threshold concept and Sullivan's (2019) description of deep reading as a threshold concept.

In order to transform our practice, we need to shift the focus. Instead of asking what academic reading skills students lack, we should be asking what problem-solving skills students are bringing to college classrooms that we are failing to help them translate into academic reading skills. Our students are sophisticated problem solvers, capable of everyday acts of analysis and synthesis that would no doubt surprise most of us. So why are they not succeeding in applying those skills to academic texts? Perhaps the problem is not with them but with us. Perhaps we see apprenticeship as unidirectional and cannot foster the forward transfer needed to help students succeed in college.

Manarin and colleagues (2015) suggest that some student difficulties may arise from students holding a transmission model of reading rather than a transactional one—that is, seeing texts as sources of information rather than sites of negotiated meaning. Perhaps, just as students suffer from misconceptions of the nature of reading, faculty suffer from misconceptions about the nature of reading instruction and the relationships between reading instruction and content knowledge or disciplinarity. By surveying postsecondary instructors who have engaged with Reading Apprenticeship professional development, we hope to learn what insights instructors can add through their experiences teaching reading about the core understandings necessary for transformational reading instruction. The faculty in our survey described several aspects to their change in understanding, all of which are both transformative and troublesome: first, to understand struggle as productive for learning, second, to recognize that students are capable of learning through productive struggles, and finally, realizing that students' authentic ideas and contributions, surfaced through productive struggle, add value to the academic enterprise.

METHODS OF INVESTIGATING THRESHOLD CONCEPTS

Researchers have used a range of approaches for identifying threshold concepts, with many studies incorporating crowdsourcing of knowledge and consensus building among experts in a disciplinary literacy practice through a range of methods, such as interviews, questionnaires, surveys, examination of student work, and classroom observation (Barradell, 2013). Barradell (2013), in her study of threshold concept methodology across a range of disciplines (e.g., economics, engineering, healthcare) suggests some key shared practices in the development of threshold concepts: (1) rigor in identifying threshold concepts, such as by deciding on minimum salient features they must share; (2) including inquiry among teachers, students, educational developers, and even the wider professional community, a practice of transactional curriculum inquiry (Cousin, 2009); and (3) using consensus building to engage with, refine, and prioritize within a preliminary list of threshold concepts.

Many of these practices have been employed by threshold concepts researchers across disciplines. Meyer and Land (2003) conducted initial interviews with economics faculty before building wider discussions with practitioners from across a range of disciplines and institutions. Within writing studies, Adler-Kassner and Wardle (2015) crowdsourced disciplinary experts, followed by collective participant sharing of information and perspective, ending with a consensus-building process to decide on "final for now" concepts. The Association of College and Research Libraries (2015) similarly inquired with the information literacy disciplinary community to identify central concepts and associated practices needed for interdisciplinary engagement with information literacy, which was followed by a feedback-gathering process, engaging researchers and higher education professionals. In another information literacy threshold concept study (Townsend et al., 2016), researchers used the Delphi method—an extended process of survey, participant interaction, and revision to refine and build consensus—among occupational therapy, sustainable agriculture, and community service experts. All of these studies engaged in an extensive process of gathering and fine-tuning expert feedback.

Within threshold concept research directly focused on the thresholds faculty have to cross as teachers of disciplinary reading, Graff and colleagues (2022) transcribed discussions among first-year communication, first-year seminar, literature, and a variety of math and science faculty in a Reading Apprenticeship faculty learning community to consider the development of faculty understandings of disciplinary reading, teaching, and learning. To make sense of those data, researchers used an iterative process of coding, comparing codes, rereading transcripts, and discussing ongoing patterns within the learning community transcripts to find the most common reading conceptualization struggles for faculty in grappling with their role as disciplinary literacy leaders.

In the current investigation of conceptual thresholds encountered by faculty working to support disciplinary literacy, our team shared surveys with over 700 experienced Reading Apprenticeship educators in higher education, that is, faculty who had participated in one or more intensive professional learning experiences, such as a Reading Apprenticeship focused online course, seminar, or learning community, or the Leadership Community of Practice in Reading Apprenticeship. Authors followed up individually with approximately 100 of the most experienced practitioners and encouraged them to participate in the survey. In total, 86 responded to the survey (about 12% of the larger group). Through the survey, practitioners were asked to reflect on meaningful teaching experiences, breakthroughs, and related impacts when leading disciplinary literacy experiences with their students using the following three prompts:

- Describe a meaningful experience in your teaching using Reading Apprenticeship.
- Describe a breakthrough you have experienced in your own thinking about reading or in your work with students through your Reading Apprenticeship practice.
- Describe how that breakthrough impacted you personally or professionally.

After initially considering the responses and collectively deciding on some common themes for Reading Apprenticeship teaching breakthroughs, team members individually coded entries based on those themes and then in pairs discussed patterns, reread responses, and adjusted coding to reflect shared understanding. We then refined the code categories based on our discussion and narrowed our focus to the most prevalent patterns that emerged. Through this process, we identified some preliminary teaching thresholds that instructors may grapple with as they lead disciplinary literacy experiences with their students and one overarching concept that unifies those thresholds.

Tensions of Academic Apprenticeship

The one overarching "metaconcept" we discovered that characterizes Reading Apprenticeship teaching and professional learning in practice centers on the notion of apprenticeship. Although "apprenticeship" has many positive associations related to learning valuable skills, gaining skill and expertise, and being empowered, in an academic context "apprenticeship" could also be viewed as assimilative and oppressive. For example, Inoue cautions writing scholars against "reenact[ing] a whitely stance of control and agency" (2019, p. 363) in their work with student writers. If the nature of the "apprenticeship" is simply the "disciplining" of student bodies and minds into predetermined, preapproved ways of reading and making meaning, then we would indeed be reinforcing what Inoue calls the "steel bars of white language supremacy" (p. 364) in writing studies, and other calcified understandings and traditions in other disciplines. For Reading Apprenticeship to be the equity pedagogy we believe it to be, the understanding of "apprenticeship" that can occur through metacognitive conversation must treat both teachers and students as having valuable perspectives to share and recognize that each can benefit from engagement with the other. In other words, **reading apprenticeships, when faculty have crossed these thresholds, are reciprocal**.

One participant explicitly named this troubling and transformative concept:

> Apprenticeship isn't about molding students in our image. Rather it's about making visible disciplinary ways of reading, writing, and thinking. And when those things are transparent and visible,

students can engage in metacognition to make their own decisions about how they will weave their cultural selves and ways of being into the discipline.

While no other participant mentioned apprenticeship explicitly, most referenced some aspect of the tension between students' authentic and original contributions and our disciplinary traditions and the idea of "right answers." This is a tension described by Etienne Wenger (2000) as a characteristic of communities of practice, such as academic disciplines, as "reification" versus "participation." Without the "reification" (preservation, repetition) of distinct ways of thinking, questioning, researching, writing, and reading, disciplines would not continue to exist, but at the same time, without dynamic participation from stakeholders, especially new potential members of the community of practice (outsiders), reification becomes congealed and the community is no longer "alive." The respondents to our survey who remarked upon students' assets and funds of knowledge were wrestling with the troublesome notion that their job is not to "pass on" knowledge and traditions, but to create the conditions for participation so that students can bring new life to the knowledge and traditions.

This formulation relies on several strands of understanding. First, it presumes that although academic disciplines are animated by shared practices—ways of questioning, researching, problem solving, communicating, and sharing ideas—these are not set in stone. Rather, disciplines are always contested and as such they are "alive" communities of practice, not repositories of "content." It also presumes that students bring assets and funds of knowledge to their academic work that are of value. In fact, what students bring to the work of academic disciplines is precisely the infusion of new perspectives and ongoing participation that keeps the discipline "alive."

This metaconcept echoes and weaves through the three distinct themes in faculty responses that we consider to be potential threshold concepts: Reading is a problem-solving process, students must be entrusted with the work of making sense of texts, and reading is social and personal. It is also relevant to recent work in higher education which aims to reform institutions to be more "student ready" (e.g., Kezar, 2014; Garcia, 2019; McNair et al., 2016). Acknowledging the assets and funds of knowledge that all students bring to their academic endeavors, understanding academic discourse communities to be dynamic, shifting, and contested spaces, and making instructional decisions to support participation and interaction in the work of the discipline (as opposed to "covering content") are all transformative and troubling ideas for college instructors.

Reading Is a Problem-Solving Process

Beneath this overarching concept, we identified as a first threshold for literacy instruction the idea that reading is a problem-solving process. For many readers of this collection, the idea that reading is a problem-solving process is unlikely to be a surprising insight. As others have observed about writing in the disciplines, however, reading in the disciplines seems "transparent" to faculty in the disciplines outside of composition (Carter, 2007), a basic skill that can be assumed rather than taught. In the introduction to this part of the book, we describe this threshold concept, articulate its relevance to Reading Apprenticeship, and provide evidence suggesting that it was *transformative*, *troublesome*, and *integrative* for faculty.

Students Must Be Entrusted With the Work of Making Sense of Texts

Following closely from the understanding that reading is a problem-solving process is an acknowledgement that teachers must allow students to engage in that process independently. Of all the patterns that we noticed in the data, perhaps the strongest signal relates to the idea that students need to take charge of their academic work. Across the 86 respondents, the idea that faculty had to change their teaching to allow (and encourage) students to take responsibility for the work arose among 26 (30%). A few discuss this shift concretely as one wrote, as "shifting from the sage on the stage to student-centered learning based on metacognition." But it was clear for these faculty that the idea was transformative. They use words and phrases like "completely flipped my concept," "shifted radically," "completely transformed," and a few repeated the word from the prompt, "breakthrough." The faculty in our survey described several aspects to their change in understanding, all of which are both transformative and troublesome: first, to understand struggle as productive for learning; second, to recognize that students are capable of learning through productive struggles; and finally, realizing that students' authentic ideas and contributions, surfaced through productive struggle, add value to the academic enterprise.

Reading Is Social and Personal

Allowing students to do the intellectual work in the classroom does not, however, mean asking students to work alone. Although the stereotype of a reader is someone sitting alone with a book, it was transformative for the faculty who responded to our survey to recognize the profoundly social nature of reading and how much reading is bound up with personal identity and the malleability of that identity. Eighteen respondents (21%) mentioned the idea that reading is social as a breakthrough concept. Three respondents characterized the idea as "meaningful," "powerful," and "profound," which indicates that they considered the new understanding of reading to be transformative ("opened my eyes").

OUTLINE OF THE BOOK

In this introduction, we have reviewed research on threshold concepts, postsecondary reading instruction, and challenges that students encounter when reading in college. We have suggested that effectively engaging students in disciplinary literacy and learning requires a transformation in teaching practice, a kind of transformation consistent with crossing thresholds of understanding about teaching reading. And we have proposed a metaconcept and three thresholds that our inquiry has suggested are meaningful for faculty to cross in their teaching of disciplinary literacy. The remainder of this collection will attempt to offer readers encounters to help them cross those thresholds.

To facilitate those encounters, we have separated the contributions into five parts. The first digs deeper into Reading Apprenticeship, with chapters providing background and detail about the framework and describing what the application of that framework looks like in various contexts—science classes, noncredit English as a Second Language classes, and peer education. These chapters combine explanation and elaboration of the framework with educators' stories.

What follows are parts that illustrate the concepts we describe in the introduction through the classroom stories of working college faculty—part time and full time, contingent and tenure-track, in community colleges and four-year universities, in English and across the disciplines. These stories sometimes take the form of conversations, sometimes as reflections on growth as teachers of reading, sometimes as descriptions of particularly effective lessons, sometimes as snapshots of classroom experiences. We offer these contributions in four parts, organized around our tentative metaconcept and the three tentative threshold concepts. Although the real work of teaching effectively with text involved many different kinds of breakthroughs for faculty, we have tried to group these stories according to the threshold concepts we derived from faculty surveys. We precede each part by describing each tentative threshold concept with reference to the survey responses we received and by contextualizing the chapters in that part in the scholarship about postsecondary literacy instruction.

Part II comprises two chapters that explore the metaconcept that academic apprenticeships necessarily evoke tensions between the professional contexts of the disciplines and the personal and cultural funds of knowledge (Moll, 2019) that students bring with them to academic situations. Parts III through V explore the three concepts we have proposed as thresholds for faculty to cross in teaching reading or teaching disciplinary content through reading. In the annotated table of contents, we provide brief summaries of each of these chapters.

We close this collection with an afterword, in which we return to the theory of reciprocal apprenticeships, reconnecting the stories and strategies throughout the collection with the theoretical landscape of higher education. While we hope the chapters themselves will offer guidance and new directions in teaching for our readers, we close with implications that we see from this synthesis—both for teaching and for additional scholarship.

PART I

What Is Reading Apprenticeship?

This collection features contributions from educators who have been heavily influenced by their work with the Reading Apprenticeship framework (Schoenbach et al., 2012; Greenleaf et al., 2023), so the first part of the book aims to provide background knowledge on what exactly Reading Apprenticeship is and what it looks like in college contexts. The first chapter provides a history of the professional learning communities that inspired this book, and the next three chapters provide overviews of what Reading Apprenticeship looks like in a variety of higher education settings: college STEM courses, noncredit English as a Second Language classes, and tutoring/learning assistance centers. While each of these chapters offers insights that connect with the threshold concepts our survey results suggest, their emphasis on Reading Apprenticeship in action makes them ideal to help readers gain a deeper understanding of the framework before they engage with chapters that focus less explicit attention on that background. In addition to their illustration of the Reading Apprenticeship approach, the chapters in this part also connect to scholarly research about how to support learning and literacy achievement in the disciplines.

Chapter 1

Making It Real: Reading Apprenticeship in College

Nika Hogan

As we established in the introduction, there is robust research available on how to support learning in general and literacy development in particular, but it is not easy for college faculty to integrate this knowledge into their teaching practices. Even when evidence strongly supports active and social learning techniques, the prevailing culture of disciplines, departments, and institutions can stand in the way of changing the long-standing habits of "doing school" (Bransford et al., 1999; Hammond, 2015; Immordino-Yang et al., 2019; National Academies of Sciences, Engineering, and Medicine, 2018; Pearson et al., 2020). Faculty often report that they don't feel supported to engage in efforts to transform their teaching (Bathgate et al., 2019), and studies show that students sometimes dislike active learning techniques even when they learn more from them (Deslauriers et al., 2019). Looking for effective ways to engage students in collaborative, inquiry-based, text-rich, and culturally responsive learning experiences, the participants in our study all turned to Reading Apprenticeship professional learning. This chapter describes what the Reading Apprenticeship framework is and how it works in classroom and professional learning settings. As the director of college-level Reading Apprenticeship programming since 2010 and a faculty member who has experienced personal and professional transformation through my apprenticeship into this work, I also describe what I see to be the distinct practices and innovations for professional learning that have best supported instructors to persist with the risky and difficult project of changing our teaching.

Reading Apprenticeship is an instructional framework that focuses on four dimensions of classroom life—social, personal, cognitive, and knowledge-building—in order to facilitate students' active engagement with texts (see figure 1.1). The framework encapsulates principles of how learning works, including culturally responsive, inquiry-based, problem-based, and constructivist pedagogies, with a focus on text, represented by "extensive reading" in the background of the framework and "metacognitive conversation" at the center. Designing learning experiences with the four dimensions of the framework in mind helps instructors from any discipline to orchestrate meaningful literacy instruction in context.

In Reading Apprenticeship classrooms and professional learning, this process begins by building up the social and personal dimensions in order to alter the usual, established culture of school. As Greenleaf and colleagues point out in *Reading for Understanding* (2023), "The tables have to turn—from valuing correctness to valuing struggle, from valuing right answers to valuing the processes of coming to know and learning how to learn" (p. 57). The

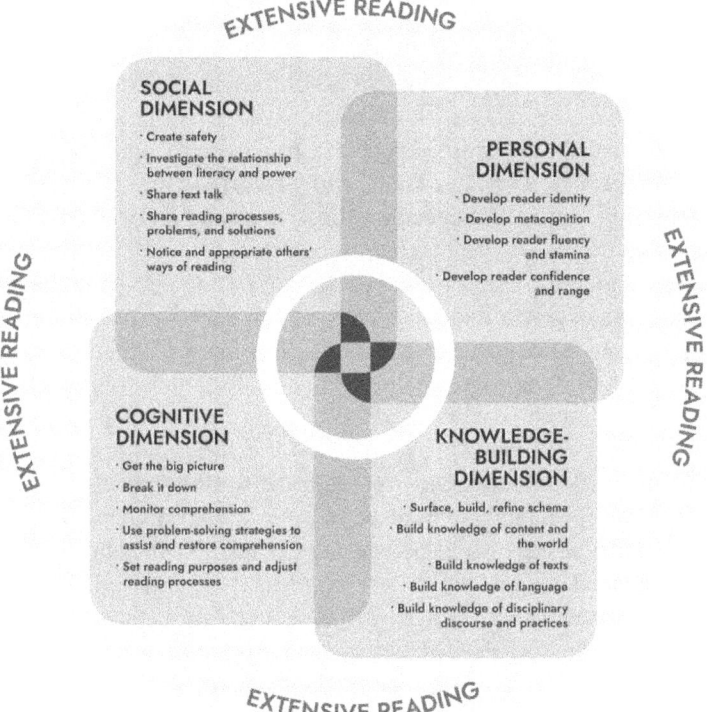

Figure 1.1. The Reading Apprenticeship Framework
Greenleaf et al., 2023

social dimension is focused on "nurturing a social environment in which students can begin to reveal their understandings and their struggles, as well as to see other students and their teacher as potential resources for learning" (Greenleaf et al., 2023, p. 30). To accomplish this, it is essential to lay out ground rules for social interactions and to establish a robust inquiry into how reading works so that it becomes "normal" to discuss struggles, confusions, insights, connections, and ways of making sense of texts. The personal dimension, developing reader identity, metacognition, fluency, stamina, confidence, and range "develops within, and in turn, adds to the development of the social context of the classroom" (Greenleaf et al., 2023, p. 33). Learners are encouraged to reflect on their personal responses, preferences, and values, to recognize and build on their own funds of knowledge, and to set goals for their own learning.

With the groundwork laid for taking intellectual risks, learners are encouraged to dig into making meaning with texts through the cognitive and knowledge-building dimensions. The cognitive dimension focuses on increasing the repertoire of strategies for reading, problem solving, and thinking deeply that learners have available. Monitoring comprehension, marshalling focus, breaking texts down into manageable chunks, getting the big picture, and setting and adjusting reading purposes are all cognitive strategies that are introduced and practiced in context in Reading Apprenticeship classrooms and professional learning settings. In order to utilize such strategies meaningfully in specific disciplinary contexts, knowledge of that context needs to be built. The knowledge-building dimension focuses not only on disciplinary content but also on building knowledge of disciplinary discourse and practices, of disciplinary language, and of disciplinary texts. Importantly, knowledge building always relies on a foundation of surfacing and refining the schema that learners bring with them. "As they engage with text, readers call up whole worlds of knowledge, networks of mental connections triggered by particular ideas, words, or situations, and by their own social and cultural experiences and traditions" (Greenleaf et al., 2023, p. 40). Building from what learners already know reinforces the social and personal dimensions, as all members of the learning community are resources for their own and others' learning. Indeed, all of the dimensions overlap and reinforce one another on a continuous, recursive basis. This is especially true of metacognitive conversation, which relies upon and integrates all four dimensions and which is central to this teaching approach. At the heart of Reading Apprenticeship, everyone—teachers and students—is reflecting on, surfacing, and sharing their meaning-making processes.

The Reading Apprenticeship framework was developed and piloted in the mid-1990s as the animating force behind a new 9th-grade Academic Literacy course for 200 students at Thurgood Marshall Academic High School in San Francisco. The impressive and lasting literacy gains for students in that first study inspired multiple large-scale studies, scores of research articles, and several books, including three editions of *Reading for Understanding*, which describes this work in much more detail (Greenleaf et al., 2023). At WestEd, a nonprofit educational research and development organization, Reading Apprenticeship professional development has also been continuously developed and disseminated in cycles of research and practice over the past 25 years as a large evidence base has established the efficacy of the approach in middle school and high school contexts (Corrin et al., 2008; Greenleaf et al., 2011a; Greenleaf et al., 2011b).

The first college instructors to engage with Reading Apprenticeship professional development did so in the context of teacher preparation programs, where the focus was still on middle and high school instruction. But a national movement to improve so-called basic skills instruction opened the door to discussing the role of reading in college learning and soon inspired funders and college instructors to invest in exploring how Reading Apprenticeship might help to support students at the college level. In 2007, the first professional development institute designed specifically for college instructors was offered, and in 2011, the California Community Colleges' Success Network (3CSN) established a statewide community of practice (CoP) focused on Reading Apprenticeship. Other states, notably Washington and Michigan, also made large investments in Reading Apprenticeship professional learning, although not with the same commitment to a CoP model. In California, projects focused on Reading Apprenticeship in STEM contexts and in Writing Studies attracted participation from educators in the California State University system, continuing to expand the reach and to generate more examples of innovations with this framework across a wide range of contexts: from academic support to upper-division courses, from humanities to math, science, and engineering, and from pen and paper to fully digital and online modalities. Colleges have connected Reading Apprenticeship professional development to increased retention and completion by women and students of color in math courses, to accelerated progress in adult basic education, and to significantly higher rates of retention for first-year students (Renton Technical College, 2011; College of San Mateo, 2013; UCLA Social Research Methodology Evaluation Group, 2015; Edmunds, 2017; Campaign for College Opportunity, 2017; Hogan & Rose, 2018).

WHAT DOES READING APPRENTICESHIP LOOK LIKE IN (CLASSROOM) PRACTICE?

In Reading Apprenticeship classrooms, students engage in routine discussions about *how* they are making sense of a broad range of texts—not only traditional textbooks but also graphs, equations, problems, proofs, primary sources, simulations, videos, and more. These metacognitive conversations invite all students to bring their own perspectives into the academic context, giving their instructors a window into their unique sense-making processes and background knowledge. At the same time, through instructor modeling and participation in metacognitive conversations, students gain access to the "insider moves" that contribute to fluency and flexibility in knowledge building in the disciplines.

For example, an instructor might select a section of text and think aloud for a couple of minutes, orally narrating their sense-making process. Then, they could ask students, "what did you notice me doing?" and make note of the reading strategies and background knowledge that students identify. It is common practice in Reading Apprenticeship classrooms to routinely revisit and add to a collaboratively generated "Reader's Strategies List" as new texts and contexts are explored and discussed. Having begun to make some invisible reading moves visible, the instructor might invite students to continue thinking aloud with the text, either taking turns in the large group or working with a partner, followed by another whole-group metacognitive conversation about the different kinds of reading strategies and background knowledge that students brought to the task. All of this could happen relatively quickly, setting the stage for more engaged homework reading or for other kinds of collaborative work. Not all reading discussions must be metacognitive conversations, but routinely discussing reading processes and strategies normalizes authentic and constructivist learning. *Reading for Understanding* contains numerous "Classroom Close-Ups" describing how this kind of routine, low-stakes engagement in metacognitive conversations builds students' confidence and fluency with texts in general and supports disciplinary learning in particular.

As the college instructors who have authored chapters in this collection make clear, there are infinite ways that metacognitive conversations can be designed and set into motion. In "Reading Historically Through Metacognitive Logs," history professor Chris Padgett describes his use of double and triple entry metacognitive notetakers to support students in practicing and mastering the "cognitive subroutines" required for historical reading and thinking. In "Feel-the-Text," English professor Sue Lee describes an adaptation of Reading Apprenticeship's metacognitive annotation strategy, talk to the text, which further scaffolds engagement by focusing specifically on emotional connections and reactions to text. Andréa Pantoja Garvey describes the way that she supports metacognitive reflection in her fully online and asynchronous psychology classes, and in so doing creates the conditions for what she calls "restorative pedagogy." In "The Early Bird Special," Caren Kongshaug also describes her approach to establishing and maintaining the social and personal dimensions of learning, what she calls "courageous collaboration . . . a safe and inclusive environment where students feel welcomed, want to come to class, and engage in learning." Finally, Nanda Warren's "Snapshots of First-Year College Reading" notes (among other things) the importance of extensive reading to her college composition class, which is characterized by time spent "reading during class in pairs and groups, and text-based discussions . . . focused not on getting a 'right' answer but on posing and pursuing questions about a text." The Reading Apprenticeship framework provides concrete goals and guidelines for designing instruction but must be brought to life by the instructor's expertise and decision making about texts and tasks to focus on.

WHAT DOES READING APPRENTICESHIP LOOK LIKE IN (PROFESSIONAL LEARNING) PRACTICE?

Designing for this kind of instruction is time consuming and involves a lot of trial and error. Therefore, Reading Apprenticeship professional learning is experiential, inquiry-based, and problem based. Instructors are engaging in activities that they might consider integrating into their instruction, such as collaborating to create a "living list" of community agreements, reflecting on and discussing personal reading histories, capturing their reading processes and contributing to Reader's Strategies Lists, and practicing metacognitive routines such as think aloud and talk to the text. Practicing these routines as learners addresses the experience gap that poses a barrier to actually implementing such activities in our instruction. We tend to teach how we were taught, and most of us were not taught in active and constructivist ways, so immersing ourselves in the learner experience helps us to truly understand the mechanics, affordances, and limitations of instructional moves. Other activities in Reading Apprenticeship professional learning ask us to switch gears, to relinquish the "student hat" and put our "teacher hats" back on—these activities help instructors learn to design and facilitate text-based metacognitive conversations skillfully. Faculty practice analyzing the complexity and demands of particular texts and tasks for their fit with specific learning needs, and use student work and class discussion as ongoing formative assessment shaping instructional next steps. Reading Apprenticeship professional learning supports instructors' adaptive expertise as they learn to integrate discipline-specific reading strategy instruction into their teaching practices.

Access to Reading Apprenticeship professional learning is varied. In general, colleges and universities don't have consistent and predictable budgets or practices for supporting professional learning, and investment in faculty development by states and institutions tends to happen in fits and starts and with shifting foci. There is also a common, kneejerk negative reaction to the idea of supporting college reading among many stakeholders in higher education—as though literacy instruction should happen in primary and secondary contexts and *stay there*. This uncertain landscape has led to innovation and ingenuity for instructors and program developers trying to find ways to sustain and spread all kinds of professional learning, including learning about Reading Apprenticeship. A straightforward way to learn about the framework is simply to read the publications about it, namely *Reading for Understanding* and *Leading for Literacy*. However, for many faculty, as noted above, actually *practicing* metacognitive conversation as learners in community has been essential to developing a fuller understanding of the framework and the courage to actually implement new practices in the classroom. This can happen in a variety of ways.

The first college-focused Reading Apprenticeship professional development offerings by WestEd were in-person institutes and seminars, held at WestEd offices or hosted on college campuses and funded either by grants or by registration fees. In addition to opportunities to read about, practice, and discuss community building and metacognitive routines, a hallmark of these professional learning experiences is the use of classroom video case studies to support inquiry into effective teaching practices and metacognitive conversation in action. In 2011, WestEd partnered with college faculty to create an asynchronous online course that would support a deeper learning experience and also be much more accessible to instructors nationwide. Now known as "RA 101," this seven-week course asks participants to learn about, practice, and then try out core routines in their classes. These weekly "Making It Real" assignments—both the direction and scaffolding to try new classroom practices and the supportive community to discuss what happened—have become another hallmark of Reading Apprenticeship professional learning.

Several different face-to-face seminars and online courses have been developed to meet the needs and priorities of stakeholders over the years. An investment in STEM professional learning led to the development of STEM-specific in-person seminars and asynchronous online courses, featuring STEM college classroom video cases. Highly successful programs integrating Reading Apprenticeship into first-year experience contexts (summer bridge programs, first-year seminar courses, etc.) led to a "Reading Apprenticeship for FYE" seminar to help others create similar programs. When the Covid-19 pandemic forced all classroom and professional learning into remote formats in 2020, another round of innovations occurred. Planned grant-funded STEM professional development was adapted to an online learning community model that moved forward as a hybrid of two-hour synchronous (Zoom) workshops and asynchronous (Canvas) assignments over a period of 10 months, with an option to continue engaged for a second year in a learning community focused on honing facilitation skills. Though developed under duress, this model proved to be very effective at helping college instructors to implement meaningful, equity-centered, and culturally responsive pedagogical changes. The fully online format allowed for much greater participation across various groups of faculty than the face-to-face version could ever support. Evaluation of the two-year grant that funded this programming showed that participants experienced a robust sense of community in a virtual environment, shifted their perspective on the role of text in learning, significantly changed how and how much they used text in their classrooms, and reported greater transformational changes to their practice through sustained participation over two or more years (Hogan et al., 2023).

Clearly, sustained learning experiences are essential to support college faculty to uptake significant pedagogical changes. Just as clearly, funding for professional learning is not ample or consistent enough at the college level to reliably support sustained engagement. An understanding that college faculty must find ways to embed ongoing learning and engagement with the Reading Apprenticeship framework in their unique institutional and disciplinary contexts has always been foundational to the college programming designed by WestEd. The "Leadership Community of Practice" professional learning course is meant to support instructors to do just that—to design and facilitate Reading Apprenticeship professional learning in their contexts. It is critical to develop leaders and facilitators who can devise methods of maintaining the kind of sustained engagement that will lead to classroom and culture change. For example, Reading Apprenticeship leaders at California State University, Monterey Bay provide "Deepening Our Practice" workshops through the university's Center for Teaching, Learning, and Assessment (TLA), bringing faculty together to share their ongoing practice implementing Reading Apprenticeship routines in their classrooms. At other institutions, such as Pasadena City College and Fitchburg State University, integrating Reading Apprenticeship into the professional learning required to teach a first-year seminar course means that new faculty are introduced to and supported to implement the framework every year. These examples provide helpful insight and direction for other faculty and institutions, but in truth it can be quite difficult for faculty to find the combination of resources, collaborators, institutional will and vision, leadership aptitude, and facilitation skills to establish this kind of programming on campus. In the final section of this chapter, I will describe two of the distinct practices that distinguish Reading Apprenticeship professional learning and that have supported the personal and professional transformations described in the chapters that follow—and my own.

PERSONAL HISTORY AND POWERFUL PRACTICES: FACILITATION APPRENTICESHIPS AND COMMUNITY OF PRACTICE APPROACH

I came to Reading Apprenticeship professional learning for the first time in 2007 well aware that my doctoral work on the novels of Toni Morrison, Philip Roth, and Chang Rae Lee had not prepared me to teach English composition at an open access community college. I knew I had a lot to learn about everything, and especially about the mysterious territory of how to support my students as readers. However, I also had very low expectations for the five-day professional learning experience I had signed up for and was mostly engaged in planning to explore the San Francisco bay area with my wife. I hadn't read the preparatory materials sent to me in advance of the institute, hadn't done the homework reading, and showed up late to what I assumed was a "conference." I was stunned to have my socks knocked off by rigorous, relevant, inquiry-based, hands-on learning activities that were clearly research-based and rooted in equity principles. I had never experienced this kind of learning. At the end of day 1, I went back to the hotel room and did my reading homework. I was hooked.

My first attempts to incorporate Reading Apprenticeship into my teaching were, as most people find, very uneven. Most of the social and personal activities worked well, but those were the dimensions where I already did pretty well as an instructor. I was good at building relationships and trust, but struggled to support my students to push themselves academically, to dig into challenging texts and tasks. The cognitive and knowledge-building dimensions were areas where I needed to work. Unfortunately, those were the areas where I flopped early and often. Introducing my students to think aloud for the first time, I was immediately daunted by their bored, heavy-lidded stares and abandoned the activity with a sweaty feeling of "never again." The first time I implemented a structured protocol for discussion, which took 45 minutes when I did it as a participant in the summer institute, the students each said about three words and were "done" in three minutes. I was a novice. I didn't know how to scaffold engagement, how to coach students to reveal their thinking in useful ways, how to explain the relevance of activities, and how to adapt wonderful lessons created by others to my students, context, and learning goals.

After several years of continuing to show up at different Reading Apprenticeship professional learning opportunities and continued classroom trial and error with inconsistent results, I was accepted into a new grant-funded program to develop faculty leaders in the California community college system. This turned out to be an extended years-long apprenticeship as a Reading Apprenticeship facilitator. We began as participant observers in summer seminars. We had access to the facilitator agendas that described the professional learning in great detail, and as we participated, we kept notes on what we noticed in terms of table or whole-group interactions. We would stay after each session with the facilitators to review participant feedback and to discuss our observations. Gradually, we were invited to take on the role of facilitator, choosing small parts of an agenda to lead, and continuing to participate in the reflective debrief after each session, where it was normalized to discuss the successes and the difficulties in facilitation and to use participant feedback as formative assessment to plan for the next day's learning. Working with the facilitation agendas, I came to deeper understanding of why and how metacognitive conversation works. Leading other faculty in beautifully designed inquiries and learning sequences, I got to experience what happens when they go well, and my confidence back in the classroom soared. Through my facilitation apprenticeship, I actually learned how to teach.

The transformational facilitation apprenticeship experience that I had is difficult to replicate for other faculty. The leadership program culminated with the development of a three-hour in-person introductory workshop, which those of us who had apprenticed as facilitators traveled around the state to offer at various community colleges. Facilitating Reading Apprenticeship professional learning on campuses other than my own further developed my leadership and confidence, and the workshop itself was effective at raising interest and awareness in the approach. But a three-hour stand-alone workshop was not effective in helping instructors to truly understand the framework or meaningfully change their instruction. The truth is that it takes years of learning and study as well as sometimes painful practice to change how you teach, but our institutions continue to offer "one and done" "tips and tricks" kinds of professional learning offerings. We are trying to take apart and rebuild an engine, and we receive coupon after coupon for free oil changes and windshield wiper fluid refills. How do you invite colleagues into deeper and more sustained social learning, when it is not part of their job description, not compensated, and not easy?

In 2011, about six months after I was invited by the developers of Reading Apprenticeship to continue my apprenticeship with them by leading the college-level work for WestEd (in addition to my teaching load), the director of the California Community Colleges' Success Network (3CSN) invited me to take a break from teaching and to build a statewide community of practice (CoP) in Reading Apprenticeship for the 116 California community colleges. As it turns out, the CoP approach was the perfect way to try to pass on, at scale, the intensive professional learning I had experienced. 3CSN invested in deep professional learning such as the Leadership Community of Practice for cohorts of faculty and also sponsored many introductory Reading Apprenticeship workshops around the state. In combination, these activities provided the opportunity to grow a cross-disciplinary leadership team and to extend facilitation apprenticeships to many other faculty. The emerging leaders produced new innovations and enlivened the work in their classrooms, on their campuses, and within our CoP. The college-level work on Reading Apprenticeship grew exponentially, and 3CSN flourished as the framework and the best practices around facilitation that we learned from WestEd permeated the way we approached all professional learning.

3CSN developed several statewide CoPs based on promising educational frameworks and practices, and as coordinators, we studied best practices for this kind of social learning. Wenger (2000) defines a CoP as something "alive," which, as we mention in the introduction in the context of "apprenticeship" into academic disciplines, aims to balance "reification" (building shared language, discourse, and understanding about a topic) with "participation" (infusing new and diverse perspectives into the community's engagement with a topic). Studies have shown that effective CoPs create an environment that combines the familiar with the new, emphasizes sustained collaboration, allows for organic evolution, fosters dialogue among diverse perspectives, and provides a space for practitioners to share their problems, needs, and knowledge (Wenger, 2000; Reed et al., 2014).

The Reading Apprenticeship framework works beautifully as a CoP focal point. This stable framework maintains the necessary reification for the community, while the innovations required for instructors to utilize the framework in their contexts continue to breathe new life into the community. Furthermore, in Reading Apprenticeship professional learning, a focus on the social and personal dimensions of learning nurtures relationships and encourages all learners to fully participate. Metacognitive conversations, which focus on the process of reading and thinking, promote new insights and different perspectives. Structured participation routines help to break down hierarchies and disrupt the common dynamic of a few voices dominating the conversation. These conversations can also address tensions that arise due to "discourse mismatch" (Paulson, 2012, p. 7) by surfacing confusions and negotiating meaning. The emphasis on making the invisible processes of reading visible is extremely helpful for efforts to collaborate across different discourse communities, such as academic disciplines or roles on campus, educational institutions and levels, and different cultural backgrounds.

Building and maintaining the Reading Apprenticeship CoP in California, and extending that work nationwide over more than a decade, we have learned a lot about how to sustain social learning in community. We have observed a methodology that supports individuals to cross the conceptual thresholds that enable the shifts in ontology and identity—how we understand ourselves and our work as educators—that in turn underlie true transformation of educational practices (Costino, 2018). Changing how you teach is like changing how you parent. We read powerful and convincing theories about it, we make plans and have excellent intentions, but in the moment, especially in high-stakes, crucial moments, we tend to revert back to old muscle memories and well-worn cognitive pathways. We do what was done to us. We model what was modeled for us. We can change, but it takes a long time, a lot of routine metacognitive reflection, continuous knowledge building, low-stakes opportunities to practice, and a supportive community around us who get what we are trying to do. At best, when we focus on enacting what we know to be true about how people learn, we understand how much we need each other to try to make sense of an overwhelming world. We know we are not just "covering content" but inspiring and enabling new ideas, insights, and practices. We aren't teaching in our disciplines simply to replicate them, but to pass on useful ways of thinking, problem solving, and communicating, to see what we know brought to new life in the form of better insights, better solutions, and better institutional structures.

Communities of practice are built to evolve. External forces, including the Covid-19 pandemic, continue to change what the opportunities for college instructors to participate in Reading Apprenticeship professional learning look like, and that's as it should be. Our work as educators doesn't happen on stable ground. The world changes around us as we work. Still, the chapters in this book represent one of the core ways that we keep our CoP alive, nurturing our current participants and extending an invitation outward to newcomers. In this collection, we tell our stories, we share our assignments, we explain the latest hacks we have developed. These are ways we have relied on a common framework, and enlivened it with our innovations, so that we can do the work we came here to do. To locate and reach for our own potential. To help students and colleagues do the same. To make the promise of higher education real.

APPENDIX—READING APPRENTICESHIP ROUTINES AND TERMINOLOGY

Capturing the Reading Process

This activity is a first step toward discussing reading strategies. Readers engage with a short text in order to understand it, then reflect on the process and strategies they used to make sense of it.

Golden Lines

By golden lines, we mean a phrase or sentence or group of sentences that struck you as interesting, surprising, key, or perhaps lines you would like to hear others' opinions about.

Metacognitive Log, also known as Evidence/Interpretation Notetaker or Double Entry Journal

Metacognitive logs provide a place for students to think and write about their own reading process with extended assignments, such as textbook chapters, whole books, the texts for a course project, or for other media such as videos, math problems, observations in a science lab. The Evidence/Interpretation Notetaker is one kind of Metacognitive log.

Personal Reading History

Remembering and sharing our own journeys toward our current state of literacy can be a great way to build community. This reflective activity provides prompts for students to consider regarding their own development as readers, then provides opportunities for sharing in pairs and sharing insights as a whole group.

Norms, Also Known as Community Agreements

In this activity, participants in a learning community collaborate to generate a working list of agreements for how they would like the learning community to function. For example, students might be asked to freewrite about past learning experiences that were particularly powerful, enjoyable, or productive and to generate a list of qualities that were present in the learning space. They can then suggest actions, attitudes, or processes to create that kind of positive learning environment in the current class. Norms or community agreements are usually considered to be a "living list," frequently revisited to fine tune the agreements and to make the "rules of engagement" transparent and explicit.

Think Aloud

Think alouds ask readers to verbalize their thinking as they read. Readers interrupt their reading to talk or think out loud about the text, visualize the text, make connections, sort through puzzlements, make predictions, and ask questions about the text.

Talking to the Text (or talk to the text)

This routine is similar to a think aloud because it is a reading process analysis, and it is done while reading a text. Most importantly, talking to the text (TttT) is first completed individually or as a private reading experience. Readers are asked to mark their texts so that they have a means of revisiting their thinking. Also, readers have time to process their text, reread for comprehension, make detailed annotations on the text, question the material, and draw inferences and conclusions, which take time to derive.

Think-Pair-Share

Think-pair-share is a discourse routine we use to refer to reflective thinking about text, pairing up to listen and further reflect on the text, and then sharing our thoughts on the text. This routine supports metacognitive conversation as readers learn about the reading processes of others.

Reading Strategies List

A Reading Strategies List is a group-generated compilation of strategies that readers identify as part of their process in working through comprehending a text. Prompts that help readers identify their strategies can be open-ended, such as:

- "What did you do to make sense of this text?"
- "Where did you encounter challenges?"
- "What did you do to help with these challenges?"

As participants offer their responses to these open-ended questions, skillful teachers can probe further with follow-up questions that help deepen understanding of the diverse kinds of thinking/reading processes. Samples of effective probing questions on participants' reading processes include:

- "Where in the text did you use that strategy?"
- "How did it help you?"

Through these probing questions, Reading Strategies Lists can reflect more nuanced kinds of reading processes. This list helps provide a common classroom language for discussing how to approach various texts as it captures the reading processes of a classroom. These lists should be posted in the classroom; students will refer to these strategy lists when their texts demand more academic and varied reading skills. Rather than a static list of recommended strategies, a Reading Strategies List is a living document coming out of specific reading experiences that all members of a class community can add to over time.

TAPPS (think-aloud paired problem solving)

Developed by James E. Stice at the University of Texas at Austin, TAPPS is a routine in which students in pairs support each other in articulating their problem-solving processes. A listener prompts a problem solver to think aloud as the reader talks through a problem—of reading, chemistry, math, or any other domain.

There are many other routines in *Reading for Understanding*.

Chapter 2

The College STEM Reading Apprenticeship Classroom

Theresa Martin

I began my career as a professor of biology at College of San Mateo in 1995, after earning several science degrees. During my work as a graduate student, I was fortunate enough to be a teaching assistant and take a certificate program on college teaching. This inspired a career in teaching and a focus on making iterative improvements to my teaching to adapt to the needs of students each semester. However, much of the early professional development that I did was done as one-off workshops, and the changes I implemented were done in isolation, behind the closed doors of the classroom. In 2012, after hearing about Reading Apprenticeship for the first time, I enrolled in a three-day summer workshop. Little did I know that the connections formed during that summer would lead me to more than a decade of involvement and career enhancement in the Reading Apprenticeship community of practice (CoP).

Learning about Reading Apprenticeship was like seeing a ray of light coming through the darkness. I had long worried that my method of providing all the content to students, and not requiring reading, was doing a disservice to students. How would they gain independence and skills that would allow them to learn autonomously beyond my classroom? But when I considered ways to coach students through developing critical thinking skills and problem-based learning, I struggled to find a curriculum that could support that type of learning in STEM.

Reading Apprenticeship filled that gap by providing training and support that allowed me to help students learn by constructing their own knowledge from the reading. I began by incorporating the Social and Personal Dimensions (Schoenbach et al., 2012; Greenleaf et al., 2023) into my teaching. This intentional support of students' academic identity and collaborative learning led to classrooms that included rich discussions of prior knowledge and thought processes around texts. With students encouraged to "make their thinking visible," a generative cycle of finding confusions, addressing them, and exploring further took place. I also got to see strengths each student brings to the class.

Working on changing my classroom practices, and sharing my struggles and successes with a community of STEM faculty at my college, led to greater leadership roles on campus. Excited by the work happening in the sciences, our academic senate declared Reading Apprenticeship to be their highest-ranking institutional priority in 2013, and I was asked to serve as professional development coordinator and to present a proposal to institutionalize Reading Apprenticeship to the Institutional Planning and Budget Committee. Throughout all of this leadership development in my campus, I was continuing to be supported by the Reading

Apprenticeship CoP, continuing with leadership professional learning and being "apprenticed" as a facilitator. I was invited to help lead a community of practice for STEM faculty in California from 2014 to 2017 and also served as a lead facilitator for a grant project supported by the California Learning Lab called "Equity in STEM through Deeper Learning and Metacognitive Conversation." This grant, designed for community college and CSU faculty during the Covid-19 pandemic, created a structured learning community model for sustained engagement in Reading Apprenticeship professional learning. The program consisted of monthly Zoom workshops focusing on shared readings, collaborative curriculum development, and sharing outcomes and reflections from experimental teaching approaches. Participants had the option of participating for one or two years.

Evidence gathered from this STEM learning community suggested its effectiveness in reshaping practitioners' understanding of text's role in learning (Hogan et al., 2023). Some of the highlights of the program included participants reporting they felt supported to adopt student-centered disciplinary literacy activities. Their projects centered on surfacing metacognitive strategies used to comprehend complex STEM texts, and co-constructing understanding of the disciplinary practices used to solve problems. This approach, apprenticing students into discussions about texts and metacognitive strategies, was anecdotally reported to have nurtured students' confidence and proficiency in the disciplines.

The Reading Apprenticeship seminal work *Reading for Understanding* (Schoenbach et al., 2012), and the subsequent *Leading for Literacy* (Schoenbach et al., 2017) highly recommends practitioner classroom observations to support the work of faculty communities of practice (CoPs). However, while our learning communities offered mentorship and coaching, logistical constraints limited opportunities for classroom observations within the community, hindering the potential for valuable insights from this practice. In order to provide support to CoP instructors, and gain insights into how the CoP supported faculty in the classroom, I took a sabbatical semester to serve as a peer observer in several CoP instructors' classrooms and online courses. My primary inquiry was understanding how STEM faculty incorporated the tenets of the Reading Apprenticeship framework into their teaching practices. My investigation goal was to see how CoP practitioners used scaffolded work around texts to create active, student-centered construction of understanding in unique STEM disciplines. Using the Reading Apprenticeship framework (Schoenbach et al., 2012, p. 25) in a nonevaluative, appreciative manner, the observations aimed to uncover faculty skills in text selection, task design, and facilitation of robust student discussions, crucial for deeper learning and disciplinary literacy development.

METHODS

I adopted a Classroom Observation Protocol from *Leading for Literacy* (Schoenbach et al., 2017, p. 182). This protocol prescribes a collaborative, inquiry-based process, and ensures a safe and comfortable experience for the observed. This was important because being observed is often feared by faculty, who can be reticent to expose their teaching practices to others (Graham et al., 2021). It also allowed for shared reflection on the teaching practices, and offered guideposts for both observer and observee by asking each to reflect on "What a Reading Apprenticeship Classroom Looks Like" (Schoenbach et al., 2012, pp. 337–338). The protocol includes a pre-observation conference, where the instructor shared

- background information about the class;
- their plan for the lesson, including what text they were using, and how they would use it;

- content and metacognitive goals for the session; and
- framing questions for the observer.

Additionally, the two faculty review "What a Reading Apprenticeship Classroom Looks Like," which provides guiding signposts for both the instructor and the observer.

During the observations, I used a two-column notetaker for evidence and interpretation and recorded the audio during in-person classes. I had the goals of noticing

- how instructors incorporated reading or texts into the learning session;
- alignment with "What a Reading Apprenticeship Classroom Looks Like";
- instructor practices that supported metacognition;
- student talk and/or moves that showed they were being metacognitive and considering ways of knowing in addition to learning the content of the lesson;
- evidence of collaboration; and
- classroom dynamics that showed shared power of disciplinary content and disciplinary literacy.

I also considered the framing question of each instructor and noted evidence to provide the instructor about the framing question.

Each observation was followed by a post-observation conference that allowed us to jointly reflect on the experience and consider implications for moving forward in their practice. The post-observation debrief protocol is especially effective at creating a trusting collaboration between observer and observee. It addresses the framing questions of the instructor, requiring the observer to consider the needs of the observed faculty member. It also asks for joint reflection on how the class activities aligned with the Reading Apprenticeship framework, impressions of the session from the instructor's perspective, and a joint reflection on the observation process itself.

RESULTS

I was able to coordinate peer observations with seven members of the STEM CoP from institutions across the state. Four observations were from community colleges and three were from California State Universities. Disciplines observed included math, computer science, biology, chemistry, and environmental science. A couple of the observations were in the online environment and were thus limited in their observation scope.

Findings

How Instructors Incorporated Reading or Texts into the Learning Session

STEM textbooks often follow a prescribed plan of learning with subsequent lessons building on prior ones. Since many STEM courses are themselves prerequisites for other courses, these textbooks often serve as a proxy for the course curriculum. However, many STEM instructors, in spite of requiring a textbook, and assigning reading in the textbook, often lecture on the same content as the textbook, and don't incorporate lessons on how to use or understand the textbook.

The instructors from our Reading Apprenticeship CoP diverged from the traditional method of "covering" the textbook content in lecture in a number of ways. Most of the CoP instructors assigned short sections of textbook readings prior to class. Sometimes the assigned reading was scaffolded with inquiry prompts and notetakers. Whether assigned prior to class or assigned as in-class reading, all of the observed classes had text that served as a basis for students to collaborate on shared work. The instructors' lessons invited their students to make meaning from the assigned texts and apply that understanding to problems or scenarios that built from this understanding. The class sessions were heavily focused on the texts as a resource for understanding class content, with the professors actively referring to the texts, modeling thinking around the texts, and supporting students' efforts to understand the texts.

As an example, one professor used an article on machine learning on the first day of her computer science class to invite her students into the world of artificial intelligence, which the course was about. She used the article to develop an inquiry into what students already knew and invited them to build their understanding from their foundation of prior knowledge. The routine she used was Capture Your Reading Process (Schoenbach et al., 2012, pp. 94–95), which prompted students to consider how they made meaning from the text, and note those strategies on a shared Google doc. The class was then brought back to discuss these reading strategies.

In another example, in an environmental studies class, the professor utilized a text set (Schoenbach et al., 2012, pp.144–146) to introduce students to the concept of graphs as conveyors of information. The homework text set was expanded during the class session with new data sets and graphs for discussion being added. This instructor's content goal was for students to consider how graphical elements could be utilized to convey information most effectively, and her use of varied examples created multiple learning opportunities.

How Instructors Supported Student Efforts to Comprehend Texts

At the pre-observation conference with each of the seven observed instructors, the instructors discussed their goals for their students' literacy development in the observed lesson. Every instructor had an explicit goal for addressing students' literacy skills within their course context. They shared with me how they saw their lesson plan supporting this goal. In each of the lessons I observed, the reading responsibilities that were given to the students were supported by some type of scaffolded support. In some cases, this support took the form of a notetaker with prompts that asked students to notice their thinking; for example, one professor asked her students to note surprising ideas and questions from the readings. Another class's notetaker asked students to explain how they could recognize a binary ionic compound, using the textbook as a resource.

The instructors had activities in class that also supported students' comprehension of texts. In one of the most successful iterations of this support, instructor Erin Wall, in a synchronous Zoom session for her college algebra class, modeled solving a linear equation problem, and asked students to notice what strategies she was using during her think aloud routine. Students shared their observations and reflections on Erin's methods, including how she checked for errors in her process, made predictions, and made decisions about what step to do next in the process. Erin validated their responses by writing these strategies down on a Reading Strategies List for the whole class to use, and spotlighted several strategies such as rereading, positive self-talk, verifying your work progress, and using fix-ups for errors. She followed up this metacognitive discussion with a breakout room activity in which small groups of students used the think aloud routine to work on related problems. The think aloud was supported by whiteboards assigned to each group, so that they could note their equations, notes, and plots on the board to share with the class later. As the class returned from the breakout rooms, Erin probed students' thinking using their whiteboards as reference. Some questions she used included "When you drew this line, how did you do it?" and "How did you find the height [for the area of a triangle]?" She continued to point out effective strategies for problem solving. Erin finished the session by asking students to make a video of themselves Thinking Aloud to share in a Canvas discussion about their processes and strategies for problem solving. She noted in our post-observation conference that students did very well in the discussion, surfacing their strategies and using language of metacognition.

Evidence of metacognitive inquiry into reading and thinking processes; student talk and/or moves that showed they were being metacognitive and considering ways of knowing in addition to learning the content of the lesson.

In every class, I observed students grappling with meaning making and surfacing their processes for interacting with text. It was clear that students had been normed into metacognitive inquiry as a class process and were comfortable sharing confusions and strategies with one another. A big part of metacognitive discussion is the social interaction required. Students need to feel safe to voice questions and confusions, and to offer up their thinking processes to their peers and instructor. I saw an environment of comfort and interest in co-construction of knowledge in almost every class I visited. Instructors had clearly spent time and effort creating the conditions in which metacognitive conversation can be successful.

In one biology class, students were using reading homework to answer questions from a "reading quiz." They worked in small groups to figure out the terminology in the quiz and apply it to concepts related to evolutionary adaptations of echinoderms and arthropods. The instructor prepped the students for the work by asking: "So when you don't know what something is, how do you go about figuring out what it is? Like what's your thought process or what's the actual physical thing that you do?" When a student responded "you look it up," she probed more deeply to get some more strategies and shared some of her own strategies. She prompted students to surface their own strategies as they worked through the quiz. Some of the shared dialogue I heard from students included:

- "Yeah, it's on page 17."
- "Oh . . . so internal means . . . "
- "I don't know what that word is . . . dioecious, hmm."

In another class, calculus, students worked in small groups to work on sample problems from the text. The instructor encouraged students to break down the problems and share their thinking around confusions and challenges they were having. Examples of what students said as they engaged with the problems include:

- "I was thinking it was like . . . "
- "Remember what we did last time."
- "I think she said solve for K first."
- "I'm confused."
- "Are you saying . . . ?"

A final example comes from a computer science class on artificial intelligence. Students were asked to capture what strategies they noticed themselves using while reading an informational article on artificial intelligence. They reported on their processes on a shared Google doc. The Google doc shows students reported using such strategies as skimming the text, using the headings to get their bearings, trying to "get the gist" of the article, and highlighting or notetaking on key words and phrases within the article.

What Routines, Tools, Strategies, or Processes Were Used in Service of Comprehension

Each STEM class used structured routines to support metacognitive conversations and ignite problem-solving collaborations. Think aloud was the most commonly used, along with a metacognitive notetaker to provide guidance for student thinking and talking. However, in STEM courses where comprehension of intricate concepts is required, many instructors chose to infuse a touch of flexibility into the think aloud by not timing the talk of each partner in favor of a more organic collaboration. They instructed students to work in pairs to solve problems.

It was evident from my observations that the instructors had laid the groundwork for success from the outset. Their careful scaffolding ensured that students grasped the need for effective collaboration required in these routines. In each class, I saw a hubbub of shared effort as students delved into texts and problems alike, embracing the softened think aloud routine with enthusiasm and camaraderie.

When using metacognitive logs, most instructors tailored the prompts to the content the students were reading. For example, in Becky Talyn's environmental science class, students were given two text pieces and a TED talk to "read" about data visualization techniques as preparation for the class lesson I observed. Students were asked to comment on the following questions as part of the homework:

- What is the value of good data visualizations?
- How will they help you share information with others in your Environmental Proposal and your Research Symposium presentation?
- How will they help you in ways unrelated to the course?
- What is the most useful idea from David McCandless's TED talk?

This sort of tailored instruction occurred in almost every class I observed, making me appreciate the thought instructors had put into providing support for their students in their discipline.

Other practices also caught my attention as an observer and leader of our community of practice. These practices showed an understanding of the value of metacognition and the Reading Apprenticeship framework by the instructor using them. These included reflective questions for students about how much they felt they understood after a unit, a shared Google doc for students to populate and review about their reading practices, and a text set composed of a series of graphs and data that underwent a collaborative process of analysis in class.

Evidence of Collaboration

One of the greatest takeaways from these seven observations was the spirit of collaboration that radiated from each class. The instructors had put social collaboration to work to leverage learning in their disciplines. In order to achieve this culture of inquiry and collaboration, each instructor had to create an environment in which it was safe for students to share confusions and make attempts to solve problems in spite of the danger of "being wrong." Some routines that instructors shared with me that they used to develop this sense of community and safety included Personal Reading History (Schoenbach et al., 2012, pp. 78–80), and setting up class norms together (Schoenbach et al., 2012, pp. 63–64). In the personal reading history routine, instructors also had to share their own reading history and obstacles and challenges they faced as students as a way to model the talk between students. This openness, along with being explicit about the expectation of collaboration, respect, and shared learning, sets up an environment where students and teacher co-construct understanding, with students taking the lead on understanding at some times, and the teacher taking the lead at other times.

This model of work was evidenced in most of the classes I observed, with the lead for understanding shifting back and forth between students and instructor. When students took the lead in their pair or small-group collaborations, the instructors were right on hand to provide support, probe for deeper understanding, and encourage students to persist in the face of challenges.

Two of the classes I observed were online classes, and in those classes students worked together in breakout rooms and in online class discussions. The instructors were able to see the outcomes of the breakout room work by using shared digital notetakers; in one case a digital whiteboard was used for each group, and in the other case a shared Google doc for the class. The instructors were able to give feedback and support by having a shared discussion about these products in the online setting.

One other notable element of collaboration that I observed was that one instructor asked each group of students to create a deliverable product that incorporated their understanding of the concepts they were learning. The deliverable was a lesson plan for a 2nd-grade math lesson. The lesson plan was shared in a poster that was reviewed by their peers during a Gallery Walk. The instructor modeled what good feedback looked like, and provided a format for the peer review that was done online. This additional element of collaborative work had the effect of deepening students' understanding of the concepts involved, and developing students' constructive feedback skills.

Classroom Dynamics That Showed Shared Power of Disciplinary Content and Disciplinary Literacy (i.e., Equity)

In each class I observed there were practices that promoted equity and inclusion. The list that follows spotlights each class I observed.

1. **Pairing Students for Equal Participation**: By pairing students, the instructor ensured that each student had an opportunity to actively engage in the learning process. This reduced the likelihood of any student feeling marginalized or left out, promoting equity in participation.
2. **Respect for Each Group's Contribution**: By requiring students to begin peer reviews with an appreciation or affirmation, the instructor established a culture of respect and recognition for diverse perspectives. This ensured that every group's contributions were valued and acknowledged, fostering an equitable learning environment.
3. **Fostering Social Support and Accountability**: The instructor cultivated a sense of community within the class, where students showed respect for each other and collaborated effectively. This social support system promotes equity by ensuring that all students feel included and supported in their learning journey.
4. **Confidence in Students' Abilities**: By demonstrating confidence in her students' ability to develop insights and make meaningful contributions, the instructor empowered them

to succeed regardless of setbacks. This instilled a sense of equity by valuing each student's potential and providing support as needed.
5. **Valuing All Contributions**: The instructor invited each student to share their thinking, demonstrating that all contributions were valued and respected. This promotes equity by ensuring that every voice is heard and considered in the learning process.
6. **Empowering Students to Take the Lead**: By allowing students to take the lead on developing a reading strategies list and discussing their prior knowledge, the instructor empowered them to take ownership of their learning. This practice acknowledged and valued students' existing knowledge and experiences, promoting equity in the classroom.
7. **Treating Every Student as a Valued Member**: The instructor cultivated a strong sense of community by treating each student as a valued member of the class. Learning names and using them demonstrated a personal investment in each student's success, while calling on students to describe their thoughts and processes promoted equity by focusing on individual contributions rather than right or wrong answers.

CONCLUSION

The classroom observations and pre- and post-observation conferences were incredibly valuable for understanding how our professional development community supported the work of instructors in the classroom. I am very appreciative of the work these instructors did to bring active learning and an inquiry-based approach to their students. This shift in focus from teacher-centered practice to student-centered practice is extremely challenging and requires a huge commitment to shift the instructional paradigm.

As STEM educators, many of us were trained to uphold the objective and impersonal nature of science, emphasizing the need to remove personal biases from our teaching. However, the Reading Apprenticeship approach teaches us otherwise, illuminating the profound influence of social and personal dimensions on the learning journey. Recognizing this critical concept compels teachers to redefine their roles in the classroom, prioritizing activities that foster collaboration and nurture students' development of a science identity. It was gratifying to see that instructors had internalized these elements of the Reading Apprenticeship framework by incorporating these elements into their classes. These cases highlight the effectiveness of Reading Apprenticeship in fostering inclusivity, comfort, and student engagement.

Another prominent theme that emerged from the observations of the seven faculty members was how adaptable the Reading Apprenticeship approach is across diverse STEM disciplines. The case reports showcase various classroom settings where instructors successfully implemented Reading Apprenticeship strategies to engage students and enhance learning outcomes. This adaptability underscores the versatility of Reading Apprenticeship in promoting active, inquiry-based learning irrespective of the subject matter. Additionally, it supports the notion that the professional learning and support provided by our community of practice was successful in providing the understanding and skills faculty needed to successfully transform their practice.

Lastly, it is worth mentioning a unique contextual challenge these instructors faced to transform their practice. Implementing innovative research-based teaching methods like Reading Apprenticeship runs counter to older traditional STEM education values of lecture and Socratic method, posing hurdles for educators. Of particular note is the idea of instructors being facilitators of learning by students as opposed to purveyors of content. Faculty may face resistance or skepticism to this idea as they navigate changing their practice. There can be pressure to go back to more traditional teaching methods from colleagues, the institution, and even the students. The successful engagement of students observed in these cases illustrates the strength and commitment these seven faculty had for this work. It also made me consider the importance of ongoing support from communities of practice to navigate this challenge. The success of these faculty in reforming their practice drives home how collaborative learning communities, reflective practices, and nonevaluative peer observations can serve as crucial support mechanisms. These supports aided these seven instructors in embracing and effectively implementing these methods, fostering the transformation of classroom learning toward active, student-centered learning.

Chapter 3

Exponential, Not Linear: Designing for the Four Dimensions in Noncredit ESL

Tiffany Ingle

No one engages on Zoom. It's black boxes. That is predominantly what teachers reflected in meetings and in emails about struggles over student engagement. Our 14-hour-per-week noncredit English classes had moved fully online in March of 2020. Fourteen hours is a lot of Zoom for anyone. One year later, we were at the anniversary of the pandemic closure with connection and community at a low. On January 6, the nation was rocked with an attack on the Capitol by a mob of rioters. On March 16, 2021, the fifth week of class, there was yet another mass shooting—this one targeting Asian women working at massage parlors in Atlanta. Just one semester before, the conflict with Azerbaijan and Armenia over the area called Artsakh impacted our student population due to its mix of Russian and Armenian immigrants, causing unprecedented drops from classes. Now, our Asian students were feeling unsafe in their daily lives. My students needed a space to increase their confidence in light of everything happening around them.

How can language learning happen in this kind of environment?

Building community is not linear, it's exponential in payoff. Do not underestimate how much the first five weeks of class can impact how far students can go beyond your expectations. I remember this concept from my first experience with Reading Apprenticeship. This concept pushed me to start the practice of thoughtfully designing the way that the personal and social dimensions layered into the first five weeks of class. Before this, I had been very focused on content organization and tweaking it endlessly for better results. For spring 2021, I had spent a lot of time developing how the first five weeks would build the personal, social, cognitive, and knowledge-building dimensions of the course in light of the tumultuous external environment that our noncredit students were facing.

The week one, two, three, and four "is this working?" anxiety is real for me as I see the students dealing with hard things and as our class asks more of them each week. Thoughts of "was that project just too much?" "Was this book a horrible idea?"

CLASSROOM SNAPSHOT

On March 18, 2021, it was the last day of our fifth week of class. I had been wondering to myself all week, "Did setting up the social and personal over these first weeks do what it needed to?" That Thursday, we were engaging in our weekly reading time about the book *Born a Crime* (2020) by Trevor Noah. It was a heavy section, and students completed reading logs to bring to class on Zoom and have discussions about golden lines that represented difficult passages for them. We discussed a few things and then after a breakout room session where students were with a partner discussing their golden lines and what they had written in their evidence and interpretation logs, a silence happened, and a brave Asian student, Hannah (this name has been anonymized) started a discussion.

Hannah asked, "If I speak with an accent, do Americans really think I'm less intelligent?"

"Let's make sure everyone is with us because this is a big conversation. Are you on page 49? Where it is talking about speaking differently and racism? Can you read the passage that you're talking about, or would you like me to read it?" I clarified.

Hannah continued, "Yes, because is this saying that Americans will see me as not smart no matter what I do? I've learned a new language to be here but if they see me as not smart . . . and those women were shot just because they worked at that massage parlor. I can't do anything."

"Wow, yes, and we have talked about that shooting a little bit this week, too. Let's all read this passage and then talk about it. I'll read it for us. Can everyone find page 49 and find the part that starts right after the word 'tricked?' Let me know you're there with a thumbs up."

I read from page 49, "'If you're racist, and you meet someone who doesn't look like you, the fact that he can't speak like you reinforces your racist preconceptions: He's different, less intelligent. A brilliant scientist can come over the border from Mexico to live in America, but if he speaks in broken English, people say, 'Eh, I don't trust this guy.' 'But he's a scientist.' 'In Mexican science, maybe. I don't trust him.'"

A discussion started that included a lot of questions and connections to the things in the text, clarifying, deepening, making connections. The text was on the screen and students were pointing out different parts of it. I asked if anyone was willing to share whether they'd had an experience like this. And I started by telling an experience I'd had when I lived in Asia and said some really incorrect things and was thought to be stupid. Students added experiences and continued to deepen the connections to the text and other parts of the book. Finally, the student who had started the discussion said, "But teacher, can you just tell us your direct opinion, as an American? Is this how it is here? Will people always see us as stupid? Or less smart than someone with a better accent? Be direct, please."

At that moment, I thought about all the work we had done to be connected as a class, to know each other beyond ice breakers and into a social dimension where we knew who each other was and where we were all from. I thought about how much of the personal dimension was unseen until we got into metacognitive conversations about texts that challenged who students want to become and how they hope this new life can be. What have they gotten themselves into, moving to a new country? And I paused and said, "To be honest, some people always will, but many won't. The right people will see who you are and find out more about who you are. Others will put you in a 'box' and not let you out of it. This is true for everyone whether it is accent, clothes, weight, race, car, anything. But finding the right people changes everything." The conversation extended much beyond the intended time, but turned into recognizing—how can you recognize the right people? And how can you know your worth beyond these labels? They shared about how they had met "right people." They also shared things that made this class feel like a special space where they could believe we were right people. They questioned whether that was really safe to believe about each other. And we discussed what it would take for that to remain true.

All during this conversation, they were using advanced vocabulary and grammar structures that we had learned to grapple with complex ideas that they were experiencing in English. They were also providing examples from their lives that supported various points or counterpoints. But without the social and the personal foundation that we actively built in our first five weeks, this conversation would have been very different.

SETTING UP THE FIRST FIVE WEEKS

Thinking through what I hoped for the students in spring semester, I wanted them to experience the four dimensions: personal breakthrough in their English learning confidence—"English identity," community with others who were like them, opportunities to deal with ambiguity together, and a clear sense of building skills and knowledge related to their goals.

When I first started making a shift to using a Reading Apprenticeship approach, this layering was one of the most challenging parts. Managing all those dimensions all the time overwhelmed me. Over years of trying things and reflecting, things became more natural. The increased metacognitive conversation that students engage in became clear feedback to help the growth moves in each subsequent semester of teaching.

The Personal Dimension: Don't Wait!

The pre-course welcome letter serves as a perfect personal connection between teacher and student. Students receive a letter welcoming them and asking them to fill out an intake form so that I can prepare for the first day of class. This is a warm and fun intake form, asking some questions to help me understand the student's goals for learning English and next steps they'd like to take in the United States. The intake form helps me gather what I need to frame a norming activity for the first day that is already based on real concerns and expectations that connect personally to the students. Getting to read about some proud moments of the students from their past education and some things they expect a good teacher to be allows me to collect and chart the expectations into a first day norming conversation. Asking about concerns the students have gives me a chance to personally respond to students with big concerns before the first day or on the first day.

Students have complex reasons for wanting to learn English. And past experiences might already have impacted their English identity. The sentence, "Oh teacher, my English is poor, please excuse my grammar mistakes" is a precursor to many conversations with students one on one. Maybe they were told their accent needed improvement or they make a lot of grammar mistakes. This English identity can change and shift to become a confident English identity, but it often requires space to develop that identity.

Students from cultural backgrounds that define success in education as perfect scores can face conflicts with what happens in a Reading Apprenticeship classroom: embracing confusion, tolerating ambiguity, learning from mistakes. My pre-course intake form seeks out some personal expectations students bring with them so that the norming process as a group can support breaking down any barriers that exist in those expectations themselves. The form prompts students to share their understanding of the teacher's role versus the students' roles with each other in learning, then asks students about their personal role in their own learning. When I ask these things and really listen, I can start a personal connection with the students before the first day.

The Social Dimension: Don't Give Up!

Constantly wondering, "is it working?" is normal! Designing for the social dimension in the first five weeks stretches my own ability to tolerate ambiguity. Trying once and giving up will usually end in a difficult social dynamic. Continuing to layer the social dimension into academic or content-related activities is essential during and through the whole course of those five weeks.

Starting with a discussion about what brave spaces for learning means in practice. We read about brave versus safe spaces together as an academic exercise in some vocabulary-deepening strategies. And then we identify and chart out differences in brave versus safe spaces using that vocabulary. In weeks two and three, students reflect individually on their weekly check-in quiz about any barriers to the brave and safe space. Those reflections become a whole-group conversation with anonymized comments from those reflections.

My students experienced norming on day one, but as we started using things like breakout rooms more and had real reading assignments, the need came up for shifting those norms.

At the end of week two, I noticed in some check-in reflections that students reported lacking time to read the book outside of class due to their busy schedules. Everyone had access to the book, but they lacked access to *time* to read.

Many had a little time before class started, so we decided during our check-in about the book that I'd host a Zoom with some portions of the audiobook playing before class each day. Some students purchased the audiobook themselves, and others came a half hour before class every day to listen together and follow along. Even students who had read on their own came to the audiobook time to enjoy the portions again and gain access to pronunciation of certain words. For one student, this was the only way he was able to manage reading the book. This norming conversation created momentum and made the book more accessible. It also apprenticed what it means to have time to read when you're busy into a broader definition. Best of all, all of the students were able to engage in the group discussions about the reading during our Book Club Thursdays at some level.

If the social is not gelling, I get very anxious, but I try to engage ongoing norming creatively, finding ways to deepen the social around protecting the benefits I've designed into the learning environment. My students were coming to class not having read, but I engaged them as a group to identify barriers to reading and connect around those. Many of us commiserated about the things that often got in the way of reading, but the truth was we all wished we'd had time. Then we got creative together and resolved them as a group. My teacher self could have shut down in a sense of, "Oh no, I knew they wouldn't read," or, "This was the wrong book choice." That would be the giving up choice. Not giving up looked like bringing it back to a question of who are we and how can we know each other well enough to find community in our situations and goals, Weekly reflections, quick re-norming conversations as a class, can help turn the social dimension into a creative problem-solving connecting point.

The Cognitive Dimension: Don't Forget!

Complex assignments that really stretch students into new places require problem solving. My students experience complex assignments in my ESL class. To be able to attain a great product that showcases their learning in a way that builds their identity as a confident English speaker, they need support to engage the assignment in ways that will get them all of the benefits.

As we start a complex assignment, they experience doing the assignment together during class time, then sharing about how the assignment benefits them and their learning. With our book, *Born a Crime*, the first complex assignment was a vocabulary log modeled on vocabulary work from Keith Folse and Cheryl Boyd Zimmerman (Folse, 2004; Zimmerman, 2009). This log takes students through a series of six mini-activities with words they identify from a mentor text (book, article, video, etc.). The six mini-activities involve finding examples of the word in use, creating an image to associate with the word, translating the word with nuance into their preferred language, finding English synonyms and antonyms that they already know, and generating some sentences using the word to connect to something they are familiar with. As we read, students were supposed to choose 3–4 words a week to work with in this deep way, and their assignment's goal was to reach about 50 words through the course of the whole semester. Students expressed that they had never done vocabulary in this way and expressed doubt that it was worth their time. Shouldn't they be memorizing lists of 25–50 words per week? To kick off the assignment, we read a small text set about receptive vocabulary and productive vocabulary development together with the directions of the assignment. I also provide some student models of work showing different ways students had organized themselves for the assignment.

Doing the first week's worth of this vocabulary log, students try out dictionary tools and an English Corpora, thesaurus tools, and now AI tools, that could help them deepen their understanding of the words in breakout rooms. If they didn't know how to use the tools, they could problem solve together or call for help in their rooms.

After doing the assignment and getting feedback from peers and the teacher for four weeks, students prepared short presentations of a word that impacted them most from the text and how the routine of this assignment was changing their vocabulary development. To layer the social dimension into this assignment, they shared their presentations with small groups, and rotated around to three different groups in class. This way they had three meaningful conversations with groups of three to four and continued building their ownership of their productive vocabulary.

When we got to week five and had the lesson from the reflection, the students engaged the vocabulary that had come up to have this complex conversation. Some of the words students had worked with were bias, racism, stereotype, insurgency, and shame. These were not teacher-chosen words listed on the board. These were words that students identified and worked with because they realized they were words they needed to be able to use in order to discuss the book together.

In the past, assigning something like this and just letting students do it alone as homework was my norm. It's easy to forget the value of what the cognitive dimension can do to deepen learning and protect the value that I had so carefully designed into assignments. Often students working alone aren't getting the value that I designed into the assignment unless they get feedback and redirection around how they are engaging the assignment. Don't forget that when students struggle to do a complex assignment, slowing down, scaffolding, and developing the cognitive dimension reengage the value that you dreamed of and designed into the assignment.

The Knowledge-Building Dimension: Don't Stop!

"But I don't know how to do that." "This is confusing." "I didn't learn about this part of history in my country." "I'm really bad at grammar." It's always something different, but it hits different students at different times. They identify a barrier to their ability to do something, but this is where inquiry can start.

On March 18, the class started to show they had owned the idea of inquiry by having the most authentic inquiry we had had up until that point. And that brave space to inquire about an area that was impacting them directly opened the door to our ESL class being a place where it was OK to explore relevant inquiry, not just practice or canned inquiry with a correct answer.

To build their curiosity for inquiry, students need opportunities in the first weeks to use their prior knowledge and expertise. Our ESL class is designed to stretch their learning and confidence with English, so they will hit new information and things they don't know. Busy students can become overwhelmed or feel hopelessness creep in if they feel there is too much to learn and no roadmap.

When introducing the book in week two, we did an activity called *reading a book by its cover*, making predictions about what it might be about. Together we started to list topics that might be related to the book. In this case, it is about dynamics of racism in South Africa, Apartheid, Trevor Noah the comedian, comedy in U.S. politics, and perspectives on racism in the United States. Students started to share what they knew about these topics and how they compared to things in their prior knowledge, their culture, or their experiences.

After they started the book, in weeks three and four, they began keeping track of topics they may want to learn more about because they are areas of curiosity or confusion in their real lives. Some students pointed out language-related topics, like grammar choices that Noah made in the book. Others chose historical facts about South Africa or culture. And to my surprise, the book developed a great curiosity about the linguistics of swearing in English and how to know when it is appropriate as a language learner. A lot of this stemmed from the idea of respect and being perceived as a native speaker of English. Several were doing gig work delivering food orders and received a lot of messages from customers full of profanity. They didn't know if it was supposed to be funny or angry. But the book's use of profanity for the sake of comedy helped them realize there was real nuance and situational meaning that helped their comprehension of everyday experiences. This created an opportunity for a social gathering, outside of class of course, with a guest speaker—who definitely didn't recommend profanity in a professional setting! But the conversation helped students with a fundamental curiosity about how to improve their comprehension of tone and nuance when experiencing that kind of language via text and in a conversation.

When students were stuck in wondering why Noah told a story a certain way, their confusion allowed for grammar lessons that were based on curiosity for meaning rather than a checklist of grammar points. From time to time, students would struggle with comprehension of the text, and this gave us chances to build knowledge about using routines like talking to the text and thinking aloud, as well as learning other ways to annotate and summarize to track comprehension.

Any area of feeling stuck or confused allowed me as the teacher to see where the learning edge existed for the students. And the confusion surfaced the existing schema students came with and allowed students to build new knowledge onto that foundation. Designing opportunities to surface confusion in the first five weeks opens up a desire to build relevant knowledge.

Weekly reading journals and the vocabulary project helped students to track their growing knowledge and see that their knowledge was building to something measurable. They weren't just coming to class and practicing English; they were growing their English. More powerfully, they were growing their skills for learning in English.

All of this led to a final reflective writing about their experience reading *Born a Crime* and what they had learned beyond the book because they didn't stop at the first sign of confusion.

When I got to week five and saw all of the dimensions at work in the conversation about being perceived as stupid, it was clear that we had a learning space that wasn't mine anymore. It was the students' space to learn in. And the way we continued, students who started low or intermediate ended high. Students who started high ended extremely high. The growth was exponential, not linear.

Chapter 4

Peer Educators as Reading Apprenticeship Practitioners

Crystal Kiekel

Professor bell hooks writes, "To teach in a manner that respects and cares for the souls of our students is essential if we are to provide the necessary conditions where learning can most deeply and intimately begin" (hooks, 1994a). She reminds us that education deeply involves the "souls" of our students, referring to the whole student and not strictly their ability to perform discipline-specific tasks. She emphasizes that respect and care are prerequisites for deep, intimate learning. They are also at the heart of the social and personal dimensions of the Reading Apprenticeship framework; their importance is underscored again in literature about the "affective domain," culturally responsive teaching and learning, and in any exploration of cognition and learning (Cantor, 2020; Hammond, 2015; Schoenbach et al., 2012).

One of the most important and often underappreciated resources students have to support their success is other students. In colleges and universities nationwide, peer educators, like tutors and supplemental instruction leaders (SILs), have been quietly creating powerful learning spaces that are strengths-based, student-centered, and rooted in care. These spaces inherently address the social and personal dimensions of learning while simultaneously offering support with content instruction. In these spaces, students can feel connected and included while they engage in inquiry about how learning works. There is a deep, inherent connection between the Reading Apprenticeship framework and learning assistance, and within this connection lies tremendous potential to bridge content and care in peer-centered communities.

I was first introduced to the Reading Apprenticeship framework in 2011. I was a coordinator for a professional development organization known as the California Community Colleges' Success Network (3CSN), which had established a statewide community of practice (CoP) focused on Reading Apprenticeship (California Community Colleges' Success Network, 2023). I was also the director of the tutoring center at Los Angeles Pierce College. Along with two of my amazing colleagues, Danny Pittaway and Mark Manasse, who were also 3CSN coordinators and learning center directors, we established a Community of Practice (CoP) called the Learning Assistance Project (LAP). LAP was focused on empowering peer educators across California to participate in similar kinds of rigorous, high-quality, ongoing professional learning offered to faculty and staff.

We found ourselves partnering with the Reading Apprenticeship CoP often, easily drawing parallels between the work done in these two communities. We began to articulate these connections more clearly, actively exploring ways in which peer education already parallels the Reading Apprenticeship framework, and experimenting with new ways in which the framework could improve our ability to connect more meaningfully with students. In the years that followed, we had the pleasure of hosting multiple peer-educator-led conferences and workshops; meeting numerous inspirational faculty, staff, administrators, and peer educators; and participating in many wonderful conferences and events put on by learning assistance and Reading Apprenticeship leaders.

What we have found along our journey is that well-supported, well-trained peer educators have the ability to facilitate activities and environments that cultivate metacognition and the four interconnected areas of learning—social, personal, cognitive, and knowledge-building. They are in a unique position to be able to create learning spaces that provide safer, braver, and more caring communities where students are empowered to work together to become stronger, more independent learners.

To build and sustain these highly effective academic spaces, rigorous and ongoing training and support for tutors are essential. The ability to nurture this type of deep care and learning does not come naturally to peer educators simply by virtue of the fact that they are students themselves. At the same time, colleges and universities already dedicate a tremendous wealth of resources to train peer educators. We are tasked with teaching students, many of whom have no history of paid employment, a staggering amount of information. Most training programs include lessons on the role of peer educators, student support techniques, learning theory, policies and procedures, professionalism, and compliance standards, to name just a few (Schotka et al., 2014). We teach all this and much more in a relatively short period of time, within the confines of a semester or quarter. Given all that is already required of leaders in these centers, taking even more time to cultivate these deeper, interconnected, inquiry-based connections can be challenging, especially at first.

However, my colleagues and I have found that the time invested has had tremendous benefits. Peer education can be a space where we can strengthen metacognition, holistic education, and equitable learning, but we need a place to begin. We can start by cultivating curiosity and openness with ourselves and with each other. We can share successful practices from colleges and universities that are currently engaging in this type of deep professional learning. We can prioritize the process of continuously reflecting upon and revising our own peer educator training and support programs. My hope here is to honor the tremendous work that's already happening in the field of learning assistance, and to empower practitioners to explore more ways in which the Reading Apprenticeship framework can uplift and enrich peer education.

CONNECTING READING APPRENTICESHIP AND PEER EDUCATION

The Reading Apprenticeship framework is made up of four interconnected areas of learning—the social, personal, cognitive, and knowledge-building dimensions. Students can explore the interconnected and complex nature of these areas through metacognitive conversations. These conversations help students reflect and expand on the learning process.

"Peer educators" refers broadly to peer-led support for college and university students. This chapter will focus specifically on two types of peer educators, tutors and SI leaders. These are peer educators who provide "learning assistance," which refers to peer-led services that provide academic support outside of the classroom with the aim of helping students succeed in their coursework (Aschenbach et al., 2021). The centers where these services are housed are designed to be thriving, student-centered spaces in which "all students can come to study, congregate, collaborate, and learn in a social, academic-oriented, and 'un-lectured' learning environment" (Aschenbach et al, 2021). "Tutoring" refers broadly to peer-facilitated support that can be conducted one-on-one, in groups, or in labs and classrooms. Supplemental instruction refers more specifically to peer educators who conduct regularly scheduled study sessions with a focus on integrating content and effective learning strategies (University of Missouri–Kansas City, n.d.). Trained peer educators support students by making learning visible, empowering them to surface and strengthen their own learning processes, and creating peer-centered learning communities based on inquiry, strength, and care.

The peer education model inherently parallels the Reading Apprenticeship framework in several key ways. These sessions can blend content-based instruction with connection and care, and they can address metacognition and all four interconnected areas of learning. Rather than "giving answers," peer educators can be trained to ask questions that facilitate student-centered, self-reflective conversations that strengthen students' ability to learn. For example, tutors at my college have shared these techniques for facilitating a learning dialogue:

- "When students ask me yes/no questions, instead of answering, I ask them what they think the answer is and why. This helps in two ways. If they know the correct answer, explaining it to me will help them remember it. If they don't know the correct answer, I can see their thought process, where they're getting it right, and where the misunderstanding is." —Biology Tutor
- "In both tutoring and on my own, I ask, 'How would you start/approach this problem?' Just trying to think about how to start it has helped me overcome being overwhelmed." —Math Tutor

If peer educators are provided with professional learning designed to emphasize these skills and concepts, we can more deeply cultivate this inherent connection. While the training programs vary by institution, many widely recognized training programs (e.g., College Reading and Learning Association, CRLA; University of Missouri–Kansas City, UMKC; and Association of Colleges for Tutoring and Learning Assistance, ACTLA) are rooted in self-reflective learning, student-centered routines, active student engagement, and inquiry around how learning works, the same principles inherent in the Reading Apprenticeship framework. If trained and supported on an ongoing basis in this fashion, these students improve their own learning while also learning to be role models, apprentices, and learning partners with their peers.

METACOGNITION AT THE CENTER OF PEER EDUCATION

At the center of these interconnected dimensions of Reading Apprenticeship are metacognitive conversations, where students are invited to explore their own thinking and learning processes (Schoenbach et al., 2012). Metacognition is one of the core principles of learning assistance. Peer educators ask questions and facilitate activities that help students make their thinking and learning visible, thus supporting them as they reflect on and strengthen their own learning strategies.

These student leaders have tremendous potential for facilitating these kinds of reflective dialogues, but again, the ability to facilitate these activities is learned through training, practice, and ongoing support. Many learning assistance leaders have recognized this and have thus put metacognition at the center of their peer educator training programs. For example, at Los Angeles Pierce College, we train new tutors to structure their session around the "KWL" routine. This routine invites peer educators to start the session by asking the student to write down or talk about what they already know (K) about the topic they came for help with. They are then invited to write or describe what they want to know (W) about that topic. The tutors then use that information to guide the activities of the session. At the end of the session, students write or discuss what they learned (L) about the topic. Thus students, not the tutor, become the driving force of the inquiry. The peer educator is a guide who invites the learner to access their own prior knowledge, generate questions, and reflect on and celebrate new connections.

PEER EDUCATION IN THE SOCIAL DIMENSION

Addressing the social dimension is essential to create a safer environment for students to connect in ways that allow them to share their confusion and difficulties with learning (Schoenbach et al., 2012). Because of the collaborative, peer-led nature of learning assistance, this dimension is inherently at the core of this work. Learning assistance strives to create student-centered spaces. They shift the power dynamic and put students at the heart of the learning, thus creating safer, braver, and more comfortable learning environments. Here, students can connect, ask questions, surface and discuss questions and confusion, see themselves as a part of a community, and productively struggle together.

There are many excellent training programs that prepare peer educators to strengthen this dimension. For example, at Cal State University, Long Beach, SILs learn that connection and safety are necessary for learning to begin. They facilitate brief, low-stakes, collaborative exercises to help build trust, safety, and connection with students at the outset of the session. They begin sessions with amusing, preplanned icebreakers and rapport-building routines like "Dad Jokes," "Riddle of the Day," or questions about trends or their current moods. They model different versions of these activities in training, and SILs are encouraged to try out ones that resonate most with them. Similarly, one SIL in an "Approaches to University Writing" course at California State University, Northridge starts each session with a "question of the day" exercise, where she begins by asking students to reflect on a question about their lives and perspectives. These exercises create space for students to connect with each other as well as with the course content (DeTemple & Sarrouf, 2020). At the same time, these SILs norm a more lively, less formal learning environment while inviting students to participate as learning partners alongside peer educators, cultivating safety and inclusion at the outset of the sessions.

PEER EDUCATION IN THE PERSONAL DIMENSION

When we address the personal dimension, we leverage skills students have outside of the school setting, including their interests, identities, self-awareness, sense of purpose, and learning goals (Schoenbach et al., 2012). Because peer educators often work individually or in small groups of students, they have unique opportunities to help students make connections between their lives and experiences and what they are learning in the classroom. A trained peer educator "meets students where they are." They can create environments in which students talk not just about instructional content, but also about their learning goals, past successes, histories, and their skills and interests in other areas. In this way, peer educators inherently address the "soul" of each individual student and not just the content area that they seek to improve.

We have seen a multitude of ways in which peer education training programs have focused on strengthening the personal dimension of learning. For example, tutor training at Mount San Jacinto College emphasizes students' need for positive relationships and a safe environment in order to take the risks that come with learning and engagement in difficult tasks. After examining Zaretta Hammond's "Ready for Rigor" framework, tutors generate session strategies that affirm and validate students' lived experiences and build collaborative partnerships (Hammond, 2015). Some examples of tutor-generated strategies include inviting students to talk about their overall educational goals; offering their own educational stories, including their academic struggles and successes; asking students about what they are curious about or want to learn, even if it's different from the assignment; or simply sharing a joke or a smile. When peer educators and students can talk about their lived experiences as part of academic conversations, they normalize that connection and allow themselves to feel seen, heard, and understood. Because these are peer educators and not faculty members facilitating these conversations, they empower learners to create essential networks of peer support that are for, and by, students.

PEER EDUCATION IN THE COGNITIVE DIMENSION

Addressing the cognitive dimension invites students to investigate mental processes, comprehension, and problem-solving strategies (Schoenbach et al., 2012). This is also at the core of the learning assistance domain. Peer educators are, first and foremost, academically successful students. They are selected in part because of their ability to successfully navigate course requirements and to identify and implement appropriate, high-impact learning routines. A peer educator's primary expertise is their own ability to learn and succeed. It follows then that one of their primary roles in learning support is to assist students in identifying and strengthening their own study strategies so that they can improve their learning.

Many learning assistance centers have created excellent training modules to help peer educators cultivate and refine these skills. For example, educators who lead the SI program at Chaffey College train SILs to explore the cognitive dimension by using the "Think aloud and paired problem-solving method" (TAPPS) in their sessions. With guidance from the SI leader, one student "thinks aloud" with a selected text or problem. They verbalize their mental process and problem-solving strategies alongside a partner. The partner may ask probing questions or make note of different problem-solving strategies that the student uses. Then the students switch roles, so each student has a turn as a thinker and an observer. Finally, the partners discuss the problem together to make sense of the problem or text. They discuss the problem itself as well as the strategies they used to solve the problem. In this way, the SILs shift the focus away from giving answers to a more productive and inclusive conversation about how learning works. Students can surface their thinking and learning strategies while applying those strategies to a difficult problem. This strengthens and expands students' learning toolkits in ways that make them more aware and in control of their learning process.

PEER EDUCATION IN THE KNOWLEDGE-BUILDING DIMENSION

When we attend to the knowledge-building dimension, we are scaffolding knowledge about the language, text structure, and discourse practices specific to a given discipline (Schoenbach et al., 2012). Again, this is also central to learning assistance. Peer educators act as a "discourse bridge" between the student and the course material (Paulson, 2012). Their role is to assist students in making connections between their own knowledge, the discourse-specific vocabulary and concepts, and discipline-specific practices of inquiry and knowledge generation.

We've seen numerous examples of learning assistance centers that invite peer educators to address the knowledge-building dimension. For example, at Los Angeles Pierce College, tutors can work in partnership with professors to create "directed learning activities" (DLAs) for use in tutoring sessions. Tutors work with discipline faculty to identify particularly challenging ideas, vocabulary, and texts. Then, with guidance from the instructor, they create short handouts that include a brief summary of key terms and concepts and an activity to apply them. Tutors use these DLAs in sessions by either working alongside students one to one or by pairing up students to work through them together. One embedded animal science tutor at LA Pierce College has created a growing collection of DLAs over several semesters. He makes them available to students in advance through the class's course management system a few weeks before the test as a way to encourage students to reflect on their prior knowledge and their remaining questions, and to seek support. Tutors can revise and add new DLAs each semester, continuously reflecting on and improving on their ability to navigate discipline-specific concepts.

CONCLUSION: SUPPORTING, SHARING, AND EXPANDING THIS WORK

We see many phenomenal examples of colleges and universities that explicitly address these deeper, interconnected dimensions of learning in their training programs. At the same time, with the overwhelming amount of training, logistics, and supervision necessary to run these programs, leaders in these centers don't always have sufficient support and resources to easily begin to explore these opportunities. Since the benefits to peer educators and students far outweigh the initial challenge of getting started on this journey, my hope here is to identify ways to make these opportunities more accessible to more peer educators and learning assistance professionals.

There are a few key ideas that have helped my colleagues and me deepen and explore this work:

- Start by recognizing and honoring the important and unique role peer educators can play in higher education as student leaders, role models, and thought partners.
- Commit to exploring interconnected, metacognitive frameworks like Reading Apprenticeship as opportunities to deepen our potential to build caring, student-centered spaces.
- Explore well-established peer educator training certification programs that are rooted in metacognition, student-centered learning, and equity. Many of my outstanding colleagues have used UMKC, ACTLA, and CRLA to structure training.
- Create and attend professional learning opportunities, both in person and online, where we can exchange ideas, explore frameworks like Reading Apprenticeship in community, and normalize the practice of continuously evaluating and revising our training programs.
- Collaborate with peer educators themselves as learning partners and leaders, inviting them into these conversations and creating avenues to share their unique and invaluable lived experiences as both students and as educators.

The learning assistance field has tremendous collective expertise and agency. Colleges and universities participate deeply in professional networks and communities made for and by learning assistance professional programs, like ACTLA, UMKC, CRLA, IWCA (International Writing Centers Association), and ACTP (Association for the Coaching and Tutoring Profession). We can also participate in conversations related to our field. For example, we can engage with the Reading Apprenticeship communities, culturally responsive, socio-emotional learning, and equity-based communities, and other networks where conversations about interconnected, self-reflective teaching and learning take place. Not only can we learn from these parallel discussions, but we also have a tremendous amount of expertise and experience that could make meaningful contributions to these related fields.

Our students deserve the kinds of communities of care that only their well-trained and well-supported peers can provide. Our peer educators deserve the opportunity to recognize, celebrate, and strengthen the tremendous student-led, holistic, care-based learning spaces they facilitate. Learning assistance practitioners deserve to feel empowered to explore deeper connections, cultivate our craft, and share our contributions broadly to the world of higher education.

PART II

Equity Matters: Tensions of Academic Apprenticeship

As we suggest in the introduction, a deep resonance among the responses in the survey underlies the three threshold concepts we describe. We call that resonance a metaconcept that establishes the equity basis for Reading Apprenticeship: **reading apprenticeships, when faculty have crossed these thresholds, are reciprocal**. Below, we review some of the comments in respondents' answers to the survey that hint at this metaconcept and then introduce the two chapters in this part that elaborate more explicitly on the concept itself.

What seems clear from reading faculty comments in response to meaningful experiences and breakthroughs in their teaching of reading is the notion that equity matters to these faculty. Of the 86 respondents to our survey, 8 (9%) explicitly used the word *equity* in their responses. Some attribute that focus to their experience with Reading Apprenticeship. One writes, "Today's focus on equity gaps and social belonging are nothing new to RA practitioners." Others comment about the context in which they encountered Reading Apprenticeship (an equity institute) or the equity-minded reputation they have developed as Reading Apprenticeship practitioners.

Less explicit in their comments, though still present, is the tension we describe. This arises in comments about expertise and modeling, bringing students into disciplinary communities. One respondent commented that "I also spend the first few weeks discussing and identifying what disciplinary writing looks like, how it differs, why it differs, and how they can immerse themselves in that language. The Insiders & Outsider Tobias text is an important text in engaging student discussion. Students enjoy this, and it bakes in equity: students feel seen, their experiences acknowledged and voiced." Notice the tension here: in this framing, disciplinary writing exists independent of the students. They must adapt to it and find their place within it, acknowledging insider or outsider status and hoping to move to greater insider status.

Yet faculty also describe their growing awareness of students as individuals who bring important expertise, funds of knowledge, and life experiences into disciplinary conversations. One respondent writes, "Learning has become so much more authentic! Students are in constant dialogue with texts and connect what they read/watch with things they know and ideas or questions brought up by others. This is a high-level skill that I was actually hindering before I started implementing RA strategies." The faculty member's use of *dialogue* highlights the interaction involved in study—that students are not simply making meaning from texts; they are making meaning *with* texts.

The tensions implicit in these responses are the topic of the two chapters that follow. Servais takes it on explicitly, describing her personal educational history to frame her stance that we should cultivate practices that invite students into "conscious apprenticeship." Acknowledging the privilege and power that can be conferred through membership in disciplinary discourse communities, she advocates that we help students to make informed decisions about how they will assimilate, challenge, or seek to change those academic spaces. In their discussion about the synergies and tensions between the Reading Apprenticeship framework and Zaretta Hammond's Ready for Rigor framework from *Culturally Responsive Teaching and the Brain*, Lee, Lopez and Shelton similarly focus on empowering students to take on the "heavy lifting" required of academic work by offering tools, processes, and orientations that support a vibrant learning community, and by leaning into the cultural wealth that students bring to their higher education experiences. Both chapters emphasize the way that all four dimensions of the Reading Apprenticeship framework are required to enact the personal commitment, social relationships, cognitive labor, and dynamic knowledge building that they envision.

Chapter 5

Consciously Apprenticing Students

Lauren Servais

My conscious teaching apprenticeship started in 2001. I walked into a developmental English class feeling like I had arrived as a teacher, as I had just printed copies of an assignment I "created on my own." After the usual welcome and check-ins, I moved us into our first activity, which I prefaced with, "as a student I always hated doing this, but . . ." Before I could finish the sentence, my students erupted in near-unison with "then why are you making us do it?" I thought, "this is what we do in an English class," but I could not bring myself to say it. The students in this class were exceptional. They were fun, wild, and lovely, and together they created the best community of learners I've ever experienced. It was in their question that I realized I had somehow become the English teacher I never set out to be.

Until that moment, not once did I consider the kind of teacher I wanted to be, nor did I consider the ways that as a student I was compelled to contort my body and language to fit my teachers' expectations. I consciously strove for a BA, and then an MA in English, but unbeknownst to me, I was being apprenticed into the teaching of English, throughout the many assignments and class activities that disciplined my speech, writing, interactions, and more. I also learned what it means to teach and be taught. My schema for teaching and learning in English classes are heavily influenced by my experiences as a student. My unlearning started with critical reflection to surface my unconscious apprenticeship, and then a commitment to ongoing reflection and action to be not only the educator my students deserve, but the educator I needed back when I was a student.

LOOKING BACK

My apprenticeship in school English began in the 7th grade when, upon the advice of my 6th-grade teacher, my parents enrolled me in a parochial K–8. I felt my linguistic difference for the first time when a classmate teased me for speaking Hawaiian Creole. The 7th grade was also my first experience with white teachers, who implicitly and explicitly communicated linguistic and cultural values that students were expected to emulate if they wanted to learn and succeed in their classes. The 7th grade taught me that Hawaiian Creole—the language and connected values—was not welcomed in school.

My apprenticeship in higher-education English started in my second junior year at the University of Hawai'i. I was still unsure of my major when I enrolled in a 300-level class on John Milton. I remember reading and highlighting *Paradise Lost*, and still being completely confused. Getting to class early and hearing the other students grumble about how difficult a text it was to understand saved me from internalizing my struggles as deficit. Instead, I blamed John Milton for writing such a difficult text. After my professor arrived, he would ask questions, and very few of us, if any, would respond. Out of what I am sure was exasperation due to our silence, he started taking us through the reading. He would say things like, "here Milton is alluding to this historical event . . ."; "here I am imagining . . ."; "I am making this connection . . ." He did this for several class periods, and then we got to a section of the text when my professor said, "and now, in my mind, I am seeing the Son standing on the pin of a needle" and, for the first time, I could see it too. I needed my professor to show me how he reads, and that invited me to insert myself into the text and myself back into school. I needed to imagine, to make connections, and to talk story with ideas, texts, theories, and more. I became an English major because of my professor and John Milton.

My apprenticeship in teaching started in graduate school. Teaching was the last thing I wanted to do, and the idea of being in charge of something that caused me so much discomfort was unimaginable. While still at the University of Hawai'i, I was offered a teaching assistant position in Ethnic Studies, and I refused it. Then, I started my MA in English program at the University of Colorado, and I could not pass up on the tuition waiver and stipend from teaching a section of Composition. I walked into class that first day, and students thought I was playing a practical joke on them. They were convinced I was a student pretending to be the teacher. I had to show them the syllabus with my name on it for them to quiet down that first day, but they, and I, still spent the entire semester mystified and amused I could be the "teacher." The syllabus and assignments were given to me; all I had to do was figure out what to do during class and then grade assignments. I delivered assignments and content, as if who I am and who students are did not matter, and as if learning were merely transactional. I was so busy working on my MA that I never thought about what I was "teaching." Being real here: My students were white and at the University of Colorado, Boulder. Most succeeded despite me and already possessed the skills and met the outcomes of the class before we even started.

In Whose Likeness?

Already possessing the skills necessary to be successful and being able to succeed despite my teacher was certainly not my experience as a first-year composition student at the University of Hawai'i, and this was not the experience of my students in that developmental English class. I finally voiced what I had never dared to utter previously, "I always hated doing this as a student" because my students showed me what a classroom could be, and they invited me into a learning community beyond transaction. Learning doesn't have to be sterile; we don't have to hide our identities, we don't have to pretend to be someone else's ideal student/teacher, and we can examine and speak our truths.

When they asked me why I'm assigning a topic that I have always hated, I was forced to reckon with the fact that at that moment, I was emulating the very teachers I struggled with in the past. Teachers who told me "you have such wonderful ideas, but your grammar is really atrocious" and who demanded an implicit adherence to linguistic rules in discussions and essays. I was disciplined as a student to understand thesis, paragraph, and so on, and here I was playing the role of "teacher" who asked students to engage in literacy acts as if those acts do not communicate values, reify systems, and enact/maintain power.

Since 2001, I have been grappling with my role as teacher/learner. So why was I trying to emulate the white English teachers of my past and why wasn't I allowing the experiences, knowledge, and identities of my students and myself to inform the "what" and the "how" of learning? What's the point of school and what's the point of composition? What am I apprenticing students into and for what? What does it mean to be literate? What power am I enacting as a teacher when I make instructional decisions and whose interests are served when I do? How do I invite students into powerful learning in ways that honor who they are and that offer them agency, choice, and sovereignty over their own learning? What should be my role as "teacher" and what ought I be accountable to and for? How do my decisions reify power?

Learning Is Apprenticeship

In addition to acquiring skills and knowledge, dispositions, worldviews, and epistemologies are learned, which makes the learning process an identity-forming endeavor and a constellation of political acts. No one told me that at the end of my apprenticeship, I would take on the teacher dispositions I did, nor did I ever think that in the process of learning and participating in the Englishes of K–12 and higher education, I had become a tool for the status quo, and yet there I was in 2001 unconsciously parroting my perception of what an English teacher does. Once I realized I was attempting to manifest the status quo in the classroom, I needed to engage in a process of figuring out how I got there and then figuring out what to do instead.

The calls to center racial and linguistic justice have many educators in knots over what to teach, and this question is especially apparent in first-year composition classes where linguistic gates have been called out. However, I struggle when people with advanced degrees grapple over whether to teach academic English and "the standards" to first-generation, low-income, and/or linguistically and culturally diverse students. It is the advanced degrees and the acquisition of academic discourse that conferred the power to be in a position where they are deciding if their students should have access to the very same power they are wielding. This is another form of gate-keeping; it is well intentioned, but no less a power move. It is not that we shouldn't be asking questions about what students should learn and how students should be allowed their own languages, but that these decisions are not for teachers to make. Students should have the right to make their own decisions about the languages they acquire. As teachers, it is our responsibility to invite students into conscious apprenticeship, where students have access to literacies that confer power, agency to make their own choices, and opportunities to critique and reflect.

INVITATIONS INTO CONSCIOUS APPRENTICESHIP

Over my years of teaching, I have landed on practices that help me invite students into a more conscious form of apprenticeship—one that seeks to hold a space of critical engagement, community, self-reflection, and action.

Mutually Agreed-Upon Safe and Brave Space Expectations

Building upon the Reading Apprenticeship Setting Norms Routine, we engage in collaborative inquiry to establish our safety and brave space needs in the class, and out of this process of curiosity, dialogue, and negotiation, we make transparent our expectations for each other and ourselves (Ali, 2017; Strano, 2023). We inquire into what "safe space" means, and we surface our expectations to be invited and welcomed into a learning community that allows us to bring the fullness of our intersectional identities into the classroom. We simultaneously inquire into what "brave space" means, and we surface the kind of learning community we need that allows us to take learning risks, make mistakes, and grow, without shame, blame, and/or guilt.

When I ask students to reflect on their experiences of safety, I do so too. Geneva Gay taught me that I need to be willing to do what I ask my students to do, and so I have adopted a co-learner paradigm and I have tried to lead the way by modeling the vulnerability of learning throughout my teaching practice. Before I ask students to think about their experiences of safe and brave space, I am transparent about mine. I limit myself to sharing one experience of safety and one experience of brave space, so I leave room for student experiences. I share my experience of feeling physically sick each time my 8th-grade teacher asked us to take turns reading aloud in class. I would count to see which paragraph would be mine, hoping for a short paragraph and looking to make sure I knew how to pronounce each word because I was so fearful of being laughed at by my peers. I share my experiences of safety too, like being in the 5th grade and learning the ukulele with a teacher who praised students for creating new notes and songs, rather than chastising them for playing the wrong notes.

We take our experiences and convert them into requests and expectations that are needed for us to create a learning environment that establishes safety and invites vulnerability. Through this process, we also come to agreement about how we will let each other know when one of our shared requests and expectations for safe and brave space are not met; we also frame this failure as an expected part of the learning process. It is not a matter of trying to avoid failure; rather it is to be expected that in learning to achieve safe and brave space, we will all need loving reminders. Our safe and brave space needs, expectations, and reminders are added to a living document that is revisited and revised throughout the semester, and most importantly, it sets the aspirations we will work to embody together in the classroom, and they become foundational to the vision of community that we will hold ourselves and each other to cultivate together.

Naming Our Ideal Community

The term *community* is a schema, a conceptual map, that helps individuals make sense of, and participate within, the world. This conceptual map is developed over our lifetimes, both implicitly and explicitly, and determines how we interact in "community" spaces. When we lack community norms and/or fail to uphold those norms, then we invite those with power and privilege to determine the kind of community we create together.

How many of us have been in situations where some people in the meeting are raising their hands to speak next, while others just blurt out to command the airtime? In these situations, we either didn't take the time to decide how we'll engage together or we did, and some are choosing to disregard because their preferred experience of learning in community is one in which individuals jockey for power and assert the power of speaking.

I ask students to consider their seminal experiences of community and to reflect on multiple questions: What is valued? Who is valued? How do members interact? What connects members to each other? What/who are members accountable to? How is disagreement handled? How are decisions made? How transparent is all of this and how is it taught to members?

The point of understanding one's community schema is to uncover how we have learned to engage in community and to be conscious of how aspects of our schema can enhance and/or interrupt our learning when in community.

I am transparent with students about ahupua'a, which is one aspect of my community schema. An ahupua'a is a complex ecological and social system in indigenous Hawaiian culture, and while I don't expect students to embody ahupua'a, that preferred conception is always present for me, so I surface my preference so students understand where I am coming from. I invite students to share their preferred experiences of community and their schema, so we can understand where they are coming from too, and through the process of making our schema transparent to ourselves and each other, we use this knowledge to negotiate the community we will embody together, and more importantly, we invite ongoing personal reflection and action of being students in the community of our class and more broadly the community of our college. This is important because students need to know how their schemas of community are aligning them with some classes/disciplines more than others and how they can create the conditions they need to succeed when classes/disciplines are not in alignment with their schema.

Transparent Discourse "Rules"

In graduate school, I read Lisa Delpit's (1992) "Acquisition of Literate Discourse: Bowing Before the Master?" in which Delpit situates literacy within discourse, rather than language. Understanding literacy as discourse-driven helped me understand that first-year composition invites students into a specialized form of reading, writing, thinking, interacting, and engaging in inquiry. Students do not enter my classes to learn "English"; instead, they are learning a specialized form of reading, writing, and so on, that is based on expectations and standards of "correctness" that those in power established and that composition instructors are expected to uphold to "prepare" students for the high expectations and the "rigor" that will undoubtedly follow in future classes. This is a cycle of conformity that ultimately serves the status quo, and while I would prefer to stop the cycle, whether my students will learn academic discourse and meet the expected "rigor" is their decision.

Through the Reading Apprenticeship think aloud routine, I make transparent the academic discourse, specifically English discourse, reading processes that I have acquired. I also make transparent my ways of reading that stem from talking story. I do not present these to students as the way to read, but instead the ways that I read to make meaning.

While a new teacher, I would tell students to preview, underline, annotate, etc., until I read a student's journal response that helped me understand that when I tell students what to do to be a better reader, they took it to mean that they were bad readers. I realized that each time I led with "good readers do this," my students heard "you're not a good reader." It also created the faulty notion that there is one model of a good reader, when in fact there are multiple discourses within higher education and beyond, each with multiple ways to engage as readers, writers, and thinkers. Students need to see a full range of linguistic possibilities and then practice weaving those possibilities into their own practices.

Linguistic Possibilities

"Teaching students academic discourse is racist," said my white male colleague with a PhD. Yes, and the acquisition of academic discourse is precisely what enabled my colleague to earn his PhD, attain his current position as a full-time instructor, and utilize the very academic discourse that he argued we should not give students access to. Yes, and if my teachers had not given me access to academic discourse, I do not know that I would have gained access to higher education and I would not be the educator I am today.

The decision to provide and/or limit access to academic discourse is not one for instructors to make. To wield the power to deny access is no less paternalistic than the decision to require adherence to academic discourse. Students ought to decide for themselves the aspects of discourses they will acquire. Students also need to know the history, power, and privilege embedded within discourses, so if and what students elect to acquire, they do so knowingly.

Further, as someone who grew up in Hawai'i speaking Hawaiian Creole, I make transparent how I negotiate discourses—code mesh, code switch, create, challenge, and disrupt discourses. I also show students how I negotiate the power embedded in discourses when I make my linguistic choices. I share my experiences acquiring academic discourse, how I've maintained my cultural and linguistic connections, and I challenge students to develop their academic identities in ways that weave together and enhance their intersectional identities, rather than seek to assimilate.

Choice and Agency

Think aloud helps me make my discourse choices transparent, and I invite students to use talk to the text and metacognitive logs as the primary means to consciously think through their multilingualism and multiculturalism, and then decide for themselves the discourse(s) they will embody to become both literate and change agents.

I have adopted a grading scheme that invites students to engage and to embody whatever discourses they choose, without evaluating them against "standards" and without demanding adherence to the codes and rules that I have chosen to integrate and embody.

Throughout the semester, we ask what comprises powerful writing. With each reading, each discussion, each written response, we ask: What is powerful about this writing? How has the author composed strong ideas and prose? How could I do the same?

Using a labor-based grading (Feldman, 2018) scheme allows me to give students full credit on their assignments provided they meet assignment criteria, like responding to the question. On larger assignments, like essays, I invite students to annotate before submitting. Students insert comments into their essay, while imagining that I am sitting beside them. I invite them to talk to me about why they chose to start the essay in the manner they chose, why that thesis/claim, what choices went into the construction of that sentence, and what ideas they grappled with, wanted my perspective on, and more. I record 5–10-minute video responses and I use their annotations to guide my think aloud of their essays. On rare occasions, I invite students to revise a paragraph or two, and in these instances, I ask students to continue exploring their ideas and grappling with words.

Labor-based grading allows me to invite students to grapple and play with language, and to ultimately make their own choices about how to compose their ideas; it also allows me to hold a space of deep reflection and high expectations, without judgment and without forced adherence to discourse "standards."

Focusing on Assets

When I first started teaching, I felt the need to justify my grades—why the essay earned a B or C, rather than an A. Later, I developed rubrics, but I was still attempting to justify grades. I spent so much time looking for what was wrong, I failed to lift up what students did well. And in doing this, I invited students to fear "error," even when I voiced a desire for students to take writing risks and to grapple with complex ideas. Labor-based grading, and the space it holds for students to engage without assimilation and away from the chimera of correctness, helped me pivot to an assets-based framework. In lifting up what students do well, I'm inviting them to know their strengths. Rather than perceive writing as the avoidance of error, I am inviting students to play with language to further develop their strengths and voices.

PARTNERS FOR THE JOURNEY

I walked into that classroom in 2001 thinking I had arrived as a teacher, and I left the classroom humbled. I threw my assignment into the recycle bin on my way out, and in the days that followed, I had numerous conversations with colleagues in search of texts and professional learning opportunities. I read texts by Paulo Freire, bell hooks, Parker Palmer, Antonio Darder, Henry Giroux, Gloria Anzaldúa, Geneva Gay, and more, and as I read, I participated in ongoing conversations with fellow educators, so I built knowledge while also reflecting on practice. I came to understand that along with my fellow educators (faculty, staff, students, and managers), I belonged to a community of learners centered on facilitating student learning and success.

My students have been my best partners as I investigate what constitutes good teaching and learning. Thanks to my students, I started a journey of inquiry into teaching and learning that I have come to realize will never end.

Chapter 6

Culturally Responsive Teaching and Reading Apprenticeship: A Conversation

Yhashika Lee, Salina Lopez, and Ibrahim Shelton

Ibrahim: I'm Dr. Ibrahim Shelton. I'm a lecturer at California State University, Monterey Bay. I teach in Liberal Studies and Service Learning, and I'm a faculty associate with Teaching, Learning, and Assessment, and we work at trying to build a new department within TLA, Teaching, Learning, and Assessment at CSUMB called Culturally Responsive Education at TLA, and I do some other things. That's too much. That's about me. Yhashika, why don't you describe who you are real quick, so they can know who's coming.

Yhashika: Sure, my name is Yhashika Lee. I am a lecturer in several departments: First-Year Seminar, Humanities and Communication, and Cinematic Arts. I'm also a faculty associate in Teaching, Learning, and Assessment, and I've been here at CSUMB since 2015.

Salina: Salina Lopez. I am a lecturer for Human Development and Family Science, and also a part-time analyst for the Teaching, Learning, and Assessment department here at CSUMB. I'm also a faculty fellow with TLA.

Ibrahim: And just to say another thing, all three of us work together in this, trying to build this fledgling department. That is Yhashika Lee's brainchild. We have another colleague named George Station who's not here with us today. He's dope. And we have another colleague Moana. She's our student intern, and she's awesome. Together we have formed a collective we call CRE@TLA that focuses on providing professional development to faculty and staff here at CSUMB.

Yhashika: I just wanna step back for a second, and let [our readers] know our approach, and think I'm speaking for you all when I say that the key work that we use at CRE in TLA is *Culturally Responsive Teaching and the Brain* by Zaretta Hammond. It's our reference. It's our guide. It's our touchstone, and Dr. Hammond's definition of culturally responsive teaching is "an educator's ability to recognize students' cultural displays of learning and meaning making and respond positively and constructively with teaching moves that use cultural knowledge as a scaffold to connect what the student knows to new concepts and content in order to promote effective information processing" (2015, p. 15). All the while, the instructor understands the importance of being in a relationship and having a social emotional connection to the student in order to create a safe space for learning.

Ibrahim: For me, culturally responsive teaching gave me language for stuff I was already doing.
'Cause like how I teach and how I interact with students. I always try to be my authentic self. Like I've never tried to be anything other than Ibrahim when I'm in the front of the class, for better or worse. And when we talk about things, when we talk about culturally responsive teaching in the,

the things that I teach, we talk a lot about race and power and service, and how these things like connect and, and by default the content is edging towards us understanding various oppressions, in any class I teach, teaching teachers how to teach. And we talk about things like bias and things in the classroom, these foundational things that we need to do and understand in order for us to be effective educators, right? And, and one thing that you know that I try to teach the students, the young adults, these future teachers, is that you can't teach the people if you hate the people. So you can't hate the people and the children that you say you that you wanna teach right, and if you got any of that dirt in your heart, you gotta choose a different profession, right, cause you could do more harm than you can good, and a lot of there's so many examples in society, where, you know, there's harm being done by teachers either overtly or covertly, with their unconscious biases and things like that, so a lot of the content that I deal with by default is talking about things that's at the heart of culturally responsive education right.

Yhashika: When I started with Reading Apprenticeship, I didn't realize that I was already thinking about culturally responsive teaching, and the reason why I liked the approach, the Reading Apprenticeship framework, was because it was a way to be inclusive in the classroom, and give students, who are coming into the school unprepared, an additional tool. Again, it wasn't until I started, you know, doing my research on culturally responsive teaching and learning more about the approach that I realized how Reading Apprenticeship actually fit within that framework as well. So how I use it is, one, as part of being culturally responsive, we have high standards for our students. We're giving them the tools to meet those standards, and I think Reading Apprenticeship is definitely one way, right? So I'm teaching students how to read at the college level, how to get more out of the text, how to fill in gaps that that they're coming into the school with. The other part of or the other way I think culturally responsive teaching fits in is that a part of introducing the framework, the Reading Apprenticeship framework or or approach is being vulnerable. You have to let students see that you too struggle with new information and using, and you use these tools, right? And so that is a way to build trust in the classroom for me. I do an exercise where I have the students pick something from the sciences and, as you know, my background is not in the sciences. I let my students know that I'm absolutely terrified right now. This is just not my thing. And so they get really engaged, and they'll pick things like astrophysics, and just like really heavy scientific material. Right? And then I read it in class using the Reading Apprenticeship strategies, and they can see that it works one and two that I struggle. They see me sweating. They see me struggling to understand and make sense of concepts that are just way outside of my field. So that's how I bring in culturally responsive teaching or merge it with Reading Apprenticeship.

Ibrahim: That's really cool—thanks for sharing that and if I can go next. You know our goal is to increase the intellective capacity of our students, right? So it's not just to be understanding for the sake of being understanding. It's like Professor Hammond says, we're trying to be warm demanders. Right? So we wanna use those tactics because they're authentic, right you, you and your vulnerability is being authentic, right? And whatever, however that takes place with me in the moment could be authenticity. It could be another route. Right but the goal is to win the hearts to win the minds. You know what I mean. So if, if I can win your heart, I can stretch your mind right and for me Reading Apprenticeship plays along with it because now it gives us some tools, some real things that we can do pedagogically that will have us engage your students like metacognitive think aloud, right. That's one of the things that they do on Reading Apprenticeship that I really enjoy doing. And I like teaching the future teachers how to use this right, and with the metacognitive think aloud we're thinking about what we're thinking while we're reading, so we'll read an example of x thing, but we'll be saying what we're thinking about that, displaying what's hidden in our mind right. So it's a way to uncover something that you might be thinking that you can't really explain unless you actually start physically explaining right? And, Professor Lopez, you got anything you would add, go for it.

Salina: Sure, I can add a little bit to that. One of the one of the ways I focus on Reading Apprenticeship and the tools that it has provided for me and my students is of course one of my favorite ones is talk to text, but the way I kind of marry the two together is allowing the students to be very autonomous with choosing what readings they want to explore. So since I teach in HDFS, human development, it's a lot of having to work with people–future teachers, future health educators, you know different things like in hospice settings and stuff like that. So there's a lot of works out there, writings that can seem very, very intimidating, and really not being able to understand. But allowing them first to choose the avenues that they'd want to learn more about, and then after that's chosen, then showing them the different tools that we have, that will help them to understand those avenues a little bit deeper than just what we, as all students just see on the surface. You know, we as students tend to sometimes kind of just skim through some stuff, and true, full, thorough understanding really is never had if we continue to process our readings that way. But the number one factor that I see is when they have some kind of choice in readings that's half of the battle won, because they actually want to read that specific journal article or book or, or you know text, and then, coupled with tools, it really just brings an understanding to a level that they didn't even know they could attain. So I can stop right there.

Yhashika: I guess, ready to move on to talk about how our Reading Apprenticeship reinforces or how culturally responsive teaching reinforces Reading Apprenticeship, and I was just actually thinking about what you said about building that intellective capacity. And that's really, I think for me, like one of the key areas, because when I am speaking to my students, I am, I speak to them as future scholars, and doctors and lawyers, right? And that's the language I use throughout the entire time as part of the sort of community building, trust building, just you know them understanding that I see them as being able to learn right, and I'm there as a guide to get you there, and is part of my, I teach them how to come up with their own vision statement, and and part of my vision statement is letting them know that my goal is to make sure you get to grad school or or onto your profession. So as part of that process, you know, and, and a part of a joke that I use, as I say, well, you need to, you know, if you're gonna be a doctor, you need to do the readings. Like there's no skipping the readings. And I'll actually say, "Imagine you go to your kinesthesiologist or your orthopedist. But you go to the doctor, and you and they say well I missed that part. I didn't read that part on the knee because it was kind of hard. It was hard to understand." And this is how, you know, so I let them know that this is what Reading Apprenticeship can do for you. It will help you get prepared for your profession by learning these strategies that you can use to unpack anything. This is like this amazing tool that you're learning. And a lot of us were just told to go read or go study or make sure you understand. But no one tells us like here is what you do? This is, you know the first step and then if you get stuck here. Here are some tools that you need to use. And, and then you're telling me right so that's how I use Reading Apprenticeship to support my culturally responsive approach. It's again just letting students know that I see them in this very, very positive way, and so what I'm going to do is to give you these tools to help you get there.

Ibrahim: That's really cool and I just think that the communal aspect of both the Reading Apprenticeship and like it being a foundational aspect, I think also of the culturally responsive teaching is that we gotta understand various cultural perspectives, like your individualist societies and cultures collectivist ones, right? And for me, I try to mix and match these things throughout my teaching processes, right? I don't if I don't want to rely too much on one, but I like to mix the two together, right? So I'll give students an opportunity to have individual type of engagement with sources and things like this, but also collective means and ways to work together in teams and groups, and squads, I call it, make it squads. And when, when you make squads in my class, they gotta come up with names for their teams and how they can hold themselves accountable with their squads for the work that the squads produce. And using peer feedback and things like this to give when we do these types of things, right. But I think that communal aspect is something that I think is something that we can really hone in on. And I think it allows us to have more dynamic learning experiences. When I teach, I wanna make an experience right. I don't want to just have me talking all the time. I want to follow that format that you know, Professor Hammond laid out, that ignite, chunk, chew review. That's how I'm organizing my lessons. I always got something to have a spark to have us think about something, some activity. And then we're taking small bites and bits of information in order to make it connect. And then we gotta do something with that information on purpose right? And that could be something that has to do with Reading Apprenticeship. It could be reading. It could be investigating. It could be, you know, going outside and taking a walk and contemplating what we was doing, like something that appeals to an action right. And then we gotta do some reflection about what we just did in order for it to stick right?

Yhashika: Everything that we've been talking about reflects that key definition that I think all four of us have definitely internalized right, making that emotional connection or as we talked about before being vulnerable with our students, so that they feel that they we are trustworthy. And just to pick up on that information processing and connecting it back to Reading Apprenticeship, I think that some of the routines the Reading Apprenticeship routines work well with us being culturally responsive. So, for instance, the turn and talk or talking or the TAPPS (think-aloud paired problem solving). That is something that I use in my class as well, and I know I won't speak for Ibrahim, but I know he uses a lot of other sort of experiential and interactive routines in his class, and I'm always looking for a way to, to have students use strategies to in again very experiential, hands-on kind of ways, because that's how the brain learns. The brain learns best in community. Right, in a safe community where there aren't any microaggressions, or any overt bias right? So that is something that I'm always thinking about. So like if for instance, we're reading, I make eye contact. And at the beginning of semester, I let students know that if we're reading something out loud and you don't feel comfortable reading it, that's totally fine with me. You can participate in other ways. and I don't call on students who let me know that they are not comfortable reading out loud. So when we do use the strategies and stumble and, and you know these are folks who I feel like, trust me. They've you to show that they are comfortable stumbling. They're comfortable showing how they're learning the material in real time. And that is something that only happens because we've taken—that I've taken—the time out to build a relationship with my students.

Ibrahim: That's dope.

Salina: And I think that's like a perfect segue discussing the tensions we notice. When we are talking about tensions, I think when it comes to coupling or marrying the two, a lot of tension is not really tied to one or the other. What tensions for me that I've noticed ties to specific tensions is because it's challenging, and the process that they're learning in regards to the tools that we're giving them is a brand new thing that they've never had to rely on in the past. So I think if it came to tensions it would be more of the newness or the challenging ways to navigate through readings that they didn't have before.

Ibrahim: It made me think about a couple of different things. But Yhashika, when you read that last quote from Professor Hammond right? It just makes me sum that up as win the hearts to win the mind. Or win the heart to stretch the mind right cause if we actually care, and we show that we're regular humans. We do make mistakes and the learning isn't a mistake, but the learning is taking data for us to understand what we can do to do something right, or, or make a correction, or, or readdress something. It's not like a penalty or something that needs to be a sanction for ourselves. Right. But it's a learning point right where we can step in right and, and just to like scaffold a little bit more. Right. And to build off what you said, Salina, students might not be used to the methods that we use, because they're used to being trained, or what school should look like. They're not used to having power. They're not used to having voice and choice. They're not used to being able to decide how they would like to respond to a certain thing. Right? All of my assignments. I say that the students rarely take me up on, I say, hey, you could respond in audio, video, text, rap, whatever you want to get your point across, but don't plagiarize, right. If you want to do something, cite the source, cite the author. But how you do it is up to you. And I have to keep reminding students that you have much more flexibility than what you've been using to respond to the things that you do in my class than in other courses. They might have different ways to express what they know right, and if I know that a student is an artist right why can't you draw and show me what you know but then explain what it is that you got from that right. Because that's the way you display your information right so for me that ties into my method and with Reading Apprenticeship right? Because when, when we think about reading, reading might not just be words on the page. It could be how you interpret things in your mind and give that back, and express what you know. So that type of positioning for students is different when they come to my class. They really not used to it. It takes them some getting used to, to have a professor like, look, you can use an extension of your talents to show what you know. If you can prove it, and you're being respectful of the sources, and you can show how that is like. For me there ain't no box, right, people so there's no box like I'm trying to try different things and pull what students know out of them.

Yhashika: No, I think it's definitely a part of what Hammond calls the you know, dependent and independent learners, and when we're being culturally responsive we're trying to push our students into being independent learners, and that a part of that is that choice. And that comes from that just based on what you just said, Ibrahim, and, and a lot of that is teaching them that here are these strategies that you can use, and you can use them in a lot of different ways. You're not just limited to writing an essay, or you're not limited to doing the research, however you use it in your class. Again, the point is ultimately is that you? We understand that our students come to us having spent their K through 12 years being dependent learners, not being pushed to think on their own. And in our classes, we are trying to make sure that they come out being independent thinkers, being independent learners so that they can carry the load themselves. So we're not carrying it, so you get these tools right now. Well, just actually let me just continue thinking about the tensions. So for me, some of the tension is that some of the routines that we have used can feel like they're, you know, like multiple small assignments, and, and for some students that can get overwhelming and definitely with all the other things that they're doing as well. So a part of being culturally responsive is making sure that there's meaning behind every single assignment. It's not just rote, so I've pivoted this semester and, and starting midway through semester, I've told students you know based on what I'm seeing you all have internalized these strategies. You know how to use these strategies, the Reading Apprenticeship strategies on the bookmark. So instead, we're going to do golden lines. And so you are going to pick a line from the chapter. Tell me why you picked it. Explain why you think it's important, and then we'll use that in the class, so we'll use that as part of our conversation. And so this week will be our first time actually using it. And so I think that that is something I have to be mindful of when I'm using the strategies because again we don't want to do to our students what they were experiencing before, where they're filling in worksheets, and you know, just doing this sort of rote, repetitive boring work. Instead there needs to be some sort of I, I don't know what the word is. But a way for them to feel like there's a reason for this. There is actually a connection, an immediate and direct connection to their learning into what we're doing in the classroom. So I think when Reading Apprenticeship is perhaps thinking about how to create meaning, especially for students of color. That is something that they'll have to rethink in a few sure, right. What types of routines are. Maybe there are routines that already exist. And I'm just not aware of them. What types of routines can we use in the class that students who have been sort of nickeled and dimed in the K through 12 can find this fun? Can we get their brains' attention, which is a part of reading. I'm sorry I read a part of culturally responsive teaching and the brain right? We need to get the brain's attention and we need to have students understand that you're not just doing this to check off a box. There is a there's a reason for that it process content so whatever it is that we're doing is authentic and connected I'll pass it on to someone else.

Ibrahim: Maybe we can focus on practices that help to make RA implementation more culturally responsive. What practices help to make Reading Apprenticeship implementation more culturally responsive? Hmmm.

Yhashika: This is the equity-based routines that we discussed years ago. Definitely is a part of it. So you know it's a part of my transparency. It's a part of me bringing race into everything that we do so. And you know when we're talking about our reading history, when we're talking about what reading looked like for us when we were younger, I do bring race into it. So I talk about, you know, for me for the longest time I thought reading was a sort of solitary thing that you did because I didn't really have anyone read to me, and I always used reading as a form of, you know, sole entertainment, and escape. So since I've been learning about how to teach Reading Apprenticeship and just reading in general, as I got older, I realized that reading is actually a more communal, group-oriented activity. It's not just something that you do in the couch by yourself. It's something that you can do as part of a group where you're reading a part of a book, and you know you're digesting it together, and it's hitting you, and that's come from book clubs, and, and having these conversations. And that's something I bring to my students and just, you know, hopefully letting them know that you know especially if you come from backgrounds where your parents may not have spoken English, or your parents are busy working, and didn't you know weren't reading to you every night or, or reading wasn't an active part of your life. That you can see reading in a different way. It's like having a different connection with the text. And it starts with the personal reading history. Right? That is the introduction to Reading Apprenticeship, and that is definitely the place to set the stage for why it's important for why the framework is important.

Ibrahim: If you start reflecting on your personal reading history, you can really dig up some either some old good stuff, or even some old trauma, you know what I'm saying, depending on how it played out for you right, so that can, that can cut a couple different ways. And that also shows the emotional power of, you know, thinking about what it means to read effectively, right? Because people have different experiences, and you can start unlocking the path right. And when you start telling stories right, it is through the art of storytelling that we understand our reality better, right. And if somebody can spin you a good yarn about a story that they had happen to them in the past based around something that they read, or reading or something that happened to them while reading, or how their confidence was increased or decreased or how they were told to read: all of those things could come about, right. And if we have that trusting environment, right, and they chill, safe, and they know that they part of a learning community where we want to support you and lift you up, when you do read either independently or publicly, or if you do give an answer this professor right here ain't gonna publicly embarrass you or try to make you feel like you ain't shit because you gave a response that they didn't like. Those type of things happen to us in our past learning experiences. Well, I'll say it happened to me. I don't say it happened to y'all, but people used to try to get on me for my accent, and how I talk, you know, race that. Try to get on me about how I talk and how I move right, and in my heart it probably sparks something in think like oh, like I wanna that's the type of I don't know if it made me think about being a teacher, but probably like inadvertently or clandestinely, like in the back of my mind, one of the reasons why I probably wanted to teach is because I have so many jerkass racist teachers in my past man, that really try to discourage me from, from doing excellent in my educational career. You know what I'm saying for my educational pursuit. And as I got older and I started understanding like, yo, like when you teach you, you're literally a motivator, man, like your job is to motivate others to be their best right, and if they mess up you don't kick them, you know you lift them right. And the more you can do that, it allow for people to start gaining confidence in their abilities, right, which also stretching the mind, right. So the whole point is like for me like when you had these bad experiences in the past, or, or something like that. We can reset that, or we can try to get students on the path to see like, Look, every teacher's not that jerkass teacher that you had in the past that tried to crush you because you said something in your native beautiful language and they was too racist to see what it was that you was trying to communicate. Or they tried to pooh-pooh your experience like it didn't matter, because you know your people from another place something like that right? We don't do that. You know, we, we try to lift our people up and our students up. So yeah, I guess I guess I'll stay right there,

Yhashika: Yeah, so I'm also thinking about how (just gonna pull it up from the list here), how we set norms in the class as part of that community building. One of the things that I'm doing and it's, you know, and I let them know at the beginning of the semester. This may need to be moved up a little bit further, but this is, I'm just remembering it now. As part before we actually start using the strategies we create norms in the classroom. So I've added another layer onto that because my students are in teams. They work in teams, and so I have them create team norms, and they submit it to me. So they go off, and they sit and they brainstorm like, How am I going to show up in this group in a way that I'm comfortable, and you all are comfortable, and and you know we can build trust together. And then when we come back together as a group, they pick norms from their team that they think that we should institute classwide. And that is again that that community building, that trust building that is such an important part of being culturally responsive, right? Students need to feel like they can, as Ibrahim just pointed out, mess up right, they can stumble as they're reading. They can do the hard work of processing in front of their peers without worrying that either their teacher or their peers will make fun of them, or belittle them in some way. I think the other thing, too, is that it also is communal. Right. It's collectivistic and in a part of our framework that we use the from the *Culturally Responsive Teaching and the Brain* text that requires that we look for authentic ways to create community in the class or not create community, but sort of surface the community that's already there, right, or just reinforce the community, or the communal aspect of our students' identities that are already there. And so it's creating a group within the class that's going to use these strategies together, or that will process, read a text and stumble together, and, and, and that's a part of their relationship. And they're comfortable, and it starts again with those group norms that I've started doing.

Ibrahim: That's really cool right, and if you talk about norms like what I do at the top of you know each class, every class that we have like, I call it not norms but codes of honor is what I call it. So how are we gonna honor each other, right, like I, I call it community codes of honor and you know I got something that I'm bringing to the table, what I expect, but then, you know you turn the mike over to everybody else, and like what you gonna bring to this space, right.

Yhashika: And I think one challenge I highlighted earlier, was the lack of immediate, what's the word. I, I guess sometimes students aren't aware of the rationale, for example, the reading log, or you know some of the other routines, and I think for me it's really important that I, I make these clear, and you know I reinforce it several times, that you're using the strategies because it's we're helping you learn how to unpack dense text. Like it has to be very clear to students. Otherwise it's easy for them to just kind of brush it off like, Why am I doing this right? And I, I think that's a struggle or that's an issue for me, as I'm teaching, but I, I think also as we are going forward with this new generation of students who don't wanna do busy work who don't want to do anything and they don't really have to write. They need like an immediate payoff, or they need to see like a really very clear connection between what we're asking them to do in some sort of outcome or, or you know something related to the course, that that the, the activities are maybe through hypothesis, or, you know, just done in a way that really keeps their attention, and again feels like there is a reason behind it. I, I don't know how else to express it. So I think, yeah, I, I definitely think that it ties into the, the authentic opportunities to process content. So perhaps, as we are doing this in class in the future as I'm doing this in my class, perhaps using hypothesis or some text based way of, of doing the of using those strategies. I think that would be better.

Ibrahim: Cool, for me is this remembering like some of the basics of what Reading Apprenticeship is? But once you remember what they are, you can see how well it, it kind of overlaps with culturally responsive teaching, cause I got a little cheat sheet here, and it says that you know, with Reading Apprenticeship it's those four dimensions: it's personal, it's knowledge building, it's cognitive, and it's social, right. All of those things are like at the heart of what Reading Apprenticeship is right, and it's, it's up to us then to find ways to both connect it to the experiences of our students, the, the, the, the marriage of the content that we're trying to investigate together, right having that collective understanding that we're gonna support you. But we also want to let you use your creativity to implement and put your spin and your individual flair onto whatever is you're producing as proof that you understand what we discussed right into effect. Like those things like, like come together I think in kind of a really smooth manner right? And I think that if I could just make myself remember, because I've got a lot to go to my brain that you know Reading Apprenticeship is about social, which is also about you know, culturally responsive education, personal like that's it, build knowledge, that's like building intellective capacity, and, and cognitive right really flexing the brain muscle. That's really our mission. Our mission is to win the heart to win the mind, and once you win the heart, people feel safe. Then you could stretch the minds, right. That's the whole point, right, of doing all these extra things that we do that isn't really extra for us, because it's how we teach, right. It's just us setting the stage because we know that there's an inverse relationship between stress and learning right. If stress goes up, learning goes down right, and the learning goes up stress should go down. Right. So there's an inverse relationship between those two things. If we can remember that, we'll be very, very good in implementing various ways to try new things in our classroom collective experience.

Yhashika: No, I think that as we go forward, and we're continuing to include Reading Apprenticeship in our practice, and, and we try to figure out ways to, to make the strategy more inclusive. I think one key way is for race, equity, and any discussion about, I guess, diversity to be like forefront. It's not an add on; it's completely interwoven. So we're thinking about the social dimension: we understand that lack of safety comes from microaggressions. You cannot do Reading Apprenticeship as a trainer, as a practitioner without learning this. That ties into that awareness portion of our framework for quadrant rather of the *Culturally Responsive Teaching and the Brain* ready for rigor framework. I guess we're trying to make our students prepared to do this hard work to do this heavy lifting. We better as instructors be a safe space, or create a safe space in that classroom like that is like the floor. Yeah, I think that is what I would like to end with.

PART III

Reading Is a Problem-Solving Process

In the survey of faculty we describe in the introduction, we asked faculty about breakthroughs in their disciplinary teaching as the result of incorporating Reading Apprenticeship into their practice. One of the themes that emerged from that research is the recognition that *reading is a problem-solving process*. Below, we elaborate on that theme with the specific results of the survey, making explicit connections to threshold concept theory as it is relevant. We close by contextualizing the chapters in this part in terms of related research.

When asked about breakthroughs in their teaching of reading, 14 faculty (16%) reflected on the transformation in their teaching as arising in some way from the idea of reading as a process. In response to the question about breakthroughs in their teaching, three faculty explicitly noted as a surprise their discovery that reading is a process. One wrote, "I didn't realize what a process it actually was. To extract meaning from a text." Another wrote, "This is very basic, but as a writing teacher with NO training in reading instruction, I didn't even realize that reading is a process!"

To write that reading is a process is to suggest the meaning making that happens when individuals read does not happen instantaneously but rather over time and through a series of steps. To claim that it is a problem-solving process suggests the active engagement of readers in those steps and the variation in those steps according to the particular problems being solved. Even more, the connection to other kinds of problem solving implies that learners must discover or be taught the means to solve the problems that arise in new contexts. Thus, experts and novices read differently because they have different levels of experience solving the particular problems that arise in reading disciplinary texts.

In the second chapter of *Reading for Understanding*, which describes the Reading Apprenticeship Framework, the word *process* appears either in singular or plural form over 60 times. Because of that, it may not be surprising that instructors who have experienced quite a bit of Reading Apprenticeship professional learning would regard reading as a process. Some of them noted, however, that explicitly thinking about reading as a process, and in particular a process that changed according to purpose and context, was a breakthrough understanding for them. The notions that reading is a process that varies according to context and that all readers must learn to read differently when they enter new contexts are central to the Reading Apprenticeship framework. Setting up their discussion of that framework, Schoenbach and colleagues (2012) write that people "read with reference to a particular world of knowledge and experience related to the text" they are reading (p. 18). They go on to describe not only the ways that we activate particular bodies of knowledge when we read texts in different situations but that we apply different strategies to our reading. One of the subheadings of chapter 2 of *Reading for Understanding*, in fact, is "Reading Is Problem Solving."

In the framework itself, one of the core domains is the cognitive dimension, which focuses on making explicit the problem-solving strategies used to make sense of text. If those problem-solving strategies could be identified once and generalized universally, there would be no need for extended reading instruction, but in fact different strategies are called for in different reading situations. That's why metacognitive conversation—talk about how readers make sense of text—is central to the Reading Apprenticeship framework. And Reading Apprenticeship professional development focuses a good deal of time and energy on this threshold concept, including two routines that bring it into public view—Capturing the Reading Process and Expert Blind Spot. Capturing the Reading Process is just what it sounds like: all of the readers in the professional development setting read a short, common, challenging text and make notes about how they engaged with the text. In settings that include faculty from many disciplines, the conversation that follows often surfaces disciplinary differences in how expert readers encounter texts. That insight is only strengthened with the Expert Blind Spot routine, in which faculty in mixed-discipline pairs articulate their process of trying to make sense of texts in each other's area of expertise. Such an activity highlights for disciplinary insiders the assumptions about background knowledge and reading process they bring to their reading.

Beyond the "basic" observation that reading is a process, though, a key part of the transformation for many was in noticing their own processes in relation to problem solving text and the value of sharing those disciplinary ways of being with students. Many more faculty (24 individuals, 28%) than those just noting that reading is a process identified an implication of the idea that reading is a problem-solving process as transformational—the idea that experts and novices read differently. For example, one faculty asserted, "I think the most significant breakthrough for me is realizing my own expert lens when it comes to teaching reading" and similarly, "I began to have more intentional design [to show] how to extract meaning from a text or diagram or problem." Such reflections connect back to the expert-to-novice direction of apprenticeship—the experienced readers showing novices how they work. These reflections also illustrate that faculty we surveyed remain in a **liminal** space with regard to this threshold concept: They recognize that, as experts, they bring particular problem-solving skills to their reading, but they are not acknowledging the problem-solving skills students bring with them.

Many of the faculty connected awareness of their own expert reading strategies with specific teaching practices. For instance, one respondent identified that the "'talk-to-the-text' routine made me realize the dialogue that I have with myself when reading and processing a difficult text, and that asking students to do the same would help them identify specific questions rather than saying 'I don't get it.'" Similarly, another respondent shared, "I questioned whether I had anything worthwhile to say. I assumed that my knowledge of language acquisition and disciplinary reading was common knowledge." For many, this transformation offered new clarity and relief, such as when one educator shared that "I was able to better respond to students and pinpoint their areas of confusion, rather than feeling frustrated" and another asserted that "this activity let students see or hear exactly what I am thinking which is a real eye opener for them." These quotes reveal that while instructors often share what they know, it is more unusual for them to share HOW they know it. Entering this **liminal** space means recognizing that there is a "how" to share (and perhaps to negotiate).

While many faculty identified noticing their expert problem-solving strategies to be a valuable breakthrough, the consequences of that insight for teaching seemed sometimes to be more challenging. For instance, one faculty member noted that focusing on reading as a problem-solving process has led to thinking differently about the goals of teaching: "The breakthrough for me has been letting go of what is 'right' all the time. I have seen that the value is not always in students getting to the right answer or interpretation but in making their own meaning and then watching that insight develop and deepen and change as they work with others." That idea that readers may approach solving problems differently was also a breakthrough for another faculty member, who noted, "What works for me more than likely needs to be different for others. It is my role to show different techniques and then give space for those techniques to be applied, struggled with, and finally mastered." This reflection connects back to the metaconcept—ultimately, students have to find their own ways of doing the disciplines. Note, though, that in this statement, the instructor is still the source of the different techniques. In metacognitive conversations, students too are sources of strategies from which everyone can learn.

Along these lines, one faculty asserted, "students are in constant dialogue with texts and connect what they read/watch with things they know and ideas or questions brought up by others. This is a high-level skill that I was actually hindering before I started implementing RA strategies." Another respondent offered a window into her own liminality by noting that she has "become more open" to seeing reading as disciplinary problem solving. That "new openness" suggests the change in perspective that Land and colleagues (2014) describe as central to crossing thresholds. Yet another respondent acknowledged the challenge by sharing, "the [reading] process is very personal, and . . . it is very context-specific, and . . . too often our expert blind spots can really get in the way." Still another participant acknowledged the ongoing challenge in moving past related unexamined assumptions in asserting that "it's really eye opening for students to see how they have different experiences and conclusions about reading and what makes a good reader. . . . It made me think about how much I and other educators may assume that students already know how to do these metacognitive processes, and that may not be true for students." Each of these instructors is grappling with the consequences of seeing reading as problem solving in their work with students.

Another five instructors reflected on the importance of metacognition as a breakthrough for them, sometimes in ways that suggested that metacognitive conversation is a troublesome practice to enact. Schoenbach and colleagues (2012) describe metacognitive conversation as an opportunity for both instructors and students to surface and share their problem-solving strategies and learn from each other. One instructor wrote after reflecting on how central metacognitive conversation is to Reading Apprenticeship practice, for instance, "It (metacognitive conversation) is also, incidentally, the thing that it took me the longest to actually incorporate into my pedagogy," which hints at its troublesome nature. Another wrote, "I think every metacognitive conversation is a breakthrough," and a third suggested that the modeling and metacognition involved in RA practice was at least a little troublesome: "I have been surprised at how well the think alouds work. When I first read about them, I thought they seemed so basic, but they make a huge difference, and I use them all the time now." That the faculty member finds the value of think-alouds surprising suggests the troublesomeness of the concept. This comment also highlights a pattern suggesting that embracing this concept was irreversible as well, teachers noting that they "use them all the time now" or continue to engage with practices that stem from the insight that reading is a process.

In grappling with *reading as a problem-solving process*, many educators integrated a number of elements to come to broader and deeper realizations, most commonly by offering their transformed relationship to content. For example, one participant shared, "teaching a discipline means teaching reading in that discipline, that teaching disciplinary reading strategies is maybe even more important than teaching content itself." Another faculty asserted, "my role as an instructor is to curate content, and also support students in how they interact with content/text" and "I can impact my students in far deeper and long-lasting ways than if I just deliver content." Such comments are hints at the worlds that instructors see when they have crossed this threshold.

SOME SCHOLARLY CONTEXT FOR THE CHAPTERS IN THIS PART

The chapters in this part cross disciplines in their exploration of reading as problem solving, with Slown examining reading in chemistry and biology, Padgett describing reading in history, and Leuzinger and Megwalu addressing metacognition in information literacy instruction.

These chapters, therefore, fit solidly in the context of other research on reading in specific disciplines. In that research, as in these chapters, the particulars of problem-solving reading in the disciplines takes center stage in the analysis. Padgett, for instance, grapples with teaching history students the particular ways of reading and reasoning of historians. Such a focus has occupied the Stanford History Education Group as well as scholars in the decoding the disciplines projects (e.g., Pace, 2004; Grim et al., 2004) and beyond (e.g., Pretzlaff, 2017; Wineburg et al., 2013). While Padgett has his own routines that focus on metacognition and historical argument, he shares with Grim and colleagues (2004) a concern with the appropriate use of evidence in historical thinking and with both the Stanford History Education Group and Wineburg and colleagues (2013) a concern with sourcing of historical artifacts.

When Slown discusses her use of think-aloud paired problem solving (TAPPS) with her chemistry and biology students, she is addressing a similar concern to Davies (2017), who highlights the need to help students develop reading processes for the different genres of texts they encounter as science students. Zolan and colleagues (2004) also focus on process, but their focus is on the specific process of visualizing and model-making that experts in their fields use to understand biological concepts. Visualization also plays an important problem-solving role in astronomy (Durisen & Pilachowski, 2004). Other concerns in scholarship on teaching reading in the sciences relate to the effectiveness of teaching students about the structure of scientific articles (Cook and Mayer, 1988) and whether teaching students explicitly about how to critique scientific articles improves their critiques (it does; Gyuris & Castell, 2013).

Focusing on metacognition in library/information-literacy instruction, Leuzinger and Megwalu join other library instructors who have taken such an approach both before and following the publication of the Association of College and Research Libraries (ACRL) framework in 2015. For instance, Bowler (2010) investigated the metacognitive strategies adolescents applied during the process of writing a research paper and came up with a list of thirteen: "balancing, building a base, changing course, communicating, connecting, knowing that you don't know, knowing your strengths and weaknesses, parallel thinking, pulling back and reflecting, scaffolding, understanding curiosity, understanding memory, understanding time and effort" (p. 33). Other scholars have focused on strategies to support the development of "information problem solving (IPS)" (Blummer & Kenton, 2014). Blummer and Kenton (2014) test what they call an "idea tactic tutorial" (p. 2) as a metacognitive scaffold for graduate students' research skills and Houtman (2015) argues for the inclusion of reflective activities in library instruction to build self-regulated learning.

The authors of the chapters in this part bring their expertise and experience with Reading Apprenticeship to the conversations represented by this research. They explore the value of offering students opportunities to problem-solve and bring themselves into disciplinary texts using the tools, strategies, and processes that support their professional identities and competencies. These interactions with peers and experts are the means by which students build confidence and strengthen their sense of belonging in their academic and professional communities.

Chapter 7

Reading Historically through Metacognitive Logs

Christopher Padgett

History students begin a semester with a backpack full of common expectations. Foremost among them is that their chief learning outcome will be to answer a single straightforward question, one they fully expect to be repeated ad nauseam: What happened? Tucked into the back pocket of that expectation is the dread of an exhaustive memorization of historical facts. Such expectations are not surprising given the tidy textbook packaging of the past that teaches students to read history in terms of *what?* More concerning is that a tight focus on the *what?* offers students little choice but to accept as given the larger narrative that those countless facts evidently affirm. In formal terms, this approach nurtures a pre-liminal understanding of the history discipline, where *history* is the tedious identification of that which has already happened in a story that has already been told. Students have their own colorful descriptor of this role; they call it regurgitation. Rather than limit students to the custodial duty of reading for packaged facts in an already written story, we want our students to read history as a fertile field from which they may reap new stories and harvest meaning for their lives.

Our goal is to teach students how to read historically. Most history educators keenly appreciate the need for analytical and nuanced understandings of the past, beyond the simple memorizing of facts, but too often the demands of a content-stuffed curriculum crowd out the space and time needed to teach historical reading. To help our students become perceptive readers of history, we must reallocate class time for metacognitive routines that support historical reading and thinking. To read historically means to read contextually, and to be on the hunt for meaning. Mastering the threshold concept of contextual analysis empowers students to problematize and problem-solve the past, to read the past as unfinished, evolving, and useful in the problem solving of their contemporary world. Metacognitive logs provide a framework for practicing what I call the cognitive subroutines of contextual reading and analysis. Borrowed by analogy from computer language coding, I use the language of subroutines here to mean the frequently performed critical reading operations that together constitute reading historically.

"I THOUGHT, I FELT, I WONDERED": ESTABLISHING THE METACOGNITIVE BASELINE

Before taking on the cognitive work of contextual analysis in the full metacognitive log, I prep students with evidence-interpretation notetaker (figure 7.1) and talk-to-the-text routines (figures 7.2 and 7.3). Familiar to Reading Apprenticeship practitioners, these routines introduce students to primary source reading and metacognitive reflection on their reading experience. Here students are free to surface their thinking: make summary notes, ask questions, note confusion, make connections, register complaints, establish context, and add ruminations, impressions, inferences, feelings, and interpretations. Here is where students begin to apprehend history as a problem-solving discipline, and with these routines they establish a metacognitive baseline for further inquiry and problem solving.

"METACOGNITIVE CHOREOGRAPHY": BUILDING THE METACOGNITIVE LOG

Historical reading is built upon the interplay of the three essential cognitive subroutines of contextual analysis: basic context, evidence, and interpretation. One flexible approach to reading primary historical sources involves a simple three-column format to identify and disaggregate these three subroutines (figure 7.4). Two of the columns provide space for the visible and empirical: **Column 1** identifies basic context, and **Column 2** presents evidence. **Column 3** is an expansive space for interpretation, which builds on a synthesis of the first two columns,

Golden Lines: Evidence	Interpretation: I wondered/I made a Connection/I thought
"He walks out in front, the leader, and walks at the rear, trusted by his companions."	I think that this line here shows how people at this time in history had values. They valued trust, especially in friendship as seen in the line, "...trusted by his companions." But not only does this show what kind of things were important to them in relationships, but also what kind of qualities were important to them in a leader. In addition to trust being an important quality, reliability in a leader for protection is also seen to be important. This is seen in the section that says, "He walks out in front, the leader, and walks at the rear." It gives Gilgamesh a sort of omnipresent quality, so that his people have no need to fear. All in all, this just shows that people were starting to define what values were of the utmost importance to them and their culture, specifically in what was looked for in a

Figure 7.1. A simple two-column T-Table, with quoted "golden line" (from the Epic of Gilgamesh) on the left and reader comments on the right
Chris Padgett

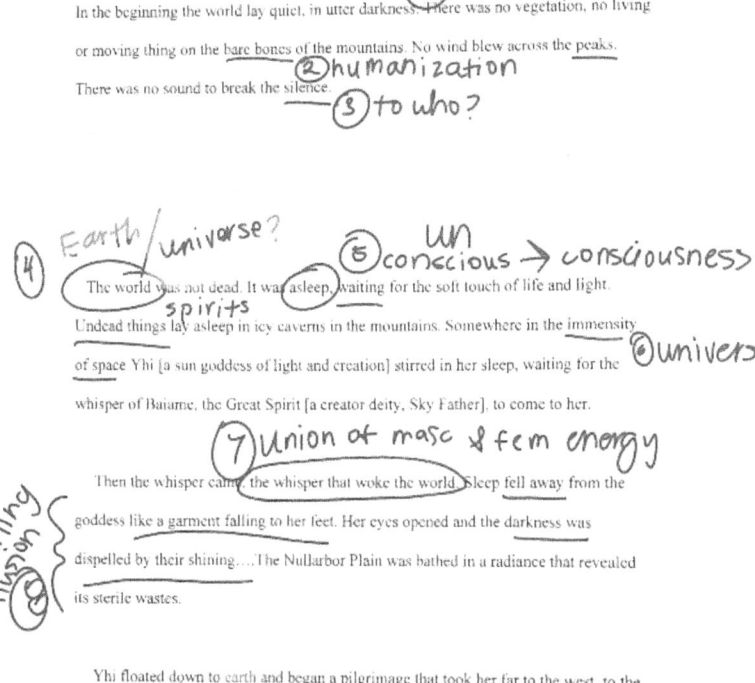

Figure 7.2. Talk to the Text with primary source—The Australian Dreamtime (sample 1)
McLeod & Huddleston, 1994

along with elements drawn from student schema, including insights from the evidence-interpretation notetaker and talk-to-the-text routines. With a simple and accessible format, these routines offer students both the metacognitive space for developing reader self-awareness, and a framework for directing the cognitive subroutines of contextual reading.

"Who, What, When, Where, and for Whom?": Column 1: The Five Ws

To say something or someone has a history is to say we discern a spatial and temporal field. History posits change across space and time. **Column 1** captures the cognitive subroutine of

Mark 1: When I read "lay quiet, in utter darkness" I thought if there was nothing to be and nothing to see, or rather no one to hear and no one to see then there wouldn't be anyway to keep track of time either. Who knows how long it was quiet and dark for while there nothing to attach a sense of time to.

Mark 2: I underlined "bare bones" and "peaks" because this specific diction indicates humanization. Something common in human stories, new or old, is to relate that which we don't quite understand to that we do, especially our own form and humanness.

Mark 3: I underlined "silence" as it again humanizes the concept of Earth or the Universe, suggesting that it can hear or sense things as we do. Perhaps suggesting an unnamed but inherent soul or spirit.

Mark 4: I circled "the world" since I was unsure if this indicated Earth, the planet, our world- or the whole Universe- the world to all things (as far as we can comprehend). Beneath that I underlined "undead things" which led me to think of spirits again and pushed me to wonder how many concepts or "things" were believed to have a spirit.

Mark 5: I circled "asleep" and underlined "waiting" written before the phrase "soft touch of life and light". This made me think of the transition from unconsciousness to consciousness. Being alive or conscious means being aware of self and environment, but how exactly did an "environment" and a "self" come to be in the first place? And then lead to consciousness? And who did it first? What is the first "self"?

Mark 6: The phrase "immensity of space" indicates to me that this has been about the Universe the whole time since space exists without Earth, but not without the Universe. But then what contains the Universe? And how did it come to be?

Mark 7: I circled "the whisper that woke the world". The whisper of Baiame to Yhi are described as god and goddess of creation. This story of creation is similar to the humans create life, usually involving the union of a man and woman. This "whisper" therefore energetically symbolizes the union of masculine and feminine energies that exist within all beings.

Mark 8: I underlined "fell away...like a garment falling to her feet" and "darkness dispelled by their [eyes] shining". This also made me think of consciousness since having open eyes is generally associated with being awake or conscious. Furthermore first part gave me a visualization of a veil being lifted, the veil being the concept that is one" or that nothing is separate- once the veil is gone and everything separated th comes awareness of "self" and "environment" and being able to distinguish between two.

Mark 9: I highlighted "earth" and underlined "the ground" since it caused me to wor if those things had always been present and "existed" or if it's very existence was dependent on it being perceived.

Mark 10: I underlined "crossed and recrossed" since it reminded me of the pattern e follows around the sun, which ensures that all parts are touched but the sun's rays, j like the story describes. This is another example of storytelling explaining real phenomenon using humanization with a figure such as Yhi.

When you are finished with this Talk to the Text exercise, save your file and upload our Canvas course site using the RA3 assignment upload link.

Figure 7.3. Talk to the Text with primary source—The Australian Dreamtime (sample 2)
Chris Padgett

basic context, where students identify the historical place and time of the primary sources they are assigned to read. Historians call this process "sourcing" the document. More than just compiling facts in a list, sourcing poses a question: *which* basic contextual facts must we first identify and prioritize from our reading to situate the source in its correct place and time? Since **Column 1** also contains the historical facts that students prefer to fudge (e.g., "in those days" instead of 500 BCE, or "why do we need to know dates?"), we may first prompt students to surface their thinking about facts (e.g., when is a fact a fact?). **Column 1** in the metacognitive log offers another opportunity for students to establish a metacognitive baseline for apprehending spatial and temporal elements, a process they have already begun with the evidence-interpretation and talk-to-the-text routines.

"What Does It Say?" Column 2: Evidence

Evidence gathering is the essential cognitive subroutine in **Column 2**. In Reading Apprenticeship terms, students here are selecting golden lines from their reading as evidence, and straightforwardly presenting them as a direct quote from the primary source itself. If the primary source features no written text, then in place of golden lines, students write descriptions, in their own words, of the non-text primary source, for example, painting, sculpture, statue, architecture (figure 7.5). Regardless of the type of primary source, history is an evidence-based discipline that requires students to show proof of what they claim. Evidence may take many forms, but is a "right there" proposition, something that can be pointed to and easily read, examined,

History 307   **Metacognitive Log**   Dr. Padgett
Format Guide

Context (who, for whom, what, where, when)	Evidence (golden line/description)	Interpretation: Big Picture (I found a connection....)
Evidence Document 1 **The 5 W's** • The name of the author/creator of your primary source document; if no person is identified, explain what sort of person might have authored it. • Who was the likely intended audience? • Identify the name and type of primary source, whether a written document, an inscription, cave painting, sculpture, etc. • Where was the primary source created or discovered? • Provide a date of origin; if there is no specified date, then describe the general time period or age in which it was created.	• If your primary source is a written source, then choose a golden line directly from the source. A golden line is an actual quoted line, so be sure to record every word and use quotation marks to indicate which exact words are copied from the source. NOTE: do not paraphrase or summarize – record here the actual words in quotation marks. • If your primary source is NOT a written text but rather a work of art, say a statue, an image drawn, etched, or painted, or maybe architecture, such as a temple, pyramid, or palace, then provide a detailed description in your own words, such that a person not seeing it would have a good idea of what it looks like.	• How does the contextual information (column 1) help us situate the evidence in a particular place and time? Why is it important for our understanding to know that? • If we did not know the proper historical context, how might we be confused or mistaken about what it meant? • What connection can you make between your evidence (column 2) and the bigger historical picture to which it belongs? How does what you learned in lecture or other assigned reading, help you make sense of the evidence you have selected? • How does the evidence help us make sense of that larger context and the people and time period to which it belongs? • Does the evidence help us understand why certain things happened at that time?

Figure 7.4. Metacognitive Log Format Guide for Students
Chris Padgett

interpreted, and discussed. Empirical, after all, means capable of being examined or observed. As a cognitive subroutine, students apprehend the primary source as the raw data from which they must contextually assess and select information in support of their interpretation. Here is where the metacognitive choreography gets activated: by referencing information in **Column 1** to inform active reading and evidence selection in **Column 2**, students begin to assume cognitive control over a selection process. **Column 2** also offers instructors an opportunity to nurture a deeper discussion with students about evidence and what they encounter in the text as they read, such as inherent or explicit bias, subtext, or context-specific language.

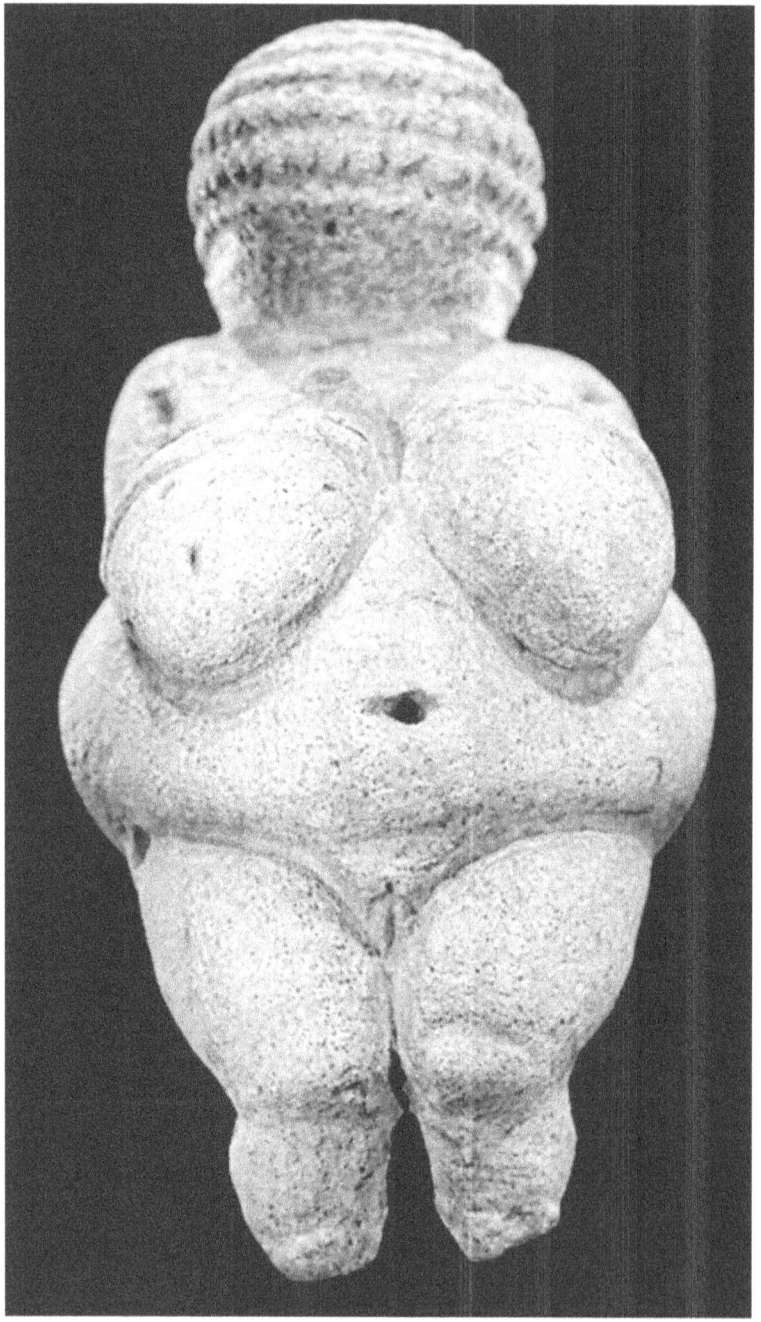

Figure 7.5. When the primary text consists of non-text evidence
Tørrissen, 2020

Identifying bias, whether a political, ideological, or racial viewpoint expressed in the text, is itself an important cognitive subroutine of reading historically, one for which a beginning history student must develop metacognitive awareness in their reading routine until it becomes a natural part of problem solving a source. To help my students find bias in primary sources, I employ a reading against the grain strategy. Using an evidence-interpretation two-column notetaker, I ask students to record golden lines from the primary source document in the evidence column. Note, for this particular exercise on bias, the golden lines in **Column 1** should reflect what the author likely intended to convey to their presumed audience. We call this reading with the grain of the document. Next, reading against the grain, I ask students to infer how we might perceive the golden line from the vantage point of a deeper contextual understanding, keeping in mind any antagonistic or contrary elements present in the author's world when the piece was written. Our primary source sample here is a runaway slave ad from a Philadelphia newspaper, 1796 (figure 7.6). In this case, reading with the grain of the document offers a familiar claim from the period of legal slavery, by an enslaver asking for the return of a fugitive enslaved servant. Reading against the grain in **Column 2** (figure 7.7) reveals how an inherent racial/patriarchal bias in the text of the enslaver's ad obscures the personhood and moral agency of the enslaved. If one were to summarize that document only, then the only evidence to help us understand slavery would consist of the enslaver's words as a literal rendering of what happened. Missing would be any sense of how his words frame a self-serving and highly

Primary Source:
George Washington - Fugitive Slave Ad
American Daily Advertiser, May 25, 1796

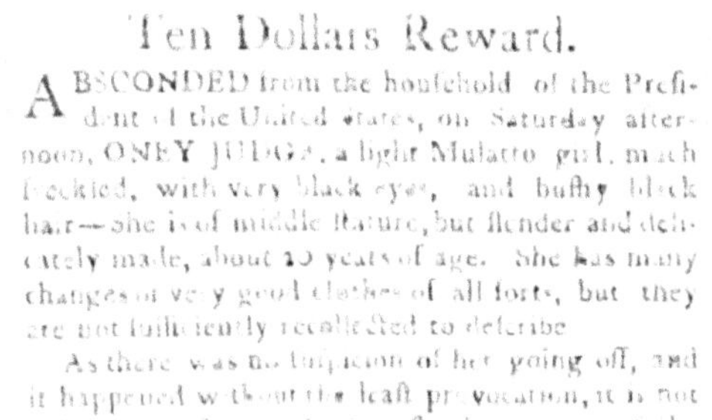

Ten Dollars Reward.

Absconded from the household of the President of the United States, on Saturday afternoon, ONEY JUDGE, a light Mulatto girl, much freckled, with very black eyes, and bushy black hair – She is of middle stature, but slender and delicately made, about 20 years of age. She has many changes of very good clothes of all sorts, but they are not sufficiently recollected to describe.

As there was no suspicion of her going off, and it happened without the least provocation, it is not easy to conjecture whither she is gone – or fully, what her design is; but as she may attempt to escape by water, all masters of vessels and others are cautioned against receiving her on board, altho' she may, and probably will endeavour to pass for a free woman, and it is said has, wherewithal to pay her passage.

Ten dollars will be paid to any person, (white or black) who will bring her home, if taken in the city, or on board any vessel in the harbour; and a further reasonable sum if apprehended and brought home, from a greater distance, and in proportion to the distance.   Fred. Kitt, Steward
May 24

Figure 7.6. Primary Source—Fugitive Slave Ad
American Daily Advertiser, May 25, 1796

History 310   Evidence-Interpretation Notetaker   Dr. Padgett

Evidence: write 3 golden lines in this column	Interpretation: Reading Against the Grain – what did the document not intend to communicate?
"Absconded from the household…."	• 'Absconded' meant to runaway, and it was a word that often appeared in fugitive slave ads to frame an illegal action in the context of the eighteenth century slavery laws. The ad intended to announce a legal claim for her return, and the free, white newspaper readers would have understood it that way as well. • Considering the frequency of such runaway ads, we may read against the grain of this document to see Ona Judge outside the bias of presumed guilt, to see her "absconding" as a deliberate act of self-sovereignty. It was her personal denial of any moral basis for her enslavement or claim on her body by the fugitive slave laws of the day.
"As there was no suspicion of her going off, and it happened without the least provocation…."	• Enslavers like George Washington, were men of public standing, conscious of their reputations as trustworthy figures. They often presented themselves as benign patriarchs, who governed their enslaved servants in a benevolent manner, befitting their own reputations as men of public trust. • Based on what we know of the often dysfunctional nature of domestic relations between free and enslaved, including abuse, sexual assault, and shaming, we may wish to see President Washington's tone of surprise here as biased toward spin control, a self-conscious deflecting of attention from any hint of wrongdoing by the enslaver. The fugitive ad draws little attention to the awkward fact of enslavement in the president's household, given his prominence as a symbol American liberty. • By presenting Ona Judge as an apparently heedless or frivolous young women, Washington by contrast seems responsible, fatherly, and benevolent.

Figure 7.7. Evidence-Interpretation Notetaker to Assess Bias
Chris Padgett

attenuated view of the enslaver-enslaved relationship. One would not get from summary alone, in other words, the enslaver's patriarchal bias and inherent legal privilege, or for that matter the counterstrategy and personhood of the enslaved, who though they were enslaved were not without volition in the negotiations of power. This is especially important since primary source documents are often fetishized as "true" on their face and treated as evidence of original intent without interrogation of bias.

Since beginning history students are more inclined to summarize their reading than interpret, **Column 2** also offers opportunity for a classroom discussion as to the difference between summary and interpretation, which are two related but distinct cognitive subroutines of historical reading. To surface these cognitive subroutines in our metacognitive classroom, we might ask students to share as reading strategies how they chose their golden lines, whether for their summary value (i.e., what the source says generally) or their value for revealing explicit/implicit bias within the source. Asking students to clarify that distinction here will make it easier to convey how summary is supportive of but not identical to interpretation in **Column 3** of the metacognitive log.

"Making the Invisible Visible" Column 3: Interpretation

Column 3 is the space for interpretation, where students construct a contextual analysis of "what it all means."

In truth, *interpretation* is an umbrella term that includes a synthesis of distinctive cognitive subroutines such as causation, connection, comparison, extrapolation, inference, and hypothesis. Simply directing students to "analyze" or "interpret" is not especially helpful unless they are able metacognitively to identify and activate these other cognitive subroutines in creating overall meaning. Otherwise, they are likely to fall back on summary. Nor is interpretation an invitation for flights of fancy. The discipline of history requires interpretation to rest solidly on a foundation of basic context and evidence. Accordingly, **Column 3** asks students to "show their work," much like math students, with explicit identification of basic context and evidence.

Figure 7.8 offers a rubric to help students assess the contextual quality of their interpretive foundation. Instructors may activate the social dimension of learning here by having students peer-assess the contextual quality of one another's interpretations. Figure 7.9 provides a formative assessment sheet students may use to assess the context-specific thinking of their classmates, based on the criteria outlined in the adjacent rubric.

With a strong contextual foundation, modeled in the rubric as fourth level, students may build read for meaning by integrating that foundation with the other cognitive subroutines of interpretation to create a "big picture" historical meaning.

"CROSSING THE THRESHOLD": CONSTRUCTING A BRIDGE TO MEANING

For all of the formal structuring, historical interpretation is also inherently creative, and rests on individual insights, assessments, and expression. If done properly, **Column 3** interpretation will surface and make explicit the threshold moment when a student accepts metacognitively the creative opportunity for reading and thinking contextually. In figure 7.10, the student's metacognitive acceptance begins with the opening line: "I made a connection."

Here the student constructs meaning by integrating the cognitive subroutines of basic context in **Column 1**, and evidence gathering and assessment of evidence in **Column 2**, with the

1st Level: Summary – Paraphrase

Restating/translating/describing golden lines into student's vocabulary.

e.g. "Chief Joseph wanted peace."
e.g. "Thomas Jefferson said all men are created equal."

Premise: Students will often fall back on summary and restating the golden line instead using it as evidence for a big picture contextual interpretation.

2nd Level: Big picture interpretation with little or no specific contextual reference.

e.g. "people were greedy"
e.g. "many were unemployed"

Premise: Students opt for non-contextually specific generalizations about the past, usually involving large and loosely defined groups and large and loosely defined actions, with little or no specific contextual content, even though they may have identified such basic context in Column 1.

3rd Level: Big picture interpretation with general context – provides a few more specific descriptors and a general sense of context.

e.g. "immigrants were arrested during WWI"
e.g. "black people in the South wanted civil rights"

Premise: here students relate their golden line to a definable historical context, but in an incomplete way, missing one or more of the basic context clues (who, what, where, when, for whom).

4th Level: Big picture interpretation with context-specific descriptors.

e.g. "the massacre of Lakota at Wounded Knee in 1890 completed the U.S. Army's mission of Indian Removal in the nineteenth century."

Premise: here the students ARE connecting a golden line to a discrete historical context, using information from Column 1. They make inferences, connections, and comparisons to the relevant context by taking what they have learned about the period from lecture, reading, or their own schema, and historically contextualizing the golden line in that bigger picture setting. This involves a leap of faith, as it were, since the contextual information is not "right there" in the golden line for the students to see. They have to make that cognitive leap beyond the literal document and its literal text to the contextual framework in which they construct meaning and significance from the evidence.

Figure 7.8. Rubric to Assess Contextual Thinking
Chris Padgett

Scoring Metacognitive Log Column 3 Samples
Note: the following Column 3 interpretation samples are drawn from student responses to the reading of the following primary source: A. Philip Randolph, The Call to Negro America to March on Washington (1941). This reading was assigned as part of the unit on the movement for civil rights and racial justice in the U.S. during WWII.

Directions:
Use the formative assessment levels 1-4 to determine the contextual depth and completeness for each of the following Column 3 analyses. Each score should be followed with a brief explanation of which contextual elements were present/not present in the statement assessed.

Sample 1: "Randolph said We call upon you to fight for jobs in National Defense."
Level _____ Why:

Sample 2: "This tells me that times were really tough for blacks, but that they were not ready to give up."
Level _____ Why:

Sample 3: "This is a proof of contradiction between fighting for equality against Nazi Germany while continuing oppression of American citizens on the basis of race, color, religion that had place since the beginning of American history."
Level _____ Why:

Sample 3: "I chose this line because it shows the problem with Americans only being able to see color in humans. It connects to the time where being a color defined who you were."
Level _____ Why:

Sample 4: "During the early to mid 1900s, discrimination was high in America. They had a policy 'separate but equal' yet blacks received much unfair treatment, and Washington is saying they are tired of waiting and will fight to get what they deserve."
Level _____ Why:

Sample 5: "Though Roosevelt did give several executive orders during the war, in 1948 President Truman issued Executive Order 9981 which gave equal opportunity and right to men in the armed forces, which was the intended goal of Randolph."
Level _____ Why:

Sample 6: "Many white Americans despised the 'negro' race and spent the majority of their time tearing them down. African-Americans were not satisfied with 'separate but equal' and being treated unfairly."
Level _____ Why:

Figure 7.9. Student Peer Assessment of Contextual Thinking
Chris Padgett

cognitive subroutines of interpretation in **Column 3**, including comparison, causation, and synthesis. Activating their schema from lecture and assigned reading, our student also makes connections and assesses causation to construct a bigger-picture historical view of the Mongol empire. What they have accomplished in **Column 3** is a metacognitive arrangement of the basic cognitive subroutines, that is to say, an intentional, self-aware, and deliberate contextual understanding. With the golden line they have chosen from reading the primary source (**Column 2**), they have begun to construct a larger meaning for Mongol history, one that is only implicit or "invisible" in the primary source itself, but that is now made explicit in **Column 3** via the various cognitive subroutines. In doing so, the student has moved across the cognitive threshold from a mere custodial relationship with 'the facts' to conscious acceptance of authorship and meaning. We see the student's interpretation of the relatively tolerant cultural stance evident in the primary source with their thinking made visible ("I made a connection") to inform what historians call the Mongol ecumene. That is especially significant considering the standard story of the Mongols—the one a beginning history student might be stuck "regurgitating"—pictures them as irredeemably bloodthirsty Asiatic conquerors. This student has instead opted for a revised narrative, by using the basic contextual building blocks from **Column 1** ("14th and 13th centuries") along with selected reading evidence from **Column 2** ("this quote describes," "the primary source document backs up") to construct a nuanced contextual, and therefore historical, meaning for the Mongol past: "they would allow foreign cultures to practice their own religion." In figure 7.10, my tracking comments highlight how and where the student models contextual thinking by "showing their work" and directing the various cognitive subroutines to construct meaning.

Basic Context	Evidence	Interpretation	
Primary Source 11.1 Mongol History from a Mongol Source Who: Juvaini, a Persian high official in the Mongolian army and a historian, writes about his observations. What: Juvaini writes about the conquest of the city of Bukhara. Where: I'm not sure where Juvaini wrote his observations. The best guess would be Persia. When: 1216 C.E	"The imams [Muslim religious teachers] And notables came on a deputation to Chingiss Khan, who entered to inspect the town and citadel. He rode into the Juma Mosque. . . . Chingis Khan asked those present whether this was the palace of the Suitan; they replied it was the house of God."	I made a connection of assimilation between this document and a quote written in, "Ways of the World" by Robert W. Strayer. The quote reads, "It was the Mongol Empire, during the 14th and 13th centuries that brought all of these regions into a single interacting network." This quote describes that the Mongols, who were under the leadership of Genghis Khan, unified the Eurasian lands through conquest. As they conquered the lands as huge as the African continent they gave the rulers of those lands a choice; surrender or continue the fight. Regardless of the option chosen, if the Mongols won (they held victories most of the time) they would allow foreign cultures to practice their own religion because they believed I 'Tengri' is what the Mongols called the lord of the blue sky above" (From lecture Genghis Khan to Columbus, pt. 2, 6:34), and regarded all religions as manifestations of their own god. The primary source document backs up that statement when Chingiss Khan brought Muslim religious teachers to inspect Bukhara, and when seeing the Juma Mosque in the freshly conquered city, he didn't burn it or destroy it because it was the house of a god (which he regarded as his own in any religious case). In this way the regions stayed unified and cultural intermix persisted.	Commented [CP1]: Metacognition: Student thinking made visible. Cognitive sub-routine: making visible an otherwise invisible interpretation-connection between primary and secondary sources, involving a number of cognitive sub-routines. Commented [CP2]: Cognitive sub-routine: evidence (column 2). Empirical 'right there' support. Commented [CP3]: Cognitive sub-routine: basic context (column 1). Commented [CP4]: Cognitive sub-routines: interpretation-causation. Explanation for why something happened, connecting lecture as a secondary source and bigger picture to inform interpretation of evidence from primary source. Commented [CP5]: Cognitive sub-routines: evidence (column 2), interpretation. Here the student reverses the "invisible" connection from evidence to inform bigger picture view of secondary sources. Commented [CP6]: Metacognition: Student thinking made visible ("in this way") in the connection of various cognitive sub-routines to create larger meaning for Mongol history.

Figure 7.10. Interpretation: Create Meaning with Contextual Thinking
Chris Padgett

CONCLUSION

When nations propagate calcified narratives of the past, with facts that are already chosen in stories that are already told, such history is often validated with seemingly authoritative claims of "who we really are." In that static frame, a people's understanding of history remains pre-liminal, leaving them with few resources to critically read or challenge the story, and therefore with only a limited historical understanding of the problems they have inherited. When students understand history as an active form of inquiry and become metacognitively proficient contextual readers and historical thinkers, they are empowered to read beyond banal mythologies and canned stories to problem-solve the past. They learn to read the limitations of received narratives and construct new understandings with real insight into the present moment of their own lives.

Chapter 8

Not a White Rabbit—Reflection on Metacognitive Conversations and TAPPS

Corin Slown

I used to think solving a problem was about finding the singular "right" answer. If I were a diligent student, then I would be able to remember this correct answer and produce it instantaneously, not unlike a white rabbit out of a magician's black top hat. Many of my students are focused on magically procuring the right answer too. Some of my students resort to the frenetic flurry of searching CHEGG/STUDOCS or any of a number of other "behind the paywall" repositories of solved problems and someone else's answers. Other students frantically enter keywords to search Google or intone the right incantation/prompt to artificial intelligence in hopes of procuring the "right" solution. All of these approaches rely on someone or something to provide an answer, which begs the question, how do you know it is the "right" answer? What I know now is that problems typically have more than one approach and often more than one solution. Rarely is solving a problem about conjuring the singular "right" answer. Problems and their solutions are not top hats and white rabbits. Instead, problem solving requires careful analysis, weighing the costs, considering the benefits and limitations, and arriving at an answer you can live with given the constraints and the context.

When George Polya designed a four-step method to solve all kinds of problems (Polya, 1945), I think he knew from experience that problem solving is not always linear or simple or obvious. Polya's four-step method includes (1) understand the problem, (2) make a plan, (3) execute the plan, and (4) look back and reflect. There is nothing in his method that suggests the first pass through the process will result in success. What will not surprise anyone with any problem-solving experience is that often when looking back and reflecting on the process, you discover challenges, which with a growth mindset (Dweck, 2006), you can frame as opportunities. You discover a small adjustment or iteration that improves the solution; you find a gap that requires a shift in thinking; or you reveal a tragic flaw, requiring you to scrap the solution entirely and start over. Problem solving is humbling and often creates tremendous potential for growth, but it is not magic. Problem solving is certainly not pulling a rabbit out of a top hat; instead, we use strategies to read and make sense of the problem in order to solve it.

Reading Apprenticeship offers four dimensions to consider when utilizing strategies to support student learning and reading in the discipline. The Reading Apprenticeship framework of four interacting dimensions of learning supports both academic and social-emotional learning: social, personal, cognitive, and knowledge-building (Schoenbach et al., 2012). Through metacognitive conversations that explore students' thinking processes, students think and talk about how they learn as well as what they learn. This collaborative work takes place within the disciplinary context of reading and problem solving. For example, in lower-division general chemistry courses, we utilize Reading Apprenticeship to support students as they develop fundamental knowledge of chemistry. In upper-division biochemistry I and biochemistry II, we use Reading Apprenticeship strategies to help students integrate knowledge across disciplines including biology, chemistry, and physics.

Think-aloud paired problem solving (TAPPS) is one example of a strategy from Reading Apprenticeship that helps when solving the absurdly complex problems we are encountering today. Introduced by Lochhead and Whimbey (1987) as a way to encourage problem-solving skills by verbalizing to a listener the problem-solving thoughts, TAPPS makes thinking visible. TAPPS helps develop analytical reasoning skills; the intellectual exchange associated with TAPPS helps to construct the contextual framework needed for comprehension (MacGregor, 1990). TAPPS also provides opportunities for students to rehearse concepts, connect them to existing frameworks, and produce a deeper understanding of the material (Slavin, 1995). In the TAPPS protocol, students are paired and given a series of problems. The paired students are given specific roles that switch with each problem: Problem Solver and Listener. The problem solver reads the problem aloud and talks through the solution to the problem. The listener follows all of the problem solver's steps and prompts for their thinking.

In my courses, this exercise takes the form of one courageous listener and one brave problem solver. I say courageous listener because active listening is not an often-practiced skill in our society. Listening to someone solve a problem often results in a strong desire to jump into the awkward silence or rescue the problem solver. It takes courage to be patient. It takes courage to elicit thinking. It takes courage to gently prompt someone with "What are you thinking?"—especially when the answer is "I wish I was anywhere else but here." It takes courage to wait. It takes courage to hear what is said and not fill in the gaps with our own thinking. It takes courage to hear a different approach and listen to make sense of what is said. It takes courage to realize that a different perspective and solution does not mean the answer is wrong.

The first time I tried this exercise was in a general chemistry class with over 100 students. Students were applying what they knew of dimensional analysis to solve for the atoms and molecules of a limiting reagent. Usually when students first try to solve this type of problem, they attempt to memorize the process and apply what they have memorized to the next problem. While this foothold in Bloom's taxonomy is understandable, the dilemma is that rarely does this strategy work. There are hundreds of variations of ways to ask a question about molar ratios. As I walked around the students talking in pairs, I began to notice a pattern. There would be a long pause, then "I don't know where to start." I walked past four pairs repeating the same pattern, with my stomach doing nervous flip flops, until I arrived at the fifth pair, same pattern, but then a tentative voice: "Well . . . what are you thinking right now? Is there a word in the problem you are focusing on?" I lingered, listening, trying hard not to disrupt their fragile beginning. "Well, maybe I could start with this number given in the problem, at least I know what I can do with those units." Inside, I was cheering like we were at the Olympics and this pair had just won the gold medal. Understanding scientific concepts, applying knowledge and skills, and analyzing process leverages more of Bloom's taxonomy (1956), but it begins with inquiry.

In addition to the courageous listener, TAPPS requires a brave problem solver. I say brave problem solver because when we are encountering a problem for the first time, most of us quail and have the internal fear, "What if they find out I am actually no good at any of this?" Plagued by imposter syndrome, worried whether we will be "good enough" to solve the problem, and terrified that our performance will not measure up to the exacting standards required to belong, we need courage to be a problem solver too.

I wonder if George Polya and Theodore Roosevelt ever met. Theodore Roosevelt's speech from Sorbonne in 1910 is one I often share with students after our foray into TAPPS:

> It is not the critic who counts; not the man who points out how the strong man stumbles, or where the doer of deeds could have done them better. The credit belongs to the man who is actually in the arena, whose face is marred by dust and sweat and blood; ***who strives valiantly; who errs, who comes short again and again, because there is no effort without error and shortcoming; but who does actually strive to do the deeds***; who knows great enthusiasms, the great devotions; who spends himself in a worthy cause; who at the best knows in the end the triumph of high achievement, and who at the worst, if he fails, at least fails while daring greatly, so that his place shall never be with those cold and timid souls who neither know victory nor defeat. (Roosevelt, 1910)

Problem solvers are brave not by nature because all of us eventually encounter a problem we do not know how to solve. Rather, problem solvers are brave because we persist in solving a problem in spite of our fear(s). By thinking aloud through TAPPS, the problem solver is sharing their starting point, their liminal zone (Cook-Sather and Alter, 2011), and their uncertainty. The beauty of this process is that often by engaging in metacognitive conversation or thinking out loud about our thinking, we can discover the sticky point. Conversations with a problem solver and a listener uncover the misconceptions, or the gap in knowledge, and often resolve confusion.

For example, in general chemistry, when talking through the problem with their TAPPS partner, students frequently discovered two critical ideas: (1) moles are the currency of chemistry—eventually anything has to be converted into moles; and (2) the balanced equation allows you to relate the moles of any substance in a reaction to another chemical in the reaction. With those two key concepts, students can solve any limiting reagent problem. Intriguingly, this strategy was so successful that students requested the opportunity to collaborate with their peers more often. We relied heavily on TAPPS, integrating this strategy six more times in class in the semester. The grade distribution improved; more students earned As, Bs, and Cs. Perhaps most encouraging though—fewer than 10% of students earned Ds, Fs, and Withdrawals (DFW) in a class that often exceeds a 25% DFW rate. These were students brave enough to try a different approach to learning. Not a white rabbit, magic out of a hat, but rather an iterative, persistent approach to learning.

I was encouraged three years later to see the same students in my biochemistry course, now an upper-division course in the major, use the strategies from their general chemistry course. "Will you walk me through how you are thinking about solving this problem? I will listen and try to make sense of your process. If you pause too long, I will ask you what you are thinking about." When solving patterns of inquiry, problems that progress from remember to understand to apply, students used TAPPS to grasp what their colleagues were thinking. And then they used TAPPS, to analyze, evaluate and create. Anderson and Krathwohl (2001) and Bloom (1956) understood cognitive progression (Adams, 2015). TAPPS can be useful when recalling knowledge from memory. Remembering is when memory is used to retrieve definitions and facts and recall previously learned information. However, TAPPS is even more useful when constructing meaning or when the problem solver is interpreting, classifying, inferring, or explaining. I think my students value TAPPS the most when applying their knowledge, the ability to use learned material, or to implement material in new and concrete situations. Students use TAPPS when analyzing, differentiating, organizing, and attributing, as well as being able to distinguish between the components or parts. Perhaps the most profound space for TAPPS, though, is when students use it for evaluation and creation of new knowledge.

I imagine that had George Polya and Theodore Roosevelt had a conversation about problem solving like Anderson and Krathwohl, one would have been listening as the other endeavored to make sense of their problem-solving process. That is what my students do when they utilize TAPPS. If they are general chemistry students, then they are applying stoichiometry and balanced equations to understand the law of the conservation of mass. If they are biochemistry students, then they are using TAPPS to elucidate how a conjugate base and an acid form a buffer or how a secondary metabolite might serve as a hormonal signal. While integrating their knowledge and pulling on new ideas, they are still utilizing the courage of the active listener and the bravery of the problem solver to build competency and confidence. Perhaps more importantly, they are building the capacity to create a sense of belonging and cultivate community.

Chapter 9

Reading into Information Literacy

Ryne Leuzinger

This chapter describes my personal development as a teacher of reading within the context of librarianship and in my role providing information literacy instruction. My first exposure to Reading Apprenticeship came through a professional development opportunity provided at the system-wide level in the California State University system for a select group of faculty who had shown an interest in experimenting with new pedagogical approaches. At the time, I was aware of my institution (California State University, Monterey Bay) invoking metacognitive learning as an aspiration, but the university did not have a clear framework for describing specifically what this looked like in practice. Through exposure to the Reading Apprenticeship framework, I came to understand that "metacognitive problem solving" could be enacted via teaching strategies such as "*talking to the text*," "*thinking aloud*," and "*developing a list of reading strategies*." These activities served as vehicles to help students understand how working through the process of evaluating sources for research projects is a unique form of reading separate from the reading strategies one might employ in an academic discipline like history.

This professional development opportunity provided me with clarity around the idea that expert reading strategies are being employed by librarians in at least two critical points in the information evaluation process: (1) reviewing lists of search results and (2) preliminary reading of articles (i.e., a cursory review of an abstract). Understanding that particular discipline-specific reading skills are being employed at these points was an invitation to apprentice students in these skills, which I quickly realized was a useful means of bringing transparency to a process that is often needlessly opaque. This shift in understanding is eloquently captured in "This is What We Came Here to Do: Literacy at the Heart of Institutional Culture Change" by Hogan and Rose (2018), who write that "we realize that as our students move into new academic contexts, they are not behind but are merely outsiders to our academic conventions, deserving to be apprenticed into them. This puts the onus on us to design learning opportunities bridging their existing assets to our academic worlds" (p. 339). My newfound understanding of myself as a reading instructor through my use of the Reading Apprenticeship framework also functioned as an important facet of viewing myself as an instructor committed to equity and inclusion through the way in which apprenticing students in disciplinary reading strategies can play a role in unveiling the "unwritten rules of college." These generally implicit rules and expectations held by faculty pose implications for equity in higher education, particularly for first-generation students and those from historically underserved backgrounds. The ubiquity of reading in college courses makes the Reading Apprenticeship framework uniquely well positioned to help instructors bring transparency to these rules and expectations, in the process helping to empower *all* students.

After my initial exposure to Reading Apprenticeship and my corresponding new insights into the broad role that librarians can play in helping students develop reading skills, I asked librarian colleagues for their thoughts regarding whether they also saw value in the Reading Apprenticeship methodology in supporting our work in information literacy instruction. One colleague said "we don't teach reading," discouraging the idea. I initially took this at face value, but upon further individual reflection I realized that discussing reading strategies was appropriate and useful in a typical information literacy instruction (ILI) session in that a three-part narrative flow can be employed in many ILI settings: (1) choosing a research question and where to search (a specific database, for instance); (2) choosing how to search (which keywords will be employed); and (3) identifying *how* to search via using specific sense-making strategies to identify the most relevant and useful search results. Reading Apprenticeship routines such as "talking to the text," in which the instructor precisely describes the reading strategies they are employing as they navigate a text that is visible to students, have helped cultivate a dialogic active learning environment in my work. In this setting, instructors can embrace an inquiry-based approach by asking students questions like "What strategies did you see me using here?" Clearly identifying these strategies via this kind of apprenticeship functions as the first step in students developing the ability to use these strategies independently. Reading Apprenticeship has helped advance my understanding that the classroom is inherently a social space and is one in which students bring the sum of their lived experiences to the work at hand. In this way, in-class dialogue regarding the strategies I have displayed are enhanced by students' own forms of expertise, as is evident in their summary of the reading strategies that I demonstrate and their corresponding questions about these strategies.

The realization that this three-part narrative flow can be employed in many ILI settings was a pivotal moment in my development as reading instructor. A significant portion of this journey was simply coming to the understanding that while I was not assigning advance reading to students, and the overall amount of reading in my classroom was modest, I was indeed a reading instructor, and correspondingly, students' utilization of particular reading skills was crucial in meeting course and major learning outcomes. These skills are also relevant to meeting the Association of College & Research Libraries Frames, a group of six central concepts in information literacy that librarians often orient their work around (Association of College & Research Libraries, 2016). Following this realization, I was able to recruit some of the librarians in my department to use the Reading Apprenticeship methodology, joining a broader group of faculty across disciplines on our campus utilizing this mode of teaching.

In continuing to develop my teaching practice as a reading instructor, I have come to better understand the social dimensions of learning both as both an instructor and learner myself. I benefited from substantive connections with other faculty in the context of a learning community that met twice a month over the course of a semester, who joined in this common effort across disciplines and collectively worked to cross two distinct learning thresholds—one being an understanding that for students reading difficulties catalyze learning and another being that reading itself is active learning (Graff et al., 2022). As an instructor, the Reading Apprenticeship framework's articulation of the social dimension of learning (Schoenbach et al., 2012, p. 24) helped me move beyond peer-to-peer learning involving activities such as think-pair-share activities into the realm of "think aloud" and "talking to the text," which was more impactful through the way in which it is a goal-oriented, inquiry-based approach in which it is acceptable to struggle and express vulnerability wherein each student has the opportunity to contribute to and potentially lead that dialogue-oriented inquiry. This approach stands in stark contrast to my experience as an undergraduate majoring in a social science discipline where there was virtually no instruction devoted to description of the mechanics of disciplinary reading. Attention paid to this was mostly accidental in terms of only having insight into a professor's approach to reading by seeing notes they had written for themselves in the margins of a photocopied book chapter. Over the last several years, my instruction has been greatly enhanced through reflection on the inadequacy of my own experience as a student and the ways in which this was disempowering, and how in turn the empowering nature of the RA framework could structure my approach to teaching reading in a mode of instruction (information literacy instruction) that exists outside of a formal discipline.

My development as a reading instructor has left me with the impression that there is a unique role for librarians to play in teaching reading instruction across the disciplines, one that helps students grapple with the complex work of evaluating sources—a crucial preliminary step in the process of deriving meaning from texts. In utilizing Reading Apprenticeship, this framework has been not just a group of activities that other instructors happen to utilize in parallel to my own work, but is instead a shared understanding of how learning works in the context of building discipline-specific reading skills.

This shared framework has the potential to play a significant role in helping address some of the shortcomings of the format for information literacy instruction led by librarians which primarily takes place in "one-shot sessions," which can alternatively be described as guest lectures that take place over the course of one instruction period. The one-shot session mode of teaching clearly has limitations, one being the limited amount of content that can be covered in this time frame. Another drawback is the way in which this type of instruction (including terminology and activities) can potentially be disconnected from the instructional approach used by the course instructor. Use of metacognitive routines by librarians helps to address both of these issues in a classroom in which the course instructor is also using the Reading Apprenticeship framework through the way in which the framework creates coherence in students' learning experience as instructors reinforce one another's work through shared language and teaching strategies. Librarians on my campus and beyond are still in a formative stage of the use of this group of "metacognitive problem-solving strategies" in an information literacy context and are working to expand upon the range of settings in which Reading Apprenticeship is used. It should be noted that while in-class instruction is the primary mode that ILI takes place in, there are also digital learning objects such as interactive video content where use of Reading Apprenticeship techniques could be applied and represents a potentially fruitful area for further experimentation with these techniques. My experience suggests that there is great potential for librarians to see themselves as reading instructors by making use of the effective, student-centered strategies in this framework that can be used to further common information literacy learning objectives.

Chapter 10

Equitable and Metacognitive Approaches to Library Sessions

Anamika Megwalu

Information literacy is a core component for successfully navigating education and citizenship. It is a set of competencies, both complex and sophisticated, that prepares students to critically think about solving problems using strategic and effective use of information. The American Library Association (ALA) defines it as "a set of abilities requiring individuals to recognize when information is needed and have the ability to locate, evaluate, and use effectively the needed information" (2023). In the higher education system, it is a common practice for liaison librarians to develop and conduct one-shot library sessions, also known as information literacy sessions, for students to develop some of those competencies. However, it is challenging to design such library sessions that engage students in meaningfully advancing their information literacy competencies.

This chapter discusses the use of Reading Apprenticeship approaches in designing library sessions. Reading Apprenticeship emphasizes techniques that are uniquely suited for diverse classrooms where students come with varied educational experiences, knowledge of campus resources, and understanding of ethics. These approaches help advance equity in education by helping students connect what they do know with the new college and disciplinary environments. They allow students to make their thinking visible for just-in-time intervention and not feel isolated in their struggles.

COLLABORATIONS AND CHALLENGES

Academic librarians, as part of their liaison responsibilities, connect with course instructors in their respective academic departments. They engage in multiple informal scoping interviews in understanding where students struggle within a particular course. Keeping the Association of College and Research Libraries (ACRL) framework in mind, librarians suggest creating library sessions where students learn about processes, resources, and applications that help them with their academic work and beyond. In collaboration with the course instructors, librarians create lesson plans for the library sessions. These lesson plans evolve as the collaboration between course instructors and librarians deepens, and feedback from student learning assessments is considered.

There are challenges to developing an engaging and effective library session. Librarians have 60–120 minutes to conduct a one-shot session with students they probably have never met before, and the likelihood of interacting with all of them after the session is less. Therefore, it is important that the session has no more than three learning objectives that are drawn from the knowledge gaps of students identified by the course instructor. Embedding metacognitive approaches in the instructional plan allows for students to reflect, internalize, and apply new materials within a short period of time. Through metacognitive exercises, students are given a space to practice the process of learning that fosters equity in an educational environment.

ACRL FRAMEWORK AND READING APPRENTICESHIP METACOGNITIVE APPROACHES

ACRL Framework

There are two main standards and frameworks of information literacy recognized by ALA. These are the AASL Standards for the 21st-Century Learner and the ACRL Framework for Information Literacy for Higher Education. The former is created by the American Association of School Librarians (AASL) to shape literacy programs in K–12 schools, and the latter is created by the Association of College and Research Libraries (ACRL) for colleges and universities and is used by academic librarians. ACRL chose to call it a framework because it is based on a cluster of interconnected core information literacy concepts rather than a prescriptive enumeration of skills. Both standards emphasize that "Information literacy requires particular attitudes, such as the awareness of a need for information and the accurate application of the information" (Behrens, 1994).

Academic librarians who teach information literacy sessions refer to the ACRL Framework for Information Literacy for Higher Education as a guide to creating their library sessions. There are six major frames in this framework (table 10.1):

Title of the Frame	Description of the Frame
1. Authority Is Constructed and Contextual	Information resources reflect their creators' expertise and credibility and are evaluated based on the information need and the context in which the information will be used. Authority is constructed in that various communities may recognize different types of authority. It is contextual in that the information need may help to determine the level of authority required.
2. Information Creation as a Process	Information in any format is produced to convey a message and is shared via a selected delivery method. The iterative processes of researching, creating, revising, and disseminating information vary, and the resulting product reflects these differences.
3. Information Has Value	Information possesses several dimensions of value, including as a commodity, as a means of education, as a means to influence, and as a means of negotiating and understanding the world. Legal and socioeconomic interests influence information production and dissemination.
4. Research as Inquiry	Research is iterative and depends upon asking increasingly complex or new questions whose answers in turn develop additional questions or lines of inquiry in any field.
5. Scholarship as Conversation	Communities of scholars, researchers, or professionals engage in sustained discourse with new insights and discoveries occurring over time as a result of varied perspectives and interpretations.
6. Searching as Strategic Exploration	Searching for information is often nonlinear and iterative, requiring the evaluation of a range of information sources and the mental flexibility to pursue alternate avenues as new understanding develops.

Reading Apprenticeship Metacognitive Approaches

Metacognition is a concept for thinking about thinking (Schoenbach et al., 2012, p. 91). It is inherently an internal process, but in the context of education, it is most effective when the process is external as well. When students express metacognitive thinking, educators can gauge students' understandings and misconceptions, and students can learn strategies from each other. But this external process of making thinking visible is not natural. In fact, it is a learned behavior.

In information literacy sessions, students can surface their initial beliefs and thinking process only when librarians create opportunities for students to express the steps involved in solving a problem. Librarians should model how to make thinking visible prior to asking students to solve a problem. Modeling is an instructional strategy where "the teacher engages students by showing them how to perform a skill while describing each step with a rationale. This provides students with both a visual and verbal example of what they will be expected to do" (University of Louisville, 2022). There are multiple metacognitive approaches. In this chapter, the following three approaches are embedded in lesson plans in the examples below (table 10.2).

Metacognitive Approach	Description
Think Aloud	Think aloud strategy involves the articulation of internal thinking verbally or through text.
Talking to the Text	Talking to the text is similar to think aloud except that it is initially done on an individual basis with students reading the text on their own privately and making notes (College of Education & Human Development, 2022).
Partner/Group Work	A structured partner/group work that gives individual students the time to think, to take notes, discuss their idea in groups or pair, and have the result of their conversation available to share during a whole-class discussion (Schoenbach et al., 2012, p. 120).

EMBEDDING METACOGNITIVE APPROACHES IN LIBRARY SESSIONS

Library Session Example 1: Apprenticing Students into Disciplinary Genres

Scenario: An instructor of a computer engineering course realizes that students in her undergraduate class are struggling with writing research proposals, especially the literature review section. They are struggling with referencing credible scholarly journal articles and extracting and synthesizing information from scholarly sources. This is also a common problem among graduate students.

Prognosis: This scenario is far too common, and these struggles are indications of students' lack of understanding of types and characteristics of disciplinary genres, their organizational structure, and its significance.

Session objectives:

1. Learning the types of disciplinary genres
2. Learning the structure/format of a typical discipline-specific journal article
3. Learning to purposefully read a discipline-specific journal article

Procedure:

1. Give students an example of a genre and ask students to name genres that they are familiar with. Take note of student responses using a tool that displays your note taking in real time, such as Google Doc or MS Word. This is called "surfacing prior knowledge." Introduce missing genres during this process.
2. A. Introduce the typical structure of a journal article. Provide a handout with a diagram of the structure for reference. Share with students a discipline-specific journal article that is selected in collaboration with the course instructor. This article should be from a recently published reputable journal and represent a commonly used style of organizing information. It is important to select an article that is relatively short to accommodate varying reading speed.
   B. Allow students to individually skim through the article with a focus on the structure, not the content, and compare it with the structure introduced in the handout. Is there anything that stands out? Are there any similarities or differences? This lends opportunities for the librarian to gauge students' understanding of the structure, clarify misconceptions, discuss anomalies, and address questions.
3. A. Now that students have an understanding of the structure, it is time to discuss and practice how to read an article with a purpose in mind. Introduce the significance of each section and what is generally discussed in them. There are many methods for reading a journal article. Using the same article, ask students to think about their approach to reading an article. Students can *work with a partner* (think-pair-share). It is important to give students instructions on the structure and ground rules for pair or group activity. For instance, allocate time for each individual to share, assign roles, and implement active listening.
   B. Building on students' responses about methods of reading, the librarian models the *talking to the text* method. Typically, readers have a purpose in mind prior to reading a journal article. Therefore, they do not read all sections of a journal article sequentially. Sometimes they do not read the complete article, and instead use headings and subheadings as a guide to find sections that serve the purpose of reading the article.
   C. Allocate time for students to practice talking to the text. Ask students to first determine and write down the purpose of reading the article. Then they can read silently and annotate the article with their own *talking to the text* comments and questions. They do not need to read the entire article sequentially, but should have a rationale for selecting certain sections.
   D. In the handout, students identify two advantages of talking to the text and one challenge they encountered. Bring the class together to discuss students' experiences.

This lesson plan is designed to help students learn to read a journal article. However, librarians can easily modify the lesson plan to introduce other disciplinary genres. Although the lesson plan does not allow a deeper dive into reading all types of disciplinary texts, students are introduced to "talking to the text," a metacognitive approach that they can apply to reading any unfamiliar text.

Library Session Example 2: Efficient and Effective Information Search Strategies

Scenario: A course instructor of a research and writing intensive course recognizes that very few students are referring to scholarly resources, such as journal articles and conference proceedings, in their writing. They extract some scholarly materials from Google Scholar, but exhibit a lack of knowledge of seminal literature. Students also complain that they cannot retrieve full-text articles on Google Scholar. They also express anxiety about the lack of published literature on their research topic. The course instructor reaches out to the librarian to introduce students to platforms or library databases relevant to the discipline, and the process of searching and selecting articles.

Prognosis: Students are not aware of library databases that can be used to search and retrieve full-text scholarly journals and conference proceedings. They are also not aware of search strategies that are helpful in efficiently finding information on library databases and Google Scholar.

Session objectives:

1. Identifying information hub for research articles
2. Developing information search strategies
3. Developing strategies to evaluate search results

Procedure:

1. Briefly discuss students' areas of research interest. They do not have to be well formed at this point. Then ask students the tools they have used or might use to find literature that has been published on their topics. This is called "surfacing prior knowledge." This is also the time to introduce library databases and discuss how they might enhance their information search process.
2. Use one of the shared research topics to demonstrate search strategies on those library databases. This instantly makes the session more real, personalized, and meaningful. It reveals intricacies and decision-making processes involved in the information search. Model creation and modification of a search string by thinking aloud the problem-solving process of searching. Engage students in metacognitive conversation and encourage students to make their thinking visible as they offer their feedback in forming effective search strings.
3. A. Model steps of evaluating articles for relevancy by using the *think aloud* process. Verbally articulate your thinking while vetting relevant articles.
   B. Allocate time for students to practice creating search strings and selecting relevant articles by using the *think aloud* approach. This could be done in *pairs* or *groups of three* where they try to find articles for their own research topic. It is important to give students instructions on the structure and ground rules for pair or group activity. For instance, allocate time for each individual to share, assign roles, and implement active listening.

One of the major goals of this lesson plan is to help students focus on their thinking process. There are multiple approaches to creating effective search strings and selecting relevant articles. Students learn that making the problem-solving process visible is beneficial because it allows them to learn from each other in a small-group setting. Students are exposed to multiple ways of solving a problem.

Facilitating a library session is challenging because of time constraints and the nature of it being a one-time session where librarians meet students for the first time with hopes that there will be opportunities for subsequent meetings. However, as educators, it is imperative that one-shot library sessions are effective in bearing opportunities for librarians to identify points of need and address them immediately. Metacognitive approaches encourage articulation of thinking about thinking, allowing librarians to identify misconceptions and lack of knowledge, and to intervene to alleviate the struggle. It also fosters a learning environment where students learn from their peers. Students are afforded practice opportunities to strengthen their information literacy competencies. They develop transferable knowledge about learning techniques that they can apply throughout their academic and professional career. Reading Apprenticeship offers instructional techniques that create opportunities for students of all kinds to have a constructive educational experience, thus cultivating equity in education.

PART IV

Students Must Be Entrusted with the Work of Making Sense of Texts

A second breakthrough revealed in the survey of faculty we describe in the introduction is the recognition that ***students must be entrusted with the work of making sense of text***. Below, we elaborate on that theme with the specific results of the survey—making explicit connections to threshold concept theory as it is relevant—and contextualize the chapters in part IV in terms of related research.

STRUGGLE IS PRODUCTIVE FOR LEARNING

In other writing about threshold concepts in teaching reading, we have proposed as possible threshold concepts about reading the ideas that "*reading difficulties catalyze learning* and *reading is active learning*" (Graff et al., 2022). Both of these concepts arise in faculty comments that we have coded in this category about faculty threshold concepts in *teaching reading*. We see versions of these ideas in our faculty survey responses, from a focus on metacognition to "the value is not always in students getting to the right answer or interpretation but in making their own meaning" and "support[ing] students in how they interact with content/text."

Recognizing the difficulties that arise for students when they take charge of their work, one instructor wrote, "One breakthrough, early on, was that students need to think and respond for themselves and NOT just spit back what is given to them in a text or an instructor." Another wrote, "Once I started to integrate metacognitive routines consistently in my classes, I realized that students were indeed capable of making sense of challenging texts. This allowed me to ask students to struggle productively with these texts." These comments make explicit the tension between the well-known research asserting that students should engage in active, problem-based, and inquiry-based learning activities (e.g., Wenger, 2000), and the actual "normal" practices in classrooms, when such "productive struggle" feels uncomfortable for most teachers and students.

The emphasis on the value of struggle and difficulty in student learning in these comments is key and represents an idea that arises repeatedly among faculty commenting on students taking responsibility for their learning. Such comments also resonate with the idea that reading is active learning. Instructors across the disciplines comment on the value of students learning from texts. One, for instance, asserted, "Students are very capable of engaging and digesting written texts—if they are taught how." This comment suggests a shift in the instructor's identity, moving away from the idea of "delivering content" and instead embracing a role as disciplinary literacy coach, teaching students how to "engage and digest" texts on their own.

As powerful as this insight has been for faculty, there is evidence in their comments that it was also troublesome—and for some continues to be so. One instructor reflected, "Through RA, I was finally able to break myself free from feeling the need to deliver content solely through speaking." The instructor's use of "finally" suggests the troublesomeness of the transformation, as does the phrase "break myself free," a troublesomeness that's echoed in the liminality of some other instructors' comments. One instructor wrote about "coming to an understanding (via the videos of expert instructors using RA in their classrooms) that using RA as a central teaching practice often necessitates less time developing detailed lesson plans/lectures through the way in which students are placed in the driver's seat for learning and making meaning from texts as opposed to the traditional passive role of students in the classroom." The juxtaposition of lesson plans and lectures in this instructor's comment suggests a challenge in seeing the need for rigorous planning in order for students to struggle successfully with their texts, while referencing the shift away from students' "traditional passive role . . . in the classroom" shows the instructor's recognition that students must do more of the work in the classroom. The concept is also troublesome in practice, as faculty refer to "pushback from students."

That the change in practice that results from this change in perspective is lasting (if not irreversible) is implied by many faculty comments about how they teach now. The instructor's comment cited early about being freed by their Reading Apprenticeship practice appears in other instructors' comments as well, including this one: "Early on, I discovered with Reading Apprenticeship that I could focus on learning rather than teaching in my classes and this gave me such freedom." Focusing on learning meant turning the lens on the students' struggles and the changes in perspective that resulted from those struggles.

Students Are Capable of Academic Work

In order to allow students to engage in productive struggle, faculty must believe that students are capable of doing the work, and that class time driven by students' thinking, questioning, and sense-making is time well spent. Respondents clearly describe a transformative and likely irreversible shift as a result of engaging students in metacognitive conversation, and thus gaining access to students' thought processes. As one teacher reported, "I had worried that my students wouldn't have the vocabulary to talk shop about how they react to reading. I was so wrong. They blew my mind with what they had to say." Another similarly reflected, "The ideas they share are beyond my expectations," and a different respondent shares the transformed understanding that "my students, even those who seem like weak readers or hate reading, are indeed readers with profound insight on reading as a skill." Understanding that students are capable of doing the intellectual heavy lifting of making sense of texts is a break from the baseline understanding that students are not capable of meaningfully engaging in text-based learning. One teacher said, "I used to mimic my professors and teachers when teaching." To describe this new teaching situation, in which students are held accountable for meaning making with texts, one person wrote: "Instead of 'covering' a topic, we are uncovering it and I am not the only expert. Students really step up. It is exciting and collaborative." Gaining access to students' thinking and problem solving "opened up my eyes," and, in one response, was "life changing."

Better understanding what students are capable of led several respondents to describe significant shifts in professional identity, including feeling better prepared to design and facilitate active learning and to do so in culturally responsive ways. For example, one respondent described Reading Apprenticeship as "equity pedagogy" because "it gives us real, practical ways to value and engage the stores of knowledge and experience that students carry as well as their own creative and problem solving capacities." Another faculty member reported:

> RA practices confronted my own assumptions about student knowledge and capacity. I have reflected on how I made those assumptions, how I learned to read and write, and how I can unpack and redesign my andragogy to invite and embrace equity through literacy. It has strengthened my teaching and boosted student success.

These comments reveal the way that instructors' engagement in metacognitive conversations help them to rethink the pervasive deficit view of student capacity. This can happen with colleagues in professional learning, as experts consider their own literacy development in different contexts. It also happens when hearing directly from students about their background knowledge and sense-making processes.

Metacognitive conversation can also help instructors to notice and begin to address their internal biases; frequently, the transformative realization of student capacity was expressed directly as cultural humility (Lekas et al., 2020). One respondent said, "That breakthrough has made me more flexible in my teaching and helped me to be a more equity minded person . . . it has made me a humbler and understanding teacher." Another instructor recounted an instance of discussing a poem: "Because the majority of my students are Marshallese and I am not, they were able to raise important cultural elements that I had never noticed in the poem before. . . . This became an example for the class about how learning is a process of building meaning together (i.e., not the banking model)." Another professor of ESL described an instance where a cultural blind spot was revealed in a discussion: "It was such a meaningful discussion to me personally, and showed ME that I had no idea how much meaning was packed into the word 'we.' I use 'we' a lot and I became aware of how often I relied on American cultural norms to be enough context to make the 'we' the correct context. But I still had so much I didn't know." When teachers hear from students directly, when students' priorities, ideas, connections, and questions drive the sense-making process in class, teachers see clearly how much we stand to learn from our students as well as how much they are capable of accomplishing. Another respondent noted that "explicitly cultivating awareness" of what is "hidden in our cognitive processes including cultural assumptions etc. . . . has helped me to become a better reader and problem solver and teacher." Another teacher shared that "Learning is humbling. I like to think that using RA keeps me humble because I am always learning from my students." Altogether, 21 participants (24%) made reference to students bringing previously unacknowledged funds of knowledge to the learning situation.

Several faculty comments suggest that this transformed understanding of student capacity has allowed them to integrate other goals and emphases as instructors. One instructor, for instance, wrote, "I was looking for ways to give students more agency over their reading as well as their writing, and RA has provided the framework to make that possible." This instructor was ready for ways to hand over the learning, and finding a framework helped them do it. Another noted the way that this insight about handing over learning to students has influenced other areas of their practice, writing, "I have found that my RA practice has changed the way I interact with students one-on-one during office hours." This comment suggests a shift in instructor identity by extending changes in interaction from the classroom to office hours.

Students Are Essential to Academic Work

When respondents did refer to the wealth of knowledge that students bring to reading and sense-making once they are invited to engage in metacognitive conversations, they also reported that students' contributions are useful to the academic enterprise. For example, a physics instructor shared, "I think the most meaningful experience I had was realizing how much knowledge and related experiences students bring to my class about the concepts we learn. I have been able to enable the hidden knowledge and build on it. It saved me so much time and effort when introducing the new physics complex concepts." This response is noteworthy because it shows a shift from the common assertion among faculty that there is "no time," especially in STEM courses, for activities that engage the whole student. Discovering that her physics students bring valuable background knowledge to the class, now the quoted instructor sees student talk about their thinking, reading, and problem-solving processes to be a time-saving strategy. Similarly, another faculty member explained, "The way I see it, RA strategies enable students to tap into the knowledge already within them and to use this knowledge as a foundation," while somebody else described that "learning itself is a conversation and [students] have both a role and a responsibility in that." In other words, having students actively engaged in constructing meaning is not just a good practice; it is now for these instructors the essential way to approach teaching and learning in the discipline. This change in perspective resonates with the metaconcept we describe, that reading apprenticeships are reciprocal. As one respondent explained:

> [Metacognitive conversation] allows me to hold in tension a public airing of the discipline, while inviting students in to make their own decisions about how to participate. I can problematize my position as English instructor to lean into what it means to invite students in to conspire, but without any preconceived notions of what that transformation entails. We create together.

Far from the "common sense" idea that the role of an instructor is to "deliver content," these comments describe a transformed understanding of participation in higher education, one where students play an important role in helping to determine the direction of disciplinary communities of practice.

SOME SCHOLARLY CONTEXT FOR THE CHAPTERS IN THIS PART

The chapters in this part take up the threshold concept mostly in the sense of focusing on supporting students in doing the work of reading and using their reading to learn disciplinary content. As such, they enter a long-standing scholarly conversation about the role of reading in learning at the post-secondary level. Broz (2011), for instance, describes strategies that professors use that support what he calls "not reading," such as lecturing about the text, teaching around the text, and summarizing the text before class activities. He suggests that if students are not reading, they "have done nothing important enough to deserve passing grades in our classes" (p. 16). While he is describing his work in a literature class for future English teachers, faculty across the disciplines expect students to engage in significant and high-level reading and report that students do not do the reading for their classes (e.g., Ritchey & List, 2022).

Rose takes up the question of students doing the reading in particular for her transfer-level English as a Second Language (ESL) students. Her description of how she helps her students develop strategies and take risks in their college reading begins to answer findings about the high-school preparation of some ESL students (Murillo and Schall, 2016; Nguyen, 2021), and the impact of self-efficacy on academic success for Latino/a students (Manzano-Sanchez et al., 2018). Rose's focus on teaching reading strategies also helps to respond to a concern raised by some research findings that reading in English alone may not improve reading proficiency for students with lower English language skills (e.g., Pichette, 2005).

As Lynch describes in her chapter in this part, however, in some disciplines, the expectation for students to read is somewhat new. Lynch notes, "My professors never assigned reading and never discussed how to read mathematics. My classes had required textbooks, but I only opened them to look up homework problems (or occasionally to find an example similar to a homework problem)." Yet as Lynch, Hogan and Purdum, and Sheeren and Wand argue in this collection, reading is an essential component of learning mathematics deeply. Similarly, reviewing research on reading in science and mathematics, Tang and colleagues (2022) note that the ability to read in math and science contributes significantly to student success in those subjects.

If Lynch focuses largely on the what and why of reading in her discipline—calculus—others in this part look more closely at her third question—how. And they have come up with different answers. For her students with diagnosed learning disabilities, Purdum draws on principles of Universal Design for Learning (UDL; Meyer et al., 2014). Kahlert (2021) emphasizes that students need to learn to engage in productive struggle, a concept that has received scholarly attention across the disciplines and in connection with self-regulated learning. Urbanek and colleagues (2023), for instance, examine the strategies students use to struggle through (or avoid struggling through) uncertainty in science reasoning. More broadly, Nilson (2013) argues that students must develop self-regulation in order to learn effectively and suggests strategies to help them do so in a variety of learning situations and from different kinds of assignments, and Panadero (2017) reviews models of self-regulated learning and describes their intersections. Importantly for the authors in this part, metacognition is a key component of self-regulation across models.

Kahlert's attention to productive struggle examines text sets as a tool for creating the conditions to allow students to struggle productively and regulate their own learning. Gamberg likewise explicitly takes up the question of self-regulation, connecting the familiar idea of revision in writing (Horning & Becker, 2006) to the possibility of learning to revise readings. Warren, though she doesn't describe her snapshots in terms of self-regulation, illustrates what self-regulation looks like (or can look like) when instructors pay attention to students' in-the-moment needs and, as Murdoch and colleagues (2020) describe, help them feel heard.

Shereen and Wand, like Warren, don't frame their discussion in terms either of productive struggle or self-regulation, but they illustrate the use of technology as a tool for helping students to be responsible for their work and learning together. Their description of social annotation connects with other research on the impact of that group of tools (e.g., Li & Li, 2023; Porter, 2022). Like Li and Li and Porter, Shereen and Wand focus on the use of an electronic tool for collaboration annotation, Perusall. Porter (2022) and Li and Li (2023) generally find that online annotation platforms increase student engagement with reading. Porter (2022) found that students somewhat prefer Perusall to Hypothes.is.

As we see in the survey results above and in the scholarship on productive struggle and self-regulated learning, students can indeed do the work of making sense of texts. The faculty in this part describe their own encounters with this concept, highlighting the strategies they used to shift that work onto their students and to support them in doing it. Their stories reveal both the importance of letting students struggle with the work of disciplinary thinking and learning, and approaches that help to make such a shift possible.

Chapter 11

Permission to Take Risk

Shelagh Rose

Spring semester starts tomorrow. As I scan the course roster for my high-intermediate transfer-level ESL reading and writing class, I determine from their names that my students originate from at least eleven different countries on three different continents. They will likely vary greatly in their ages, incomes, and academic goals. While the majority of my students are traditional students, several of them on student visas, hoping to transfer to a University of California campus, peppered in are immigrant mothers and fathers. Their children are finally school-aged, allowing them to pursue their own education or reeducation in the United States. Many of these students are planning to earn a certificate, often in health sciences, hoping to improve their family's financial circumstances without wasting precious years. Despite these differences, experience has taught me that my students often have much in common when it comes to their English language learning. Few, if any, have ever read an entire book in English. Most count years of drill and kill grammar exercises as their primary English education.

Because of this lack of opportunity to develop reading fluency, I expect that my students will experience a sense of panic tomorrow when I share that we will be reading a 264-page novel, as well as several shorter fiction and nonfiction texts that enhance the reading of the book. With AI and the ever-increasing sophistication of translation software, these students' first instinct may be to rely on technology to help them get through the reading. I can't blame them. They desperately need to earn a high GPA to achieve their goals, whether to get accepted to UCLA or our own college's RN program. With this incentive to avoid engaging in the risky business of reading, and writing about their reading, I must give my students permission to take risks while helping them acquire the necessary confidence and strategies. Fortunately, my long experience using Reading Apprenticeship in the classroom to address the four dimensions—personal, social, cognitive, and knowledge-building—has afforded me with tools to help students face their fears and grapple, maybe for the first time, with text in English.

The first step to helping non-native speakers read in English is to make sure they have the book. With the goal of zero textbook cost, I adopted a digital book for a few semesters, but soon learned of the irresistible temptation to translate instantly into their language. So now, I select a book students can find for under $10 and keep a few extra used copies on hand just in case. For the last few semesters, we have been reading *Kindred* by Octavia E. Butler. I have chosen this book intentionally because it was written by an alumna of our college who went on to become an award-winning science fiction author. When I share this information with students, they express surprise and delight at the idea that the author once sat in the same classrooms they do now. Before they start to read, I need to provide a way into the text that will build both their confidence and interest. To ensure they understand the elements of fiction, I write the words character, setting, plot, and theme on the board and ask students to work in small groups sharing their prior knowledge of these terms. This sets the precedent that we will rely on each other throughout the semester to make sense of text, while also acknowledging that English language learners often enter our classroom with a well-developed understanding of academic literacy in their own language that can be tapped into and applied to their English learning.

Many of my students come from collectivist cultures where collaborative learning is the norm; therefore, I rarely face resistance when I ask them to work together. By forming small groups early and asking students to cooperate often, the social dimension begins to develop. Creating a safe learning environment is crucial in an ESL classroom where students' affective filter, feelings of stress and discomfort in learning language, can block language learning (Krashen, 2013). In their small groups, students engage in an adapted version of the text prediction activity "reading a book by its cover." As they carefully analyze the book cover including the images, colors, title, and any other clues, they start categorizing the predictions as related to character, setting, plot, or theme. Since the book has been reprinted many times, I layer in additional covers that may confirm or reject their initial predictions. While they are predicting, it is important to emphasize that there are no right or wrong answers, just guesses informed by evidence. This helps normalize early on the idea of taking risks with the text.

With student interest in the content of the book piqued, the time has arrived to read. This first shared reading experience is critical in establishing habits that will build fluency and stamina, an important goal in any Reading Apprenticeship classroom. Before they start, I assure students that they do not need to understand every word. In fact, if they do, they don't need my class and they can just head straight to freshman composition. For those who come from cultures where anything less than academic perfection is considered failure, this can be a challenging concept to accept, one that will need to be repeated. To prevent students from focusing on vocabulary and translation, I set a goal of reading three pages without looking at a phone or dictionary. This announcement causes several students to regard me with shocked expressions. How can they possibly keep reading if they don't understand all the words? Despite their doubts, these students are accustomed to following teacher's requests, so they plunge into the text. After ten minutes of reading, students are able to share their nascent understanding of the text with their classmates and start to realize that it is OK not to grasp every word. If there are gaps in comprehension, they will fill them in together. They will soon become accustomed to these "reading sprints," and recognize their role in helping them uncover the main idea of a passage.

Once students have practiced reading fast to get the gist of what they read, this is an opportune time to introduce a metacognitive routine to help them dig deeper into a key part of the narrative. Although think aloud is my go-to method of having students share their thoughts about a text when I am teaching non-ESL classes, talking to the text is a better fit for my non-native speakers. This silent routine allows my students to engage deeply with a small chunk of text. They are able to capture their thoughts and questions about the story, but also can share their wonderings about the language such as "Why did the author choose a particular sentence structure?" or "What vocabulary words are key to understanding the passage?" By sharing their metacognitive engagement with the text with their classmates, they can see how their classmates are solving problems with the text, allowing them to expand their repertoire of reading strategies. After having practiced both fast and slow reading strategies in the classroom, I feel more confident sending students home to read independently.

As my students expand their reading strategy toolbox and become more confident at problem solving with text, they also need support with developing schema. I often choose a novel that introduces social and historical information that may be unfamiliar to my students. Although this may be a heavy lift at first, it will better prepare them for the required general education classes they must soon enroll in. In *Kindred*, the main character time travels to the antebellum South and the novel explores the effects of slavery and racial oppression in American history. By creating text sets comprised of historical images such as photographs and documents related to the slave trade as well as brief nonfiction readings and short videos, I am able to provide students with information necessary to fully comprehend the core reading selection for the course while also creating exposure to a variety of genres with distinct text features from the novel. I leverage our college's learning management system, Canvas, to house these text sets and ask students to engage in discussions online about what is new, interesting, or surprising about the history they are learning. As they share their thoughts on topics ranging from laws against interracial marriages to slave rebellions, they are actively engaged in the knowledge-building dimension. Students also reflect on any similarities or differences they notice between the history they are learning and the histories of their own countries, allowing them to connect new information to prior knowledge.

After the first two weeks, the time has come to introduce two key assignments that ensure students' active engagement with the text throughout the rest of the semester. Each week students will turn in a double-entry journal (DEJ) and every other week they will submit a reading response journal (RRJ). These two routines are the cornerstone of academic reading in the class and support both metacognition and reading strategy development. In their DEJ, I ask students to select five to seven lines each time they read and capture them on the left side of their paper. On the right side of their paper, I ask them to share their thoughts, feelings, connections, and questions about the lines they have chosen. They are encouraged to write at least twice as much on the right side as they have on the left. As the semester progresses, the comment side should continue to develop as their ability to engage metacognitively with the text evolves. Students bring their DEJs regularly to class and know that they will have the opportunity to share several of their "golden lines" from the text as they circle up with their classmates. This sharing builds the social dimension in the classroom while providing students regular practice talking about text, which greatly increases their verbal fluency throughout the semester. Every three weeks, students are formed into new groups to allow them continued access to varied approaches to making sense of the text. This also helps build community within the whole class instead of creating limited pockets of safety.

While students almost immediately express their appreciation of writing and discussing their DEJs with their classmates, the RRJ activity is often greeted with resistance at first because of the amount of work required. In this assignment, students are asked to read a longer passage of the text—from 20 to 40 pages—and write a summary, response, and a reflection on their reading process. They are also asked to choose five good words. This activity provides practice engaging in different types of academic writing about text and helps students develop the cognitive dimension of reading. Summarizing, for example, is a key literacy skill that requires deep understanding of the text in order to identify main events in the passage and distinguish them from minor ones. Students also start to understand the distinction between summarizing, which requires them to omit their own opinions about the text, and response, which asks them to share their thoughts, feelings, and personal connections. It requires practice, feedback, and provision of examples for students to master these two distinct forms of text-based writing. Students also reflect metacognitively on their reading process, noticing when their comprehension breaks down and what moves they make to problem-solve with challenging parts of the text. They identify what supports their reading fluency and stamina, noticing what works and doesn't work when they read. The vocabulary component of the RRJ asks students to select words purposefully. Students have already started to realize from their "reading sprints" that you do not need to translate or define every word in order to understand a passage. However, some words are critical to comprehension, and these are the words worth taking the time to deeply understand and remember. This requires effort. Therefore, students are asked to include a definition, sentence, and a personal connection to the vocabulary choice that will allow them to remember the word. Students often must be nudged to dig deeper into their memories to find meaningful experiences that relate to the word. Placing the new word next to this memory is an incredibly helpful strategy for remembering new words and building their academic vocabulary.

Once students have survived their first two RRJs, they start to notice an improvement in their ability to read and to write about the book. This confidence boost not only helps them realize that they will be able to successfully read their first novel in English, but that they will likely be able to handle the many other academic challenges that await them as they take first year composition as well as general education and major classes. As the semester progresses, the routines that have been put in place allow students to continue to increase their fluency and stamina in reading in English. At the end of the semester the students are asked to write a letter to a future student with advice for succeeding in the class. Their responses reveal their own sense of accomplishment in developing their reading ability and their knowledge of reading strategies. Katie, a Korean mother of a four-year-old son, shares that she would "underline important unfamiliar words and look them up during my second reading. Personally, I also found drawing pictures and writing character names while reading the book to be helpful." Another student, Patty, who was born in Mexico and hopes to be a teacher, offers these words of encouragement: "At first, when you see the book *Kindred*, you might see it as overwhelming, but as time goes on and you start to read it, you cannot put it down. Learning about slavery in the United States was sad but empowering. I wish you all the best, and I know you will be so thankful and proud of yourself when you finish your semester." Despite their doubt in their own ability to successfully read a novel in English at the beginning of the semester, these students as well as their classmates engaged fully in the risky business of reading in English and finished the semester knowing that they had overcome their fears and were ready to continue their academic journey.

Chapter 12

Reading in Calculus: Why, What, and How

Alison Lynch

When you think about math class, you might not think about reading. As an undergraduate math major, I know that I didn't. My professors never assigned reading and never discussed how to read mathematics. My classes had required textbooks, but I only opened them to look up homework problems (or occasionally to find an example similar to a homework problem). My professors lectured on everything I needed to know about the course content during class, so reading the textbook was unnecessary.

Thus, when I started teaching math, I approached reading the same way. The textbook was there to provide homework problems, and it was my role to communicate all of the course content during class time. However, I found that this approach was neither an optimal use of class time nor an optimal method for student learning. In this chapter, I share why I started to assign reading in Calculus I, what reading (and learning to read) looks like in my classes, and the benefits of this work for my students and myself.

WHY ASSIGN READING IN CALCULUS?

After teaching mathematics for a couple of years, I started assigning reading in my classes for two reasons.

First, I realized that I expected my students to make sense of mathematical texts even though I was not teaching them how. As one example, when I worked out a sample problem on the board, I expected my students to copy it down in their notes and then be able to make sense of it later when they worked on their homework problems. As another example, when I introduced a theorem statement in class, I expected students to understand the logical structure of the statement in order to discern the conditions under which we could apply it (and what it would allow us to conclude). Worked examples and theorem statements, as well as definitions, problem statements, graphs, and proofs, are all texts unique to the mathematical sciences. If I wanted my students to be successful in calculus, I needed to help them learn to make sense of these texts.

Second, as an instructor, I became dissatisfied with being my students' sole source of information on calculus. Since students came into class with no prior exposure to a new concept, I spent much of class time introducing the basics and giving students practice with them. During class, we needed to "cover" everything students would need to know to solve the homework. This left little time in class for activities that would deepen student understanding, like struggling through challenging problems or engaging in collaborative inquiry. Moreover, my students only had access to one presentation of course content: mine. I wanted them to be able to reference the textbook and other instructional resources and develop their own ways of understanding the material.

PRE-CLASS READING ASSIGNMENTS

In my Calculus I classes, I assign a class preparation assignment for students to complete before most class periods. The assignment includes a motivating problem, a reading from the textbook, and a check your understanding (CYU) problem. The motivating problem creates an intellectual need for the new content and helps students connect it to their prior knowledge. The assigned reading indicates a section of the textbook, along with suggestions for definitions and theorems to focus on or questions they should be able to answer after the reading. Then, the CYU problem(s) are short math questions that should be easily solvable if a student understands the reading.

For example, students would complete the following preparation assignment before a class on derivative formulas for basic functions (e.g., power, exponential, and constant functions). In the motivating problem, students use a method they learned earlier in the course, the formal definition of the derivative, to calculate the derivatives of a few power functions, $f(x) = x2$, $f(x) = x3$, and $f(x) = x4$. As the exponent increases, this calculation becomes increasingly challenging. However, the results suggest a pattern—the derivative of each $f(x) = xn$ appears to be $f'(x) = nxn-1$. Students are then asked to conjecture (predict) a formula for the derivatives of $f(x)= x5$, $f(x)= x6$, and the general power function, $f(x) = xn$. This activity draws on students' prior knowledge about derivatives and motivates the need for more efficient ways of calculating them. It also promotes students' sense of coherence within the content, as the new formulas are consistent with (and emerge from) ideas they have already learned.

After completing the motivating problem, students read a portion of the textbook that introduces the derivative formulas for power functions and other basic functions. Then, students solve a CYU problem that asks them to calculate the derivative of a power function, $f(x) = x10$, and two other basic functions. This allows students to practice applying the formulas from the reading and assess their understanding of when and how the formulas are used.

Students upload their work on the motivating problem and the CYU problem before the start of class. This allows me to skim through their work and identify common points of confusion. At the beginning of class, students discuss the assignment in pairs or small groups, answering each other's questions when possible and identifying shared questions. When the whole class comes back together, we discuss those shared questions, which leads into the day's activities (typically group problem solving and student presentations).

SUPPORTING STUDENTS TO READ MATHEMATICAL TEXTS EFFECTIVELY

When I started assigning pre-class reading, I hoped that the structure of these assignments would be enough to support students in making sense of the content. However, I learned that, like other aspects of mathematics, telling students what to do is not the same as teaching them how to do it. My students initially struggled to make meaning from the textbook on their own.

Some of the common complaints I heard were that the definitions were "too technical," the examples "skipped steps," and that students "got stuck" and couldn't proceed in the reading.

To help students overcome these challenges, I started using routines from Reading Apprenticeship in the classroom. I use the think aloud routine (reading the text aloud and verbalizing everything that goes through my mind) to model how I, as a mathematician, read the textbook. When I ask students what they noticed, some of the things they mention are how I reword technical phrases in my own words, add my own steps in computational examples to verify the steps presented, and keep going when I get stuck (noting that an explanation may come later). Next, I have students practice reading a sample text in pairs, with one person thinking aloud and the other person taking notes on what strategies they notice. Finally, we generate a list of strategies that they and I used as we read. Whenever we encounter a new type of text (e.g., word problems, theorem statements, visual representations), we repeat this cycle, revisiting and adding to our class strategies list.

My students also struggled to translate their confusions into specific questions. When I asked them, "What questions do you have from the reading?" a typical response was, "I don't know; I didn't understand any of it." To help students learn this skill, I give students two minutes to formulate one question about the reading in pairs. I provide question frames that might be useful, such as "Why do they _____?" "How do they get from _____ to _____?" and "What does it mean when they say _____?" Once formulated, students add their questions to a shared Google Doc for the class to discuss. This exercise not only gives students practice developing questions, but also allows them to see the breadth of questions that other pairs posed.

I also use the question-posing sessions to center the textbook as a reference. Rather than answer each question directly, I select a few and model how we can use the textbook to answer them. Then I turn some of the questions back to the class to try to answer using the textbook. After a few minutes, students share out the answers that they found, and we work as a class to answer the remaining questions. This process is time-consuming, so I only use it two or three times near the beginning of the semester, but I see a notable impact on students' ability to formulate questions and seek answers in the textbook.

BENEFITS OF READING IN MATH CLASS

Assigning and teaching reading has significantly impacted my instruction and my students' learning in Calculus I. One of the most important benefits is the extra class time it affords. As an instructor, I no longer feel pressure to introduce every definition, theorem, and strategy that students may need to know during class. My students and I can spend that time delving deeper into the most essential and most challenging. I can allow my students to struggle through solving challenging problems with their peers without fear of running out of time to cover everything. For my students, this extra time creates space to engage in productive struggle in a supported environment. It also allows them to work through confusion, practice asking and answering questions, and gain clarity before individually attempting the homework.

Another benefit is that my students have developed stronger problem-solving skills around reading mathematical texts. Over the semester, they show growth in their ability to make sense of new ideas presented in the text and apply those ideas to new problems. They also ask more sophisticated questions about the text during our class discussions. For example, early in the semester, I get many questions of the form "What does _____ mean?" However, later in the semester, I get more questions of the form "How is _____ related to _____?" and "Why do they use (one method) instead of (another method)?" I also observe students applying our class reading strategies to exam problems, annotating the problem statements to understand what the question is asking.

Finally, my students have become more independent as learners. They can use the textbook and other course materials as meaningful references rather than simply sources of homework problems. During class, I see students pulling out their textbooks and reading notes as they try to make sense of ideas, rather than calling me over with a question. They are also better able to make sense of other texts on the course topic, such as YouTube videos and online tutorials. While my students have long sought these out as references when stuck on a problem, I used to hear that they had trouble making sense of them because they presented the content differently than I did in class. Now, I hear them sharing explanations and examples from these resources with their peers (and occasionally with me). I expect this skill will be invaluable to my students in their future courses and later in life.

Chapter 13

Thinking Matters: Universal Design for Learning and Reading Apprenticeship in Math

Kristen Purdum and Nika Hogan

Open access institutions such as California community colleges are intended to serve as a bridge for all students to make progress toward a certificate, degree, career, or continued higher education. But instructors don't always feel well prepared to support all students in our richly diverse classrooms. Despite our clear equity and social justice mission, community college courses are still structured in traditional ways, from the course outlines of record we work from to the built-in grading structures in our learning management systems and the furniture we sit on. Although it is our responsibility to effectively differentiate instruction to equitably serve all students, it can feel daunting for individual instructors to meet this mandate. The authors of this chapter, Nika Hogan and Kris Purdum, worked together in a learning community designed specifically for STEM instructors to utilize the Reading Apprenticeship framework in their efforts to create active and equitable learning environments. Our conversations and collaborations have helped us to identify productive intersections between Reading Apprenticeship and Universal Design for Learning. In what follows, we introduce these overlapping frameworks, and Kris describes the way they are operationalized in a statistics course designed specifically to be supportive for learners requiring accommodations for learning differences documented through the college's Disabled Students Programs and Services (DSPS) office.

THE FRAMEWORKS: UNIVERSAL DESIGN FOR LEARNING (UDL) AND READING APPRENTICESHIP

Universal Design for Learning (UDL) is a framework developed by CAST (formerly the Center for Applied Special Technology) to support educators in establishing equitable and inclusive learning environments for all (https://www.cast.org/). The fundamental principle behind UDL is that learning and learners are variable; therefore instruction should be intentionally designed to meet that variability. The UDL framework (figure 13.1) focuses on creating multiple and varied ways for learners to engage, interact with information, navigate a learning environment, and express what they are learning. Each of these three framework elements (engagement,

Thinking Matters: Universal Design for Learning and Reading Apprenticeship in Math 111

Figure 13.1. The Universal Design for Learning Framework
CAST (2018)

representation, and action and expression) comprises further guidelines and "checkpoints" for instructors to consider in their learning design.

The Reading Apprenticeship framework (figure 13.2) is complementary and supportive to enacting UDL while keeping a strong focus on disciplinary learning. Reading Apprenticeship's emphasis on both instructors and students making their thinking visible is at the heart of UDL's promise to provide appropriately differentiated learning experiences for all students. Only through accessing our students' thinking can we design next steps—including accommodations in some cases—for each learner. While both UDL and Reading Apprenticeship can feel, when first presented, like an overwhelming amount of work for instructors, the practices central to each framework are supportive for *all* learners; therefore, they needn't be conceptualized as "additive" or "extra." At best, these frameworks can help instructors to establish a new norm, so that the way we design and facilitate learning experiences is truly equitable, while enhancing students' mastery of disciplinary concepts. The description of Kris's Statistics 10X class that follows exemplifies the way that both frameworks support well-established best practices that are within reach for instructors. The bottom line is a rigorous focus on connecting with students, helping them to connect to each other, and finding ways to access students' thinking.

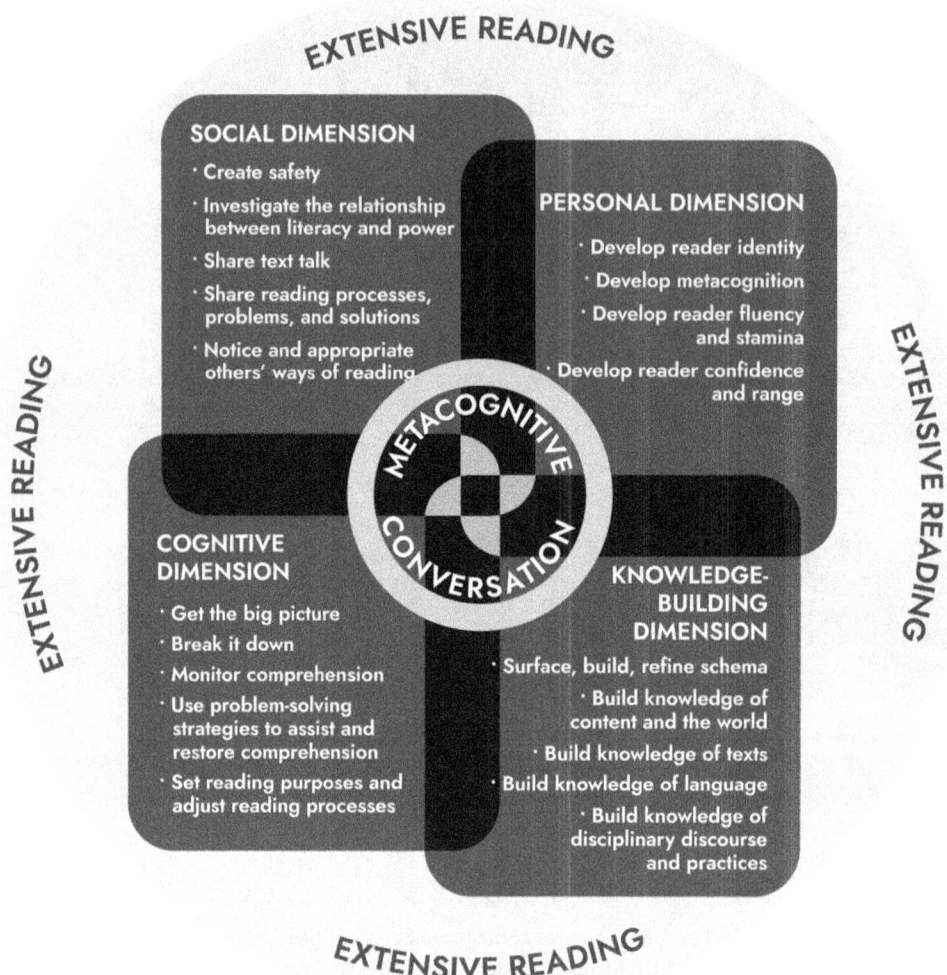

Figure 13.2. The Reading Apprenticeship Framework
Greenleaf et al. (2023)

FRAMEWORKS IN ACTION: KRIS'S ELEMENTARY STATISTICS COURSE

I teach a course at Mission College in Santa Clara, California, called Math 10X: Elementary Statistics with Additional Support. This class is intended for students with disabilities as well as for students who struggle with math. It is a six-unit class (four units transfer credit, two units corequisite), and we meet four days a week for an hour and a half every day. This gives me two extra hours a week in class, so I generally use that time for doing metacognitive routines and additional hands-on lab activities.

Disabled Students Programs and Services (DSPS) directs as many of their students into my Math 10X section as they can. The general education counselors know that this section is mainly for DSPS students, but they will also refer students who have severe math anxiety or have struggled with math in the past. Essentially, my section of Math 10X is an entire class of students who have documented DSPS accommodations, math anxiety, or some other gaps in learning that make math difficult for them.

Establishing Engagement and Supporting Active Learning

UDL's "engagement" area recommends creating a strong sense of social connection and safety in the classroom community, which maps closely to Reading Apprenticeship's "social dimension" and classroom routines such as creating community agreements and establishing routines for productive partnerships and collaborations. This groundwork is important for students in Math 10X, many of whom require additional help with basic math and executive functioning skills and lack the confidence to attempt work independently. The "engagement" area also emphasizes building on students' personal interests, motivation, autonomy, and sense of self-efficacy, which overlaps with the focus in Reading Apprenticeship's personal dimension of building on students' background knowledge, strengths, and interests, and supporting them to consider their personal and academic identities as "available for revision and refinement" (Greenleaf et al., 2023, p. 95). In Math 10X, I work to establish a safe classroom community at the beginning of the term through a "learning pact" that includes expectations I have for students as well as what students can expect from me (table 13.1). This learning pact is posted to a discussion board, and students use the discussion space to agree to the pact and add to it as well. The discussion around our learning pact helps to create a classroom environment where nobody is berated or made fun of for making mistakes during class. Mistakes are opportunities to learn, and students are asked to respect that from day one.

Our Math 10X Learning Pact

This course is a two-way street. To be successful, it requires clear expectations and a commitment from me and from you.
Please take a moment to read our pact below. It communicates what you can expect from your instructor and what she will expect from you. You will be asked to agree to our pact or build onto it.

Here's what you can expect from me:	Here's what I will expect from you:
1. I will be actively present in your learning, and available via email, office hours, and by appointment if you have questions or concerns.	1. You will actively and regularly participate in this course. Plan on spending about 12 hours per week for this class (4 hours of in-person classwork, plus 8 hours for reading the textbook, reviewing notes, working on assignments, etc.)
2. I will respond to all communication from you within 24 hours (my goal is 12 hours) Monday–Friday, and within 48 hours on the weekends, and I will let you know if more time is needed due to unforeseen circumstances.	2. You will respond to my messages within 24 hours (Monday–Friday) or let me know if you need more time due to unforeseen circumstances.
3. I will grade assignments within 5 days of the due date and will inform you if more time is needed. I will provide constructive and supportive feedback on graded assignments to help you learn.	3. You will do your best to meet the due dates for all assignments. If you are not present for an in-class assignment, you will make it up within 72 hours. Seek help from me or the tutoring center if you feel like you are falling behind.
4. I will do my best to create a safe, inclusive learning environment, both in-person and on Canvas.	4. Treat your instructor, embedded tutor, and peers the same way you would like them to treat you. You will use positive and supportive language in all communications, both written and oral.

(continued)

Our Math 10X Learning Pact *(continued)*	
Here's what you can expect from me:	**Here's what I will expect from you:**
5. I want you to be successful in this class. If your attendance or Canvas presence begins to decrease, I will contact you to better understand how I can support you.	5. We are all human, which means we can and will make mistakes. Use mistakes as learning opportunities.
6. I will be as flexible as possible to support your individual needs.	6. Be patient with the instructor's (and your classmates') ability with technology. Be flexible if there are technological issues, and be willing to help if you know how (or think you know how) to solve a technical problem.
7. Do you have anything you would like to add to this list? Send me a message!	7. Do you have anything you would like to add to this list? Send me a message!

Most of the students in Math 10X prefer to learn in a more "hands-on" and interactive way and not solely through lecture and examples. I emphasize ongoing collaboration and communication as students dig into the course content and concepts. Both the "representation" area of UDL and the cognitive and knowledge-building dimensions of Reading Apprenticeship recommend helping students actively make sense of and decode texts in ways that build comprehension. Both frameworks emphasize activating and/or building background knowledge as well as highlighting patterns and relationships in disciplinary texts and discourse, and both frameworks recommend authentic, mastery-based assessment of specific learning goals. Finally, both the "action and expression" area of UDL and Reading Apprenticeship's central practice of "metacognitive conversation" describe ways to support information processing through instructor modeling and student-guided practice of disciplinary thinking and problem solving. The practices that I rely on to bring together all of these principles and to best support my Math 10X students include metacognitive reading logs, low-stakes partner quizzes, exam corrections with error analysis, and metacognitive "exit tickets."

Metacognitive Reading Logs

Many times, even when the textbook is free, students don't utilize it to enhance their learning in math class. They might expect that in a math class, the teacher will provide notes and there is no need to read. However, the textbook is one of the ways that information is represented and engagement can be fostered; they need to get into the habit of reading before class and understanding the relationship of the textbook to the classwork. I ask students to do "preview reading" assignments before each class. They read the section the night before they come in and make notes on a two-column notetaker. The left side of the notetaker is for their notes (vocabulary, facts, etc.). The right side is for their thoughts they noticed while they were reading. When they come to class, the first thing I ask them to do is to partner with someone and share their logs for a couple of minutes. Afterward, we do a "shout out" where they can describe something interesting their partner wrote or said during the sharing period. In addition to getting warmed up for class, this routine allows us to make space for different kinds of sense-making. For example, we talk about the different types of text, because in a statistics book there can be paragraphs of text describing things in one section and in another section the language is mostly math or graphs. When the students share their notes, it's great to hear the differences in how they're approaching these different sections of text because students approach problem solving in so many different ways. And it's kind of neat, I think, for others to see how their classmates are dealing with and processing the different types of information.

Collaborative Group Work (Partner Quiz)

I love using collaborative work in class. It gives students the opportunity to discuss mathematical ideas with each other. Students who understand the material can explain the concepts to others in the class who do not yet understand. Both sides benefit: students doing the explaining are better able to solidify their understanding and commit the knowledge to memory, while students who receive the explanations get the same material I have been teaching but from a student perspective. If a student doesn't quite understand the material from my explanation, they may understand from someone else's explanation.

In my classes, quizzes are used more as student "checkpoints" than as formal learning assessments. These quizzes are short and would usually take 10–15 minutes if students are working alone. Students are given 10 minutes to work on the quiz by themselves to see what they know. After the 10 minutes is up, they are allowed to confer with other students in the classroom to get help with what they don't know or understand fully. If a student asks me if they are "doing the problem correctly," I refer them to ask a classmate; I will only clarify what a problem statement is asking for. What I love the most is the student conversations during the collaborative time. Instead of hearing students say, "What did you get for 2b?" the students ask "How did you do 2b? Why did you do that?" Students do an amazing job of explaining their problem-solving processes to their peers if you give them the opportunity. I have also noticed that at the beginning of the semester, students tend to gravitate toward peers with the same quiz form, but as the semester progresses students will begin to stay with their friend groups and discuss problem-solving processes in general, even if they have different quiz forms.

Assessment

My approach to assessment signals to students what is valued in the course. As I tell them on day one, I don't put a lot of emphasis on the final answer. I care more about how they arrived at that final answer. So on a multipoint question, one point may be for that final answer and the rest of the points are for the process. I know getting the right answer is important, but I care more about the journey than the final destination.

Some students with dyscalculia and learning gaps may not be able to do the actual calculations very well, but if I can see they have the process, I can evaluate that instead of focusing on the mistakes or the wrong answer. If a student has their thinking process written down but calculated $2 \times 3 = 5$, for example, I can evaluate whether they actually knew how to do the problem and I can award points accordingly.

Exam Reflections, Error Analysis, and Exam Corrections

Nearly all of my Math 10X students have some degree of math anxiety, so their performance on exams may not truly be indicative of their learning. The UDL framework recommends mastery-oriented feedback and opportunities for self-assessment and reflection directly related to specific, transparent learning goals. I work hard to support students to notice and value their learning process and journey by providing opportunities to reflect on their mistakes. A lot of times with math, the exams are high-stakes "one and done" activities because we have to keep moving forward. We just can't back up and redo things like many other subjects can. However,

I want students to be able to learn from their mistakes, so on every exam they have the ability to go back and correct their errors and misconceptions.

The directions (figure 13.3) ask them to try to identify their error and then classify it. Is it a computation error? Is it a problem-solving error? Did you skip the question? What's going on? If they know what kind of mistakes they are making, they can learn to look for those in the future.

Once students have identified their errors, I ask for an error analysis/classification. If they know that they make a lot of computational mistakes, for example, maybe they could slow down and double-check their work or use a calculator to try to avoid making those errors in the future. After the error analysis, they correct the mistakes. If they do the error identification, the error analysis/classification, and the corrections, they can get up to 50% of the points missed added back to their exam score. This is often enough to bring the exam score up a letter grade. They have to do the error analysis to receive full credit, because the analysis to me is just as important as doing the corrections. The students need to know what kind of mistakes they're making if they want to improve their test-taking skills.

If you would like to make corrections to your Exam #1 and earn back up to 50% of the points missed, you will need to do the following for each question you are correcting:

1. Identify your error as best you can. State or describe your error in one or two sentences.

2. Classify your error as one (or more) of the following:

- **Careless Error** *(Writing the wrong number from the start / Not following directions / Misunderstanding the question)*
- **Computation Error** *(Adding, subtracting, multiplying, or dividing incorrectly)*
- **Precision Error** *(Work too messy to understand / Dropping a negative sign / forgetting parentheses / missing units / incorrect notation / rounding issues)*
- **Problem Solving Error** *(Not following the rules of algebra / failure to complete all of the steps / not showing your thinking process)*
- **Skipped or Omitted Question**

3. Correct the problem or justification. **If you are correcting a vocabulary term from #1-10, state the definition of the incorrect term you chose AND give the corrected answer.**

Please do your error analysis and correction on a separate sheet of paper. Clearly label each problem and staple your corrections to the back of your original exam. Exam corrections are due **by the beginning of class (9:20am) on Thursday, March 14**. If you need assistance identifying your error and/or making corrections, please ask!

Note: Exam correction points will be added directly into your Exam #1 score.

Figure 13.3. Exam Corrections
Kristen Purdum

Exit Tickets

Finally, one classroom routine that allows me to access my students' thinking is the regular use of "exit tickets." At the end of class, I give them a piece of scratch paper and have students fold it in half. On the left half I ask: "Give me all the pluses. What do you know? What do you remember? What are you confident about? What do you appreciate?" And on the right half, I'll ask for the negatives: "What don't you get yet? What questions do you have? What are you still stuck on?" If I see a pattern in the negative side, I can identify areas where I might need to rethink or revisit instruction. If one person has a very specific question, I can follow up with them individually. But on the whole, I have access to what they are thinking and how they are feeling so that I can be as responsive as possible.

Communication

UDL's recommendations for "action and expression" include providing options for how students can express themselves and how we can communicate. To equitably serve all students, we have to be flexible in how we elicit and engage with students' thinking.

In the past couple of years, I have been getting more autistic students in my classes, and many of them have some difficulties with communication. For example, I had one student who was really good with oral communication, but somehow, between talking about it and putting it on paper, her thoughts and ideas would get a little scrambled. When I assessed her work, I would often refer back to the conversations we had during office hours, and I would follow up with her: "You know, when we were in office hours, you mentioned this but you wrote it this way. You didn't write it quite correctly, but I am going to give you credit based on our discussion." I could tweak the rubric to accommodate her.

Another student with autism was less verbally communicative. He could do the math, but he couldn't tell you *how* he solved the problem. His subconscious brain wasn't letting his conscious brain speak to the process questions that I asked. Since he couldn't really give me too many details about his problem-solving process, I asked him to just write down what he could so I could at least see some of what he was thinking. His responses tended to be a little less wordy and a little more "mathy," but that's how he thinks. I needed to see his thinking process through the math as opposed to through words.

Since everyone's going to communicate a little differently, I give the whole class the option of doing a media recording rather than uploading written documents. If students have extreme test anxiety and they have difficulty sitting with a piece of paper, I will offer those students the option of an oral exam so I can assess their thinking and learning orally.

CONCLUSION

Although designing and facilitating instruction for diverse populations of learners is undoubtedly challenging, we have the benefit of strong research-based principles to draw on. We know that all learners need to connect new knowledge and concepts to existing funds of knowledge, that they need to externalize their thinking in some way, and that their learning is enhanced through metacognitive reflection (National Academies of Science, Engineering, and Medicine, 2018). We also know that novices need direct guidance and mentoring from experts to take on the questioning and problem-solving strategies characteristic of their field of study (Bransford et al., 1999). We see many more connections between UDL and Reading Apprenticeship than what Kris has described here. For example, text sets (Greenleaf et al., 2023) can be used to optimize choice, leverage personal interest, provide alternatives for interacting with information, and build background knowledge. The Curriculum Embedded Reading Assessment (CERA; Greenleaf et al., 2023) can be used to support reflection, self-assessment, appropriate goal setting, and mastery-oriented feedback. There are many more examples of how these frameworks can enhance one another. When working to establish routine metacognitive conversations about disciplinary texts in college classrooms, instructors have the opportunity to simultaneously bring the Reading Apprenticeship and UDL frameworks to life, and in so doing, support all of us teachers and learners to accomplish our goals and reach our true potential.

Chapter 14

The Role of the Productive Struggle in Authentic Learning: Why Student Learning Insights Matter as Much as Student Learning Outcomes

Shirley Kahlert

Learning cannot be measured, argues instructional designer Jonan Donaldson; it can only be described (Donaldson & Allen-Handy, 2020). However, if we cannot measure authentic learning, what does it look like when we describe it? It can, of course, best be described by the learner. In order to learn authentically, however, students must be able to break the habit of "doing school," which "refers to the structuring of and engagement in rote and shallow learning performances, which students and teachers give to each other to signify that they are accomplishing normative classroom tasks" (Windschitl, 2019, p. 8). In this bargain, "familiar procedures often stand in for the accomplishment of something valuable" (Windschitl, 2019, p. 8). As one of my students acknowledges, "Students, like myself, often do this just to get the work done instead of actually wanting to learn the material." When students move away from "doing school" toward more meaningful engagement in learning, they gain insights into their own learning processes and move from a fixed to a growth mindset where they see "error" as part of a productive struggle that improves their understanding of texts.

Understanding how students deal with a productive struggle is essential in helping them succeed. In stepping up to the struggle, students can discover their own agency and are less likely to succumb to imposter syndrome and fail to persist. In this chapter, I am going to use students' own language to describe the productive struggle they experienced in my transfer level English 1A (Reading and Composition) class at Merced College, a community college in Central California. I was able to engage my students in the process of productive struggle by choosing text sets. I hope to demonstrate that when students successfully engage in a productive struggle with difficult reading, they gain a positive self-awareness of their own learning that allows them to persist in their college education.

Mathematics educators have recognized the power of a productive struggle like this in the learning process as Murdoch and colleagues (2020) explain:

> quality mathematics teaching engages students in "productive struggle" by eliciting students' thinking around the mathematics that they do not yet understand, or are coming to understand, thereby getting learners to explicate their confusions, puzzlements, doubts and the like, verbally

or in writing. Additionally, . . . teachers' responses that reinforce students' "unproductive struggle" are those that either simplify the task, thereby under challenging learners, or tell learners the right answer.

Educators like Murdock, English, Hinz, and Tyson turned to metacognition as a problem-solving strategy because metacognitive activities like those used in Reading Apprenticeship (Schoenbach et al., 2012) often offer students a path into their challenges and promote authentic learning.

Allowing students to engage in a "productive struggle" with reading is also essential because denying students access to challenging texts deprives them of the opportunity to grow as readers and thinkers. In the words of cognitive scientist Marilyn Jager Adams, "Giving children easier texts when they're weaker readers . . . serves to deny them the very language and information they need to catch up and move on" (cited in Wexler, 2018). As a result, a steady diet of so-called remedial text serves to push students into a stagnant pool and forces them to always swim—or flounder—at the same depth.

HOW TEXT SETS CAN HELP CREATE PRODUCTIVE STRUGGLE

In *Reading for Understanding: How Reading Apprenticeship Improves Disciplinary Learning in Secondary and College Classrooms*, Schoenbach and colleagues explain that a "text set exists any time a topic is presented to students through more than one text" (2012, p. 150). They differentiate between "vertical text sets" and "horizontal text sets": "Vertical text sets present texts about a particular topic at a range of difficulty levels" and offer a "range of entry points" to the student, while "horizontal text sets" are built upon a wider theme. Schoenbach and colleagues note that "horizontal text sets are a widely used way to build interest, background knowledge, and vocabulary" (p. 145). Both vertical and horizontal text sets improve background knowledge as they create a context for ideas. Consequently, because text sets are open ended, they offer students choices, and these choices provide them with the autonomy to construct their own interpretation. When students are allowed to interpret a text rather than provide a "right answer," they can develop their own insights that lead to a more precise and meaningful interpretation that keeps them engaged in the reading. As students make these choices, they are more likely to engage in the productive struggle of authentic interpretation rather than search for a "right answer." They are more likely to recognize their own challenges as readers, and therefore more likely to experience growth as they address these challenges.

Text sets can support students to take on more challenging reading tasks. Schoenbach and colleagues (2012) list six criteria for the difficulty of a text: language, sentence length and complexity, conceptual difficulty, idea density, and relevance, or the importance of the topic for the reader. As Willingham (2017) suggests, reading comprehension also involves background knowledge, so text sets also provide students a ready-made fund of general knowledge, and a vocabulary preview may add to that fund. Many argue that when students cannot tap a fund of general knowledge, they struggle with difficult texts. Some teachers seek to mitigate this struggle by assigning texts at an "appropriate" reading level, but avoiding this struggle may prevent students from growing as readers, writers, and thinkers. Immersed in the "data driven" culture of measurement and accountability, many teachers lose sight of the complexity inherent in the process of reading as they push students to get the right answer on a comprehension test. In Willingham's (2017) words,

We might think that reading tests provide an all-purpose measure of reading ability. But we've seen that reading comprehension depends heavily on how much the reader happens to know about the topic of the text. Perhaps then, reading comprehension tests are really knowledge tests in disguise.

Text sets support students to build the knowledge they need to make sense of academic texts and topics.

Finally, text sets offer ample opportunities for metacognition as they provide students with this opportunity to engage in "productive struggle." Schoenbach and colleagues (2017) comment that "an activity that asks students to explore a vertical text set gives them a metacognitive experience of identifying the factors that make a text difficult or accessible" (p. 143). I designed this freshman-level English class (English 1A, Reading and Composition at Merced College) to allow both students and teacher to engage in an ongoing metacognitive curriculum "spiral" that encourages thought that is transparent rather than opaque. Students read about metacognition as they engage in metacognition. They also read academic work directly relating to the emotional struggles they themselves are experiencing as first-year, very often first-generation college students: Module 1 text sets focused on imposter syndrome and growth mindset, Module 2 on time management, grit, and stress management, Module 3 perfectionism, executive function, flow, and intrinsic/extrinsic motivation (Kahlert, 2021). As students engage in challenging reading assignments, many come to recognize that learning is messy for all learners, but especially for learners in a first-year reading and writing class. When we do this, students can better understand the importance of growth mindset and grit as factors in their success, and teachers can recognize that learning doesn't happen on a schedule as planned but imperfectly in flashes of student insights.

HOW STUDENTS FELT ABOUT THE CHALLENGES PRESENTED BY TEXT SETS

As described above, I used text sets throughout the course to help students make their thinking visible so that I can respond more effectively. I collected reflections from a mid-semester assignment designed to challenge students with a more rigorous "strength and endurance training." Students were assigned Michael Martinez's academic article, "What is Metacognition?" alongside two pieces on growth mindset that had been presented early in the semester, Carol Dweck's TED Talk, "The Power of Believing You Can Improve" and short article, "Brainology." Dweck's TED Talk presented the ideas clearly in spoken language for a lay audience; her article "Brainology" reiterated the ideas in print, but again for a lay audience. Martinez's article presented related ideas in academic language. The assignment asked students to connect the two concepts, metacognition and growth mindset. In addition, the students' own work on metacognition in metacognitive reading logs or "research logs" and reflections also became part of the text set.

To understand the power of productive struggle, it is important to look at how students perceive and respond to difficulty, as understanding this response is essential to helping them persist. Productive struggles often create stress for students, but this stress can lead to important student learning insights. In this section, I will report on students' descriptions of their experience engaging with the Martinez article and text set. Their reflections identify struggles with academic language, time management, and self-doubt, but ultimately speak to the possibilities for authentic learning that are created when a growth mindset supports students to persist in difficult texts and tasks.

In my class, as often is the case in the community college writing classroom, students entered with different skill levels and responded differently to the level of difficulty. It therefore came as no surprise that this group's perceptions of the difficulty of the text varied. In their reflections, 6 of 27 students reported that they noticed a difference in difficulty compared to previous reading. One noted the difficulty but recognized that the challenge was productive, describing it "a learning read." Notably, a student noticed that much of the reading he had been previously assigned did not feel like it was college level: "This reading definitely felt like a college article, over the past two semesters the articles that my teachers have made me read were not too difficult; they all felt the same as high school except this one." His response underscores the idea that providing students with a "productive struggle" helps them move toward authentic learning where they recognize the value of challenge in learning rather than making an assumption about their inability to learn.

Many students reported a large part of their productive struggle to be linguistic. In the words of sociologists Pierre Bourdieu, Jean-Claude Passeron, and Monique de Saint-Martin (1994), "The divorce between the language of the family and the language of school only serves to reinforce the feeling that education belongs to another world and that what teachers have to say has nothing to do with daily life because [it is] spoken in a language which makes it unreal" (p. 9). Students responded to the productive struggle of understanding vocabulary in several ways, one noting that he needed to "do my research" to meet the challenge. Some reported their process of finding the meaning of words they didn't understand, for example, rereading. For instance, one noted, "I also continue to do my best to figure out what each of the words meant so I can get a better understanding of the article." Others made broader connections; one student described how growth mindset helped her approach the productive difficult vocabulary words, and another connected to previous reading instruction, describing how she located "the context clues of the article so that I can connect the definition with the sentences." Finally, another described her process of rereading: "I thought about how it seemed a little bit more difficult to read. I also thought to myself 'what did I just read?' and then proceeded to read through it over again."

For many students in the group, time management was a key factor in their productive challenge because they felt pressured by the length of the article and their own time management issues. When they failed to manage their time effectively, they found it difficult to actually engage in a productive struggle. This issue surfaced when students were concerned about the length of the assignments. One student reported experiencing stress about the "endurance" aspect of the challenge. In the words of another student, "Then as I kept reading after a while I kind of became frustrated because I was wondering how long this article is going to take." Yet another perceived the assignment as "never-ending." Yet students found ways to overcome that challenge. One recognized that by persisting, she could overcome the anxiety and move toward understanding the article: "The emotions I experienced were, at first, I was a little scared because the reading seemed really long. Then I started reading and found out it was not that bad. If I focus and concentrate, I know I can understand the reading and do a good job." These students were able to connect the quality of their time management with their ability to understand a challenging article.

Although students articulated self-doubt as a significant issue, they also relied on their prior knowledge about growth mindset to mitigate those emotions. One student said, "Some emotions I experienced was frustration, anger and doubt. I felt all of these because I was pushing myself too hard and it made it difficult for me to understand but I tried staying patient with myself. This also made me doubt myself because I was having trouble understanding where the author was coming from for a bit. I tried keeping a growth mindset to get past all these frustrations."

Others reported that completing the research log and the preview definitions brought a positive result to their productive struggle. Another explains how she worked through the confusion in order to connect to the text. In these cases, the productive struggle in the text set assignment helped many students move toward ownership of their own learning because they found that their own efforts led to an increased understanding of the reading. They were able to persist in the reading task as they worked through the emotions that may have led them to give up the task in the past and perhaps succumb to imposter syndrome.

CONNECTING GROWTH MINDSET AND PRODUCTIVE STRUGGLE WITH AUTHENTIC LEARNING

When students connected their reading processes with researcher Carol Dweck's ideas about growth mindset, they were able to find a strategy to respond to the challenge of a productive struggle. Significantly, 15 of the 27 students reported that keeping a growth mindset helped them work through the challenges the reading presented. A common theme in student responses centered specifically on the link between persisting through struggle with the help of a growth mindset and authentic learning. For example, one student recognized that learning takes time and failure provided information: "I was a little stressed out but not too much. I was able to keep a growth mindset through that because I know that not understanding something the first time is okay, and that an important part of the learning process is to use critical thinking." These students were clearly able to link the productive challenge of reading a difficult essay with their own understanding of their learning, moving from "doing school" to genuine learning.

These descriptions of authentic learning show evidence of a growing ownership of both the reading process in specific and knowledge in general. One student reported that the assignment "aided me into being able to contribute my own experience into the text." Another described her reading strategy as "basically trusting myself mainly and stand on what I was interpreting into my own words because it was what I could relate to in the meaning." Another comment clearly demonstrates the growth the reader experienced; for her, the challenging assignment allowed her to "turn it into a way that I could understand and make the reading easier for me." Finally, the content of the article combined with the challenge of the reading opened up bigger intellectual doors, as one student reports: "I think that I was able to keep a growth mindset while reading this because even though I was having a difficult time reading this I felt open mind to learn all the things that I didn't know beforehand." Another student describes making the reading her own: "In my opinion I think that I was able to keep a growth mindset. Keeping this growth mindset while reading the assignment I was kind of able to take it into my own protective and turn it into a way that I could understand and make the reading easier for me."

Students may describe their challenges creatively in their own words; these words and phrases come closest to their experiences of the productive struggle. The student who described the text as a "learning read" suggests that he learned something as he read or that the "read" was an important part of his learning process. In any case, by using this phrase, he describes his own dynamic process of learning. Notably, the language of these responses is often vague and ambiguous because students are trying to put a new experience into words. Phrases like "contribute my own experience into the text" and "take it into my own protective" offer teachers insights into the working student mind as students describe their own understanding in tentative but powerful words. As students report their experiences of understanding, self-trust, confidence, and ownership, they are describing a shift from "doing school" to authentic learning via the productive struggle of interpreting a text set.

RECOGNIZING STUDENT WORK AND APPROACHING EQUITY GOALS

Reading the students' reflections helped me to see the level of stress students experienced from what I thought was a straightforward assignment, and I began to recognize that the successful deployment of text sets also depends on relational trust (Bryk & Schneider, 2003) and the teacher's perception that students are capable of doing challenging work. To create relational trust in a college classroom, a teacher must design an opportunity for authentic learning; For their part, students need to commit to responding openly and honestly. When designing a difficult assignment, teachers need to trust that students are not only capable of understanding the assignment, but also capable of maintaining a growth mindset in order to overcome their challenges. They need to understand that students entering college may question their own abilities, and as a result, their responses may be tentative and imperfect. Teachers should choose assessment methods that describe the students' journeys in this direction rather than the brutal measurement of how much "content" they banked in their memories. The most accurate descriptions are offered in the students' own words.

Designing learning around text sets asks the teacher to give up "control" of the "content" of the class. This does not suggest giving in to a pedagogical anarchy but instead to understand the power of what Donaldson and Allen-Handy (2022) describe as "learning by design": creatively designing "situations" where learning can take place rather than trying to control and measure learning the "content." This kind of instructional design can allow students to develop agency in their own education, to discover an "open mind to learn all the things that I didn't know beforehand." It opens the door to an authentic Freirean liberatory pedagogy by providing an equal opportunity for "productive struggle" for all students. As Murdoch and colleagues (2020) note, supporting "productive struggle" is an equity issue, and all learners need to be given access to opportunities to struggle productively. Text sets and metacognitive responses move students past their challenges toward equity because they generate opportunities for authentic learning. Unproductive struggles frustrate both students and teachers because they so often dead-end in the failures generated by fixed mindsets and rigid assessment of content. When built on a foundation of relational trust and respect, productive struggles result in the student learning insights that create authentic learning. These moments of student learning insights are as important, perhaps more important, to a student's academic growth as the measurement of a student learning outcome because they most accurately describe learning as perceived by the learner.

Chapter 15

Introducing Perusall to Support Reading Apprenticeship in Upper-Division Mathematics Courses in an Online Modality

Peri Shereen and Jeffrey Wand

The Department of Mathematics and Statistics at California State University, Monterey Bay (CSUMB) has gone through significant pedagogical change in recent years. One of these major changes was the incorporation of Reading Apprenticeship into many of our math courses. This shift was sparked by the chancellor of the California State University (CSU) system in 2017. Executive Order 1110 eliminated all remedial mathematics courses and declared that incoming freshmen must be able to enroll in a college-level mathematics course. For CSUMB, this meant that many of our students were potentially going to enter our math courses underprepared. In order to support our students in these courses, we incorporated equitable, evidence-based pedagogical practices that would give students the tools they need to succeed, one of them being Reading Apprenticeship. In this chapter, the authors describe two upper-division courses at CSUMB; how Reading Apprenticeship was being implemented in these courses; how that was impacted by Covid-19; and how they used Perusall as a tool to engage the social and personal dimensions of Reading Apprenticeship.

We focus on the experience of the authors in the upper-division mathematics courses: Foundations of Modern Mathematics (Math 322) and Modern Algebra 1 (Math 410). Both of these courses are required courses for the mathematics major at CSUMB. Math 322 focuses on introducing students to mathematical proof writing and is considered a gateway course to students' upper-division courses. Hence, students' ability to make sense of mathematical text in the course is pertinent to their success in their later courses. Math 410 is one of the two most challenging courses our students take in the mathematics major due to its mathematical rigor and dense content. Thus, Reading Apprenticeship is a great tool to help students be successful in this challenging course. The two courses implement metacognitive tools, such as *think aloud*, *talking to the text*, and *think-pair-share* and apply associated skills to daily reading assignments with problems and reflections. In particular, daily reading assignments were collected and generated whole-class discussions and small-group discussions. Students developed community in part due to the Reading Apprenticeship strategies implemented. Instructors were able to gauge student comprehension of reading materials during discussions using visual cues. In many ways, Reading Apprenticeship was benefiting from the in-person modality; we just did not realize it—that is, until March 2020, when the effect of Covid-19 took place, and we were forced into an online modality. In the online setting most students did not use cameras, students could not dependably attend the class Zoom session, and for those who could attend, some found it difficult to participate in virtual discussions. As a result, instructors could not determine comprehension as easily. Instead, instructors adapted Reading Apprenticeship to the online modality differently depending on how classes were structured. For example, in Math 322, the instructor continued to implement *think aloud* and found that students benefited even more from this Reading Apprenticeship tool in the online modality, as it allowed students to listen and observe the instructor's share out more equitability and without physical classroom limitations. In Math 410, while the instructor found *think-pair-share* difficult to implement, they replaced this with an initial class Zoom poll, resulting in more of a think-share activity, which would lead into group activities in breakout rooms. However, instructors were left feeling these activities were not enough. Thus, we searched for a replacement for the reading assignments that complemented the online modality—leading us to Perusall.

WHAT IS PERUSALL?

Perusall is a self-proclaimed "social learning experience" (https://www.perusall.com). More precisely, it is an online platform that allows students to asynchronously read text and/or watch video collaboratively in a community of their peers. As students read, they engage in the assigned reading with their peers by annotating words, sentences, or passages; leaving comments, questions, or observations; and engaging in discussion around the text with their peers. Everyone completing the assignment can see these annotations in real time. Thus, students are able to do the reading and interact with each other as if they were in the same room, reestablishing the social component from our in-person modality. For example, in figure 15.1, we see not only the social dimension of Reading Apprenticeship revealed, but many of the dimensions occurring providing a great metacognitive conversation among students.

In particular, the first comment is a student sharing their text talk by identifying the importance of what they read about composition of functions and relating it back to the chain rule learned in calculus. The student is developing their metacognitive skills by relating content across courses, developing both the personal and knowledge-building dimension of Reading Apprenticeship. In the third comment, the student comments that they've never heard of this way of thinking about the topic. Here the student is noticing and appropriating the first student's way of reading/processing content. In general, the exchange: student 1 recalling previous content, student 2 recalling a similar expression, and student 3 gaining a new insight is a scenario one can imagine happening in a face-to-face setting, but this is happening asynchronously as students read. On the teacher's side, instructors get real-time feedback on student confusion and comprehension. In particular, instructors can respond to student questions directly, review and "upvote" student comments before class, identify challenges that student(s) might be having with the content, and provide insight to support student(s) if necessary. For example, in figure 15.1, the instructor upvoted this comment because of the quality of the post itself and the insight into the students' current knowledge the thread provided. Students have said the following about the upvote feature: "*When the professor would give me a checkmark when I would say something helpful or ask a good question made me believe that I did understand the concepts better than I thought. This would then in turn make my attitude and engagement during class that much higher.*"

✓ Upvoted by instructor

This is relevant because we will be working with functions that have another function within itself.
My calculus teacher in high school helped us think of taking derivatives of this by saying "the derivative of the inside times the derivative of the outside."

Mar 17 8:23 am

That saying also takes me back to calc haha! Have not thought about the chain rule for a long time though so I feel like I will need to brush up on some of it to better understand this section on functions

Mar 20 2:44 pm

I never heard that saying. I appreciate hearing peoples different experiences or ways of thinking on things because at times it really does paint a clearer picture on topics, in this case an easier way to remember on how to use the chain rule .

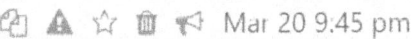

Mar 20 9:45 pm

Figure 15.1. Metacognitive Conversation in Perusall
Peri Shereen and Jeffrey Wand

As we saw above, depending on how assignments are generated and used during the course (see below for our implementation), Perusall can be made to embody the four interacting dimensions of Reading Apprenticeship: social, personal, cognitive, and knowledge-building. Assignments through Perusall are inherently social; they allow students to read a book or passage together, thus building collaboration and fostering discussion. Perusall reading assignments touch on the personal dimension since students can practice reading and, possibly with instructor and/or classmate support, build academic identity and confidence (see below for an example). The cognitive dimension is embedded in the annotation feature because students are required to break down the reading (assuming it is part of the assignment), develop their own ideas, make their own conclusions about the text, and observe how others are interpreting the reading. Finally, with some instructor help, students can build the knowledge of the discipline as well as how to read in the discipline through the readings.

IMPLEMENTATION

Before Covid-19, in both Math 322 and Math 410 students would complete daily reading assignments that had a mixture of focus questions (i.e., questions on the main content that should be answerable post-reading) and reflection questions. Like an entry ticket, the reading assignments would be turned in upon entering the class. Throughout the pandemic, however, Perusall assignments replaced the daily reading assignments. A typical Perusall assignment involves reading a section of the course textbook (usually corresponding to the next day's class activity) and making two "substantive" annotations. These annotations could be questions they had about part of the text, answering other student questions, an observation they made about the content, or answering one of the computational questions inside the textbook. In terms of "substantive," students are given the directions found in table 15.1.

Math 322	Math 410 (revised over iterations)
Remember you must do at least 2 substantive annotations. *Substantive* means that the comment is meaningful/thoughtful and either enhances the text or allows others to engage in a dialogue that will increase understanding. —Asking questions is fine as long as your annotation includes a description of why you are confused. For instance, *"This part is confusing"* is not a good annotation. *"This part is confusing me because I thought the definition of function meant that only one input may go to a unique output. However, this part of the book seems to give a counterexample to that"* is a good annotation.	You will be assessed on your completion of 3 graded annotations scored on a scale of "low, medium/high"-quality annotations with a medium/high annotation providing thoughtful comments and engaging questions. For example, comments that simply say *"I don't understand this"* would be considered low, but comments that say *"I understand that the goal is to ____, but I don't understand how we are allowed to assume ____"* would be considered medium/high. Other examples of medium/high annotations include examples of concepts/proofs that you are stuck on and that helped you to make some insight; responding correctly to a question of your peer; making connections to earlier content; providing examples of definitions; etc.

REFLECTION AND REVISION

Perusall for both courses was a welcome change. The instructors were surprised by the depth of discussion students were having about the content being presented in the course textbook. Some students would even give full proofs to student questions using the proof techniques gained throughout the course (see figure 15.2). One comment by a student often sparked several students to respond, creating a lengthier threaded exchange. Such threaded comments could be students expressing gratitude that they weren't the only ones confused by a certain passage. It could also reflect an exchange of ideas or gratitude for a classmate's explanation of a complicated passage. Perusall also made gauging student understanding very easy. Questions students asked illuminated misconceptions for the instructor and gave the instructor a great "jumping off point" when starting class discussion. The instructor could upvote any observation or comment so that the student and class could see (see figure 15.1). The upvote and annotation system allowed instructors to easily provide students with positive reinforcement, and to empower students to be confident in their ability. Although questions cannot be upvoted in Perusall, it was important to the instructor to give value to them by either commenting on

 This statement is true.

Proof: assume that a, b, c are nonzero integers such that $a|b$ and $b|c$. By the definition of divisibility this means that $c = bk$ and $b = aj$ for some $a, j \in \mathbb{Z}$. By substitution we have $c = ajk$, and jk is some integer as integers are closed under multiplication, therefore $a|c$.

Q.E.D.

Figure 15.2. Sample Student Annotation from Math 322
Peri Shereen and Jeffrey Wand

the question in Perusall or mentioning that question during the class discussion. Lastly, because every student was required to participate, instructors were able to hear what *every* student was thinking, a huge benefit to using a platform such as Perusall. In the future, the instructors plan to continue to use Perusall. From our experiences, an appropriate number of required annotations is three or four. Additionally, in Math 322 the instructor may get rid of the option to do computational questions as an acceptable annotation to promote more discussion.

Overall, the instructors found that student experience with Perusall was positive. In an end-of-semester survey of Math 410, students were asked about their experiences with Perusall. In assessing the cognitive and knowledge-building dimensions, 84% of students agreed or strongly agreed that "the use of Perusall for reading and video assignments increased [their] learning of the class content." In assessing the personal and social dimensions, 63% of students agreed or strongly agreed that "the use of Perusall for reading and video assignments contributed to [their] sense of belonging to the classroom community and increased my engagement" (n = 19, fall 2020). Although this is a small sample, we are very encouraged by the results and look forward to what future students have to say.

Covid-19 forced the instructors to look into alternative means of delivering a Reading Apprenticeship experience in an online setting. However, the other tools we utilized pre-Covid have not been completely abandoned. In fact, think-pair-share and think aloud have already been reintroduced into Math 322 since transitioning back to in-person classes. The instructors still see how such tools are great for *inside the classroom*. For the better, our courses are now giving students a highly collaborative reading tool used *outside of the classroom*.

Chapter 16

Snapshots of First-Year College Reading

Nanda Warren

What does it mean to be an educated person? Is it the possession of a degree, a certificate, a credential? Is it the ability to think, to reason, to weigh evidence and develop an informed position? For me, education is closely tied to literacy. I believe that unrestricted access to books opens the potential for continuous self-education, and that college teachers are just partners in curating texts for the curious mind. Holding this implicit educational philosophy, I fell into college teaching without having developed a pedagogical approach to engage learners who may find reading alienating, boring, or frustrating. Trained as an English as a second language and basic literacy instructor, I knew how to build support around readings. What I was not prepared for was the challenge of meshing my own unexamined theory of learning with the views of my students, all while operating within the institutional constraints of a public university.

Students begin their first year of college defining "education" in their own ways. The university, with its system of general education requirements and learning outcomes, offers its own assumptions about what learning should look like. A mismatch in expectations can result in disorientation, dissatisfaction, and a superficial performance of roles in the classroom, with each player going through the motions to obtain some external reward. I suspect that no one observes this pained performance more closely than the adjunct instructors who teach the majority of lower-division students. As a part-time, contingent instructor primarily teaching first-year students and international exchange students, I find myself working with the most peripheral and novice members of the student body. At an institution like mine, which is designated "Hispanic Serving" and enrolls large numbers of first-generation college students, the incentives for students to become educated are high, while at the same time conflicting beliefs about what it means to become educated can make the path difficult to navigate. Too many students give up and decide that college is not for them, and seeing this abandonment of a dream is one of the most painful parts of my job.

About two or three semesters into teaching first-year composition, I attended a series of workshops on reading with Dr. Nelson Graff. We started with an article by William Broz, who connects student avoidance of reading with a performance of education that is inauthentic. Broz (2011) cites Peter McLaren's observation of "teachers pretending to teach, and students pretending to learn" (p. 16). I remember feeling a pang of familiarity at this description and thinking: "That is not the kind of teaching experience I want." Since then, I have committed to working on doing something real in my classroom. But what is that "something real," and how will I know it when I see it?

My journey toward creating a more authentic experience of teaching and learning involves all three of the threshold concepts identified in this volume, but the most challenging for me to engage with has been concept 2: "students must be entrusted with the work of making sense of texts." In this chapter, I will explore the question of what I think it looks like when students truly take on the work of making sense of difficult texts, and what conditions seem to lead more often to that outcome. I offer three snapshots as candidates for authentic text-based learning. These snapshots are not meant to be raging success stories, but rather small glimpses of a still-distant goal, or perhaps signposts for myself and other instructors to watch for as we try to bring students into an academic community that was not necessarily designed for them and where they may fear they do not quite fit.

SNAPSHOT 1

We are somewhere near the middle of a two-semester first-year composition course, around the point in the year when students have lost their initial enthusiasm for college and are confronted with the reality of its difficulty. I have put students in pairs to break down their assigned portion of a scholarly article about writer's block and share their notes with the class. One of the students has recently transferred from another section of the class where she was not doing well, having barely passed the first semester. Her assigned portion of the text is one of the densest: an explanation of the author's theoretical framework using terms like "heuristic" and "algorithm." Halfway through the activity, I give everyone a five-minute break, after which we will finish and jigsaw their section notes. Some students wander outside the classroom, while others pull out their phones. The student with the theory section on heuristics and algorithms stays in her seat, rereading and continuing to take notes on her assigned passage. She persists through the break and continues until she has notes to share.

This is not a breakthrough moment of instruction. It is just an instance where I can imagine other, less desirable outcomes. The student could have copied a few words from the section and called it done. She could have relied on her partner to take the notes and said nothing about the parts she didn't understand. She could have taken an extra-long break, slipping back into the class as everyone was finishing their explanations. In the five minutes she worked through the break, though, I caught a glimpse of something I would consider authentic learning: there were new concepts to learn from a text; these concepts took effort to learn; there was a "before" and "after" in terms of understanding; and the student was the one who did the work.

The routine we were using for this activity was one that I am still not quite comfortable with: think-aloud paired problem solving (TAPPS). Unlike traditional pairwork, the partners do not collaborate on their task. Instead, they take turns being the "problem solver" and the "listener." One person tackles the text for a while and tries to articulate their thought process while the other notes strategies the problem-solver is trying and asks questions to prompt metacognitive conversation. This kind of turn-taking is challenging for me to enforce because I enjoy listening to pairs help each other. Looking back at my own reflection notes after this class, I see that I wrote, "The listeners asked a few questions, but I felt like I wanted them to do more—I need to make their role clearer next time. . . . I definitely saw some of the weaker readers struggling on their own, with their partner watching." I remember that this struggle made me uncomfortable. I felt an instinct to rescue, to support, to push toward a faster resolution of the word or structure causing the problem. The only scaffolding I provided in this lesson was modeling what to do with unfamiliar words—when to look them up, when to skip over them, and when to try other strategies. The students continued this work on their own. I wrote in my reflection: "Once they started working in their pairs, much of the work seemed to be about problem solving vocabulary, with students marking words they didn't understand and talking about their strategies to guess the meaning." At the time, I was dissatisfied with this outcome, writing, "I would have liked to see some more global strategies, like summarizing big 'chunks' of the text. I should have put up the class reading strategies list."

Looking back at this lesson, it seems that turning over the work of problem solving vocabulary may have accomplished something. The student described above did not get stuck on the words *heuristic* and *algorithm*, but rather worked until she made some sense of them. When students encounter words they do not understand, they might call the text "boring" or poorly written, or they might silently denigrate their own abilities. Entrusting students to solve the problem of unknown words opens an alternative direction for their thoughts.

To be motivated to do this work, the text needs to intrigue students. The text for this lesson, a 1980 article by Mike Rose examining the causes of writer's block, is not "interesting" by the standards of most young adults, but it does present certain intellectual and practical rewards to those who choose to engage with it. We all experience writer's block at one time or another, so we might be curious as to what the research says about why, and how to overcome it.

The student in this snapshot did not end up completing the class. She disappeared about midway through the semester. As I said, these are not raging success stories. But perhaps if I can extend some of these moments beyond five minutes in a single class, the experiences of success can accumulate and compound, and students like this one can shift their narrative about themselves and their place in higher education.

SNAPSHOT 2

It is 10:00 or 11:00 at night, a week before finals. The campus tutoring center, where I also work, is open late for our "Long Night Against Procrastination," and students are trying to finish papers that are due in the next week, or day, or (in some cases) the next hour. One of the students that night is working on the final assignment for my own first-year stretch composition class. He is part of a college support program for students from migrant worker backgrounds. Since he is working on my assignment, I choose to sit with him while the peer tutors work with other students. He tells me about a place in the paper where he is stuck, not knowing what else to write. I suggest incorporating more ideas from our class textbook, Appeals in Modern Rhetoric. *We talk a little about a particular chapter, and I suggest that he reread some of it to develop the point he is trying to make. He takes out his paperback copy of the book, rotates his chair a little away from the computer, and reads for the next several minutes.*

Students often resist spending time reading or rereading when they have a deadline approaching. It is easier to just hunt for a quotation that will get them closer to the word count, or fill the pages with vague or repeated ideas. What struck me about this moment was the calm that the student projected as he spent a good chunk of precious work time reading and thinking about the chapter before returning to the paper. He trusted that he could get something of use from the text, and he was willing to engage in the process even at that late hour.

In this case, it is difficult to separate the personal characteristics of the student from the classroom environment to say what was most influential. This was a persistent, hard-working, and positive student, steady in his class participation. Three years later, he asked me for feedback on his application to graduate school. He successfully completed college during the semester disrupted by the pandemic and moved on to the next phase of his life. Looking back on that moment at the end of his freshman year, I like to think that our classroom structure supported the development of habits that sustained him through the rest of his undergraduate experience. We spent time reading during class in pairs and groups, and text-based discussions that were focused not on getting a "right" answer but on posing and pursuing questions about a text. The norm in the class was to get something out of every reading, even if some aspects of the text remained obscure or fuzzy. As a stretch class, we had two full semesters to develop routines of reading, problem solving, and metacognitive conversation. Also important was the support of his cohort; students in that program for migrant students formed strong bonds with each other and worked especially well in pair and group activities. This social aspect of learning is essential, and I remember this particular cohort being particularly sustained by it.

Compared to the first snapshot, this was an even less "interesting" text. Students typically find the language in M. Jimmie Killingsworth's *Appeals in Modern Rhetoric: An Ordinary Language Approach* (2005) anything but "ordinary," and they find some of his examples dense with references to texts and contexts they have never heard of. At the same time, though, students often find ways to engage with this book at an intellectual level, as Killingsworth's methods of rhetorical analysis provide an alternative way of seeing and interpreting communicative events. To me, this is a key threshold for students to cross: the idea that readers can gain a certain intellectual satisfaction from comprehending a book that brings us into a special "club" of scholars who can apply disciplinary tools to better understand the world. Instructors can and should assign texts that most students would not pick up for leisure reading, and as course texts, these can form a cornerstone of university education.

Here, my own assumptions about education are apparent: to me, books are foundational to learning, and if students do not read them, they are just performing education, not truly engaging with it. Through my work in a tutoring center, I often see students try to write source-based papers without fully reading their sources, so to see someone stop writing and just read for a while satisfies my preconceived notions of what education should look like. I acknowledge my bias in this area; certainly, there are other ways to learn besides reading. But I believe in the motto I put on our class reading strategies list from César Chávez in his 1984 Commonwealth Club Address: "You cannot uneducate the person who has learned to read." In this speech, Chávez was not just talking about reading, literally, but about the ability to analyze social conditions and effect change. Those moments where I see the habit of reading take root give me hope that we are providing an education that creates the conditions for change to happen, for the first-generation college students we teach and for their wider communities.

SNAPSHOT 3

It is the second week of fall semester, so I have not formed much rapport with students yet; I barely know their names, let alone their dispositions and preferences. Students have been given a choice of texts to read to orient them to possible purposes for studying rhetoric. The texts vary in length and difficulty. The longest and most challenging is a chapter from Victor Villanueva's memoir Bootstraps: From an American Academic of Color (1993). *Only two students choose that text, and after reading, they partner up to make summary notes to share with classmates. As I circulate, I visit the Villanueva pair and point them toward places that provide clues to the writer's purpose and structure. Later, when the pair separates and each student works on explaining their text to a new group, I return to one of those students and push him a little further, asking him to go back to the text to make his summary more precise, and posing questions about some of the more puzzling passages. I start to wonder if I am pushing too much, and I say something like, "It may seem like I'm picking on you, but this is a really cool chapter, and I know you can get this." The weeks go by. Toward the middle of the semester, when they are writing a narrative essay about their research process, this student defends his own draft narrative in a peer review session, saying, "I wanted to tell the story out of order, the way Villanueva did."*

The process of education is one of change. Education leads us to see new possibilities for ourselves and our interactions with the world. A superficial performance of education is more static: we come to class, we do some things with our time, and we leave thinking and believing the same way as when we started. In this case, the student worked through a challenging text not only to unlock its meaning, but to discover a new way of writing and sharing an experience. The fact that Villanueva's chapter specifically speaks to the experience of navigating college as a student of color means that students who choose to do the work of reading it closely enough can discover possibilities for themselves to carve a place in this world of books, philosophy, and rhetoric.

To create the conditions for this change to happen, instructors need to understand our own role. We need to know when and how to push and when to step back. We need to evaluate the things we say to students in terms of whether those utterances are likely to motivate them to do the work of reading, or whether they are likely to shut down that process. I appreciate the framing of Yeager and colleagues (2014) of "wise" feedback: the standards are high, I know you can meet them, and there are resources to help you get there. This model applies not only to writing but to reading as well.

I still have a long way to go with figuring out a process for bringing first-year students into the ideal of education that I have in mind, an ideal that involves empowering individuals to read and learn for themselves across their lifetime. For instructors who have similar goals, I hope that we might think more about how to notice small moments of authentic learning and extend them into connected, meaningful educational experiences that lead to greater student success. My experience thus far has shown me some components to continue building on and some practices to incorporate in every class.

The first step is to acknowledge our own biases and assumptions about reading, and to listen closely to what students are saying for clues about their perspectives on education and their purposes for pursuing higher education. This awareness helps us be more transparent with students about our agenda and encourages us to explain why we ask them to read at all, and not to just gather the information in another way. Then, we need to set up classroom conditions that give students the space and autonomy to take on the work of reading a challenging, but hopefully intellectually rewarding, text. A continuous series of teacher judgments go into creating these conditions, from selecting worthwhile texts, to planning when and how to work in groups and when to work individually, deciding when to scaffold and when to step back, and thinking carefully about how to respond to student questions and how to give feedback. Finally, there is the close observation of students. We need to watch for signs that "something real" is happening, that students are truly investing themselves in a process that results in growing their capacity to learn, to think, to express themselves, and to use literacy to make positive things happen in the world (Lunsford, 2016).

This work is not easy, and it must be renewed every year, every semester, with new students who are as different from each other as they are different from previous cohorts. While universities like mine strive to become more equitable places where students from marginalized backgrounds can succeed and move up in the world, too many students hit a wall early in their college career. To meet this challenge, we need a more transformative approach to teaching than just going through the motions of pretending that students have done the reading. Instead, we need to set the expectation that they *will* read, that *it is worth their time* to read, and that they *can* read anything they put their mind to. Equipped with this power, students can decide what they will do with the education they give themselves.

PART V

Reading Is Social and Personal

In the survey of faculty we describe in the introduction, we asked about breakthroughs in their disciplinary teaching as the result of incorporating Reading Apprenticeship into their practice. One of the themes that emerged from that research is the social and personal nature of teaching and learning that involves reading. Below, we elaborate on that theme with the specific results of the survey, making explicit connections to threshold concept theory as it is relevant, and contextualize the chapters in part V with related research.

The idea that reading is social and personal is multilayered for teachers, and their references to its social nature took many forms, which they engaged with unevenly, suggesting the threshold nature of this concept. In this part, we'll discuss several aspects of the social and personal nature of reading that arose repeatedly in the data and one that remained mostly unacknowledged among our participants but that research in college reading and disciplinary literacy at the secondary level suggests is key to this concept. Specifically, we'll review what faculty wrote about the ways that treating reading as social has consequences for the meaning students made from readings, their development of reading strategies, and their sense of belonging and identity as readers. We'll also discuss the role of faculty vulnerability in establishing the strong learning communities that benefit the most from the social and personal nature of reading. Finally, we'll consider what seems to be missing from the responses to our survey—a strong sense of the situated nature of reading and the ways reading is changed by the contexts in which reading happens.

READING IN COMMUNITY CAN LEAD TO IMPROVED MEANING MAKING

Several of the faculty responding to the survey noted—both from their own perspective and students' perspectives—that engaging socially around the texts improved the meaning students made from reading. That seems an unremarkable claim to faculty teaching English classes; most of us include discussion of any assigned readings in our classes for exactly this reason. Yet for faculty across the disciplines, this may have represented a shift in their thinking. For instance, one faculty member wrote, "RA and Covid-19 have opened my eyes to the profound social aspects of reading and learning. The process of interaction is key to any lasting understanding." Another wrote, "Learning has become so much more authentic! Students are in constant dialogue with texts and connect what they read/watch with things they know and ideas or questions brought up by others." The latter comment suggests the transformative nature of the insight and how recognition of the social nature of reading changed the faculty member's practice. According to one faculty member, at least some students saw the benefit of social cognition as well, noting after a group activity previewing a text, "'Wow, I would not have gotten this if I just previewed this on my own.'"

CONVERSATIONS ABOUT READING STRATEGIES HELP STUDENTS DEVELOP AS READERS

As significant as the social nature of reading is for students' understanding of particular texts, it may be even more significant for students' understanding of the process of reading—or so faculty comments suggest. Several faculty commented on the value of metacognitive conversation, including the noticing of reading and problem-solving strategies, as a breakthrough for them in their practice of Reading Apprenticeship. One faculty member perhaps put this shared insight best:

> The power of observation and reflection—intentionally creating the space and opportunities where students can observe their own thinking and the thinking and moves of other readers and writers—and consciously adopt those that they find effective—that it doesn't work to just "teach strategies" but rather to surface the ones that are in the collective—give them space and opportunity to notice what others in the community (including me) "do" when they read and write.

Clearly, this also resonates with the threshold concept that reading is a problem-solving process.

Several participants pointed to the think-aloud routine as a key component of this insight for them, one connecting it to culturally responsive teaching and Zaretta Hammond's work: "It dawned on me that the think aloud routine honors the learners who prefer to verbalize their thoughts. . . . Hammond's research and analysis reveals the importance of using a cognitive routine, such as think aloud, that helps students 'chew on' their learning in ways that align with their cultural traditions." Others noted that this routine "brings students together" and appreciated how much students themselves enjoyed the routine and "liked reading together in class." Importantly, some faculty pointed to these discussions as transferring to work students did in writing and other classes. One noted, "I recently had a student reach out and share that they are applying the reading strategies to all sorts of tasks in college and classes."

READING IN COMMUNITY CAN SUPPORT STUDENTS' DEVELOPMENT OF IDENTITIES AS READERS

It should not be surprising that making better meaning of texts and learning about themselves as readers improves the classroom community and students' attitudes about themselves as readers. One faculty member relished "watching their skills improve, but moreover seeing their confidence increase." The majority of respondents in the group who referred to reading as social emphasized that reading together is a powerful mechanism for creating classroom community and students' sense of belonging. Respondents were struck not only by the realization that deep reading is supported by social supports such as the opportunity to reflect on and share literacy histories, time in class to make sense of reading together, and metacognitive conversation routines, but also by a sense that this work of reading together is a kind of "glue" that they have long searched for. Reading together "brings students together" for "being vulnerable and bonding"; "shame or fear can be aired out"; and students "feel less alone."

For many of these instructors, this recognition was the most profound aspect of seeing reading as social, recognizing the importance of nurturing a learning community and honoring students' personal relationship to reading. Faculty point to the "personal reading history" routine as key to establishing a community and supporting students' development, noting for instance that "It is particularly meaningful for students to discover that others have and have had challenges with reading that make them feel less alone" and that "students have been empowered to become more active, engaged, and self-aware students" through such discussions. One instructor even "overheard a student say something like this: 'I don't usually like reading, but this time, I'm starting to get into it!' It was just a small remark, but it meant a lot to me to provide that entry point into an academic reading experience for someone who self-identified as a reluctant reader."

FACULTY VULNERABILITY PLAYS A KEY ROLE IN MAKING THE MOST OF THE SOCIAL NATURE OF READING

Part of understanding that reading is social is faculty understanding their own role in the social environment of the classroom. One idea that instructors have raised as important is the value of showing vulnerability with their students. While this didn't arise often in teacher responses—only nine respondents (10%) mentioned it—the ways those teachers described it seems important. There seemed to be two key ways in which their modeling of vulnerability supported teaching and learning—first, it normalized struggle for students, making it acceptable for them to struggle and improve. Respondents also described it as important to the atmosphere of the class and the learning community.

This idea of normalizing struggle surfaced most often when respondents wrote about modeling think-aloud for students, a routine in which a reader reads aloud and articulates their process of making sense of the text as they read. One respondent described this insight as a result of a change in practice:

> When first learning think-alouds in RA, I modeled this with a poem, song lyrics, article, etc., that I already knew well. Doing this think-aloud with something I already knew helped me to feel more in control of the lesson. I wanted to model the think-aloud WELL, but this modeling was not genuine. Since I already knew these pieces, the think-alouds were more performative in nature. My breakthrough came when I invited students to bring in a text that they thought might be a challenge for me (something I had heard suggested in an RA workshop). One student brought in some lyrics to a Linken Park song and another brought me a section of an automotive manual. I fumbled my way through them, applying what schema I had. I was able to more genuinely be vulnerable and authentic in my think-aloud, and I think this had a positive effect on the class when it came to their work using think-alouds. I was able to show them while I was an expert when it came to some texts, I was a novice when it came to others, and that it's okay to enter into a text wherever you are. It's important to dance with the text.

That insight, that what would help students most was not a display of expertise but permission to struggle and the recognition that learning to read is always contextual, seems to be at the heart of this idea for teachers. Another specifically named it in this way: "One breakthrough for me is the power of vulnerability." That this idea was transformative for at least one teacher was evident in this comment: "The concept of normalizing struggle and modeling my strategies has significantly changed the way [I] think, plan, and approach teaching."

Modeling and showing vulnerability also became a bridge for some faculty. One wrote that they "used a think aloud in which I asked students to nominate a current popular song for which I tried to understand the lyrics. We used my experience as a starting point to discuss reading unfamiliar text before student pairs worked with a selection from the textbook." And another wrote that the modeling was a tool for persuading students of the value of reading strategies:

> I asked students to bring in texts for us to practice Thinking Aloud. They picked one for me, and it was in Spanish. With their help, I was able to think aloud in front of them all. They witnessed me engage in some of the hardest meaning-making of my life! And they saw that the routines we practice are not just to become better readers—these are the routines to read!

For other respondents, the importance of their vulnerability related to their relationships to their students and the class atmosphere. One noted that their vulnerability made them "more approachable for my students" and "sets a nice tone and some community building." Another realized, "I can share with them some of my own mistakes so that we become a community of learners and establish a trust in each other and in me."

READING IS SITUATED PROBLEM SOLVING

Faculty responses thus far have suggested four important ideas that characterize reading as social: (1) reading in community can lead to improved meaning making; (2) conversations about the strategies used to read help students develop as readers; (3) engaging with reading socially is both personally motivating and important for creating and sustaining learning communities and a sense of belonging; and (4) faculty vulnerability can play an important role in the creation of these communities. There are also hints in faculty responses that suggest there is more to this dimension of reading. One instructor, for instance, wrote something that suggests that reading changes depending on the context in which it occurs: "In my information literacy class we have a whole section on Age of Algorithms and during our initial talk to the text, students are amazed that they are encouraged to 'push back' on the text. To question parts of it, look and record aha moments and feelings, *not take the text as truth, but as a conversation in which they are invited*" (italics added). Many faculty treat as routine the notion that academic writing means entering a conversation in their disciplines. Yet the instructor is pointing here to the need to *read differently* because of participation in that conversation, an insight that points to the situated nature of reading. Recognizing that situated nature of reading remains an area for which many faculty are still in a liminal or even pre-liminal stage of understanding.

Most of the comments cited in the above sections still treat reading as an individual encounter between a reader and a text, independent in many ways of context. The idea that texts can be lifted out of the contexts in which they make sense and used to illustrate reading strategies treats reading as universal, context-independent, unbounded. Interestingly, Gogan (2017) seems to support this position when he argues that reading as transformation is a threshold concept. In doing so, he argues against the boundedness of threshold concepts, suggesting that this threshold concept crosses disciplinary boundaries and is useful across the curriculum. He writes, "reading can be viewed as transformation unbound—that is, a kind of activity that leads to transformative effects irrespective of a particular community" (p. 59).

While it may be true that reading has transformative effects across contexts, scholars in composition who study reading have come to very different conclusions about the nature of reading (e.g., Abbot & Nantz, 2017; Carillo, 2015; Horning et al., 2017; Pearlman, 2013; Tinberg, 2017). For instance, Abbot and Nantz (2017), writing about an interdisciplinary history and economics class, noticed the ways that students read and the ways the texts were organized differed significantly between the history and economics texts they assigned. And Pearlman (2013) uses Vygotsky's distinction between a tool (external focused) and a sign (internal focused—involving a change in understanding) to describe the "true goal of literacy" (p. 4).

That research in composition studies resonates with literacy research in other domains—secondary education (e.g., Croce & McCormick, 2020; Fang & Chapman, 2020; Moje, 2015; Shanahan & Shanahan 2008) and cognitive psychology (e.g., Britt et al., 2018). For instance, Moje (2015) argues that teaching disciplinary literacy is a great deal more complicated than current discussions represent. She argues for a heuristic for engaging in disciplinary literacy instruction summarized in five Es: "engage, elicit/engineer, examine, and evaluate" (p. 260). This heuristic, she suggests, helps teachers to see their job as apprenticing students into the cultural and social practices of disciplines while interrogating the disciplines themselves. Moje describes disciplines as "cultures in which certain kinds of texts are read and written for certain purposes and with or to certain audiences" (p. 257). And in cognitive psychology, Britt and colleagues (2018) describe a model for understanding reading comprehension that they call RESOLV (reading as problem solving). They focus on the ways in which readers create mental models of the reading tasks that they are enacting in different situations. Their key insight is that the contexts in which readers read shape the ways they understand what they are doing when they read.

This idea of reading as a social practice embedded in a meaningful context connects well with rhetorical genre theory and the notion of genre as social action (Miller, 1984). Soliday (2011) takes up this idea with respect to writing assignments. She explores faculty writing prompts and student success (or failure) at meeting the requirements of those prompts through the lens of genre as social action. She suggests the importance of embedding writing prompts in the social contexts in which the writing itself would act, writing, "Because a prompt embodies a social practice, we would not *give* assignments as much as we would try to *enact* them in our classes" (p. 3, italics in original). This emphasis is quite similar to Moje's (2015), who writes that we must "ask how much our daily classroom practices are like those of the disciplines" (p. 260). One of Soliday's key focuses is on stance, which she defines as position on the topic or the "authority to speak about evidence in university genres" (p. 11), and she distinguishes a disciplinary research essay in an education class from general education music appreciation (a concert review) and psychology (a "college essay"). In her analysis of student work, Soliday shows the ways student writers use metalanguage (which she calls evaluative language) that approximates (or fails to approximate) the appropriate stances.

Like Soliday, Odom (2013) focuses on the prompts that call for student response, but she notes that while we often workshop our writing assignments, we less often pay attention to our prompts for reading assignments. She describes the importance of the social action of reading when she writes, "The material they draw on from their course readings needs to fulfill a particular role in terms of their thinking and writing, making their interaction with the text far more genuine and purposeful than many reading assignments may appear to be" (p. 11). To take up Soliday's formulation, how might we *enact* reading practices in our classes rather than simply assigning reading? For example, Graff had the experience of working with an environmental studies professor whose students were struggling to engage with and understand environmental policy briefs. In our discussion, when asked how she would read such texts, she replied (something like), "Oh, I would never just *read* this kind of text. I would always mine it for evidence for some argument I was making." That epiphany about the difference between the way she was assigning the reading and the way reading such a text would fit into the professional life of her discipline led to her changing the way she assigned the texts and much greater engagement with and understanding of those texts in her classes.

Conceptual breakthroughs about the ways that texts function in "real-world" contexts and the ways that we utilize them in school contexts matter. We have grown accustomed to urgent calls for the transformation of higher education: to be more "student ready," to be more transparent, to address what the 2030 Boyer Report calls "the equity/excellence imperative" by prioritizing "transformative education for life, work, and citizenship in an age of daunting challenges in need of world-embracing solutions" (UERU, 2022, p.11). An inextricable part of this transformation must be a reckoning with the changing nature of literacy as it moves from print-based to digital-based (Wolf, 2018), as well as corresponding questions about what counts as "reading" (Baron, 2021), and long-standing questions about the role of college reading in deeper learning and college success. This is a tall order for busy instructors who do not identify as "literacy experts." The faculty who responded to our survey have articulated some of the ways that changing their instructional practices to meet the 21st-century context requires both intellectual and hands-on experiences with text. Engaging personally, socially, and cognitively in knowledge building through metacognitive conversation, instructors across disciplines and levels have found a methodology in Reading Apprenticeship to bridge theory and practice and to support active and equitable instruction that invites students into disciplinary inquiry. Readers of this collection can find pragmatic examples of assignments and activities as well as provoking vignettes of teachers and students pushing the boundaries of "doing school" and discovering the transformative possibilities of reciprocal reading apprenticeships.

SOME SCHOLARLY CONTEXT FOR THE CHAPTERS IN THIS PART

Despite the liminality of faculty understandings of the situated nature of reading, the chapters in this part enter into conversation with a broad body of research on the personal and social dimensions of learning in postsecondary contexts, including research on social and emotional learning and sense of belonging.

For instance, Lee engages specifically with research on social and emotional learning by incorporating that into metacognitive approaches to reaching. Her approach is supported well by Wang and colleagues (2012), who find that a social-emotional learning curriculum in freshman seminar can improve both students' emotional competence and their academic performance. That emphasis on emotional intelligence and developing emotional skills is also supported by research that suggests that such skills improve college success (e.g., Walton et al., 2023; Zhoc et al., 2023).

While Knighton, Stanfield, Kongshaug, and Escalante do not address emotional skills, they are all concerned with strategies for building strong classroom communities and the advantages of doing so. Such a focus connects strongly with research demonstrating the relationship between classroom community, sense of belonging, and student success in college (e.g., Lombardi et al., 2016; McKinney et al., 2006; Zumbrunn et al., 2014). Zumbrunn and colleagues (2014), for instance, suggest that supportive classroom environments can improve students' sense of belonging and thereby increase their sense of self-efficacy and engagement. Both instructor behavior—openness to student ideas, flexibility, enthusiasm—and student-to-student relationships mattered in terms of sense of belonging. Thus, when Knighton, Kongshaug, and Stanfield focus on building strong peer-to-peer relationships, they are helping to build that sense of belonging and connection, and those peer relationships can be especially important for disadvantaged groups of students. For instance, Lombardi and colleagues (2016) found that students with disabilities who reported lower satisfaction with peer support tended to have lower GPAs.

Some of the authors in this part extend that concern with the social dimension of learning into online spaces. Garrison and colleagues (1999) argue that three kinds of presence are necessary for effective online teaching and learning: cognitive presence, social presence, and teaching presence, and without naming them as such, Garvey, Gamberg, and Strickland illustrate the strategies they used to create such presences in their teaching. As Garrison (2019) suggests, these presences are deeply interconnected. He offers principles for taking advantage of that interconnection by building a community of inquiry involving reflection and group cohesion. Garvey illustrates her own engagement with such principles by describing the ways that her students engage reflectively and restore their sense of personal agency through metacognitive dialogues. And Gamberg's focus on building community and "self-regulated reading revision" also connects strongly with such principles. Their teaching, and the opportunities for online interaction they create, perhaps answers the finding of DiGiacomo and colleagues (2023) that almost 20% of students who responded to their survey suggested that online classes did not allow for a sense of belonging and inclusion.

In the previous part, Sheeren and Wand wrote about social annotation as a strategy for helping students take responsibility for their work. In this part, Strickland focuses on the *social* aspect of social annotation, which picks up on that additional dimension described by research on social annotation (Adams & Wilson, 2020; Li & Li, 2023). Adams and Wilson (2020), for instance, found that in an online course, the use of Perusall contributed to building community, with peer-to-peer interactions increasing over time. And Li and Li (2023) found that peer interaction in Perusall contributed to increased engagement with reading.

Whether online or in-person, the social aspects of learning play a key role in students' personal engagement with their disciplines. Writing about the learning of history, Polman (2009) emphasizes the important role the social plays in learning, noting the difference between mastery of skills and appropriation of the cultural norms and identities associated with disciplinary perspectives. In particular, he connects appropriation of disciplinary perspectives with transfer of learning. He tells the story of one student, Richard, who tries to leverage his rap-lover identity with historical thinking. But both he and his student assistant are unable to help him make that connection. Such a story highlights the importance of the social interaction among students in an RA classroom. Wortham (2004) similarly links social identities and learning in a ninth-grade classroom.

That concern about the role of identity in learning plays an important part in the chapters of Escalante and Bagwell in this part. Escalante recognizes the ways that students could be made to feel like outsiders by the curriculum in her class and illustrates how culturally responsive teaching (e.g., Hammond, 2015; Gay, 2018) makes a difference in her support for students. Such an emphasis on the curriculum and the room it makes for students to feel like insiders in her classroom relates to research on how the structures of different communities of practice—basketball and math class—position students in terms of their "practice-based identities" (Nasir & Hand, 2008, p. 150). Bagwell highlights the connections between the personal (me) and the social (we) and takes up the question of how our framing of the norms of our classroom communities can undermine students' persistence and achievement.

Recognizing how important the social and personal dimensions are in learning that involves reading was truly transformational for the faculty in our study and the authors in this part of the collection. Seeing how those authors enact that understanding in their classes can help readers experience similar transformations in their own teaching.

Chapter 17

Feel-the-Text: A Metacognitive Reading Strategy Where Readers Make Emotions Visible

Sue Lee

Students have a lot to say about how they *feel* about academic reading, even when (perhaps especially when) they struggle with the text. When students feel comfortable enough to be honest about why they didn't complete the assigned reading, they would confess that they were annoyed, bored, confused, daunted, or exhausted by it. Students might not always be ready to discuss their intellectual understanding of the text, but they are often more than ready to articulate their emotional reaction to the text, and that emotional reaction can be a golden opportunity for Reading Apprenticeship (RA) practitioners to foster personal engagement with the text by applying Social Emotional Learning (SEL) tools. RA and SEL are both frameworks for teaching and learning. While Reading Apprenticeship focuses on literacy development and SEL emphasizes character education, they work well together because both frameworks strive to empower learners through inclusive, structured, and collaborative practices in metacognition.

Feel-the-text, a wordplay on the Reading Apprenticeship concept of talking-to-the-text (TttT), is a learning activity that encourages students to annotate the text by noting the feelings they have while reading the assigned text. Students are given a sentence frame that invites them to (1) choose a feeling from the SEL feelings vocabulary chart, (2) pair it with the specific quote that prompted that feeling, and (3) explain their own rationale for that personal pairing. Feel-the-text can be particularly effective in helping first-year university students consider and shape their identity as an academic reader. Many of them carry the assumption that university education is about being rational, so feelings are irrelevant since they had been told very sternly that academic writing should not involve emotive words and personal pronouns. At the same time, their personal reading history is often steeped in an elixir of emotions derived from their interaction with graphic novels, social media threads, or even their own mental health journals. By abandoning who they are as a personal reader to become more "academic," students often leave behind a powerful set of tools for true academic engagement. Feel-the-text gestures to welcome that personal reader back into the classroom.

TEACHING AND LEARNING OUTCOMES

A good lesson plan should have a clear learning outcome—a SWBAT that defines what S̲tudents W̲ill B̲e A̲ble T̲o do by the end of the learning activity. An even better lesson plan would also explicate the TWBAT—what the teacher will be able to do—to make the lesson truly a teaching *and* learning activity. Feel-the-text aims to empower both the student and the teacher:

- By participating in a feel-the-text reading activity, **students** will be able to share text-based reflections by choosing quotes from the text, connecting them to emotion labels, and explaining how each quote triggered the specific emotion.
- Through facilitating a feel-the-text reading activity, the **teacher** will be able to offer discussion prompts that validate emotions as a tool in academic reading and encourage acceptance of diversity in reader response.

Of the four dimensions of the Reading Apprenticeship framework (social, personal, cognitive, and knowledge-building), the teaching and learning outcomes of feel-the-text pertain most strongly to the social and personal dimensions. Sharing text talk and appropriating a new way of reading activates the social dimension of the classroom. At the same time, labeling feelings arising from reading and validating one's own emotional connection to a text both help students develop reader confidence in their personal dimension of learning.

The SEL counterpart to Reading Apprenticeship's four dimensions of classroom life is the five core SEL competencies: self-awareness, self-management, social awareness, relationship skills, and responsible decision making. Given the metacognitive nature of a text annotation activity, feel-the-text is most effective in addressing skill development in the areas of self-awareness and social awareness. When students are able to recognize their emotional connection to the text as a strength, that awareness helps increase their sense of self-efficacy. In addition, when students see different feelings toward a text validated in a group discussion, they become more aware of how empathy and diversity work in the classroom.

Just as teaching does not compete with learning in the design of a lesson plan, the Reading Apprenticeship framework and the SEL framework do not require prioritization. Instead, they naturally work together. Both frameworks inform the design of feel-the-text, and each offers different tools to help assess and align the teaching and learning outcomes.

PLACEMENT AND SEQUENCING

Feel-the-text can be used at any point of the course to invite students to connect with the text on a personal level. However, it works best a few weeks into the semester where students have had a chance to get to know each other and the group has had a chance to establish classroom norms in terms of safety and respect in collaborative learning. I have found that Reading Apprenticeship activities like personal reading history and reading strategy list (RSL) are very useful in helping students talk about reading without feeling daunted by an assigned text, and they also help students get into the habit of sharing—giving AND receiving—what goes on in their minds.

In terms of sequencing, feel-the-text works particularly well after students have had the experience of practicing golden lines, an activity that instills the sense of agency by honoring the student's individual choice in accessing a text. Like golden lines, feel-the-text is also a way of getting students to develop metacognition by annotating the text. The difference is that feel-the-text specifically encourages students to identify and document their emotional connection to the text. Whereas golden lines aims to help develop reader confidence by encouraging students to work with what lights up their thinking, feel-the-text aims to expand the reader's range of reading strategies by empowering students to validate the feelings sparked by a text. Once students have had the chance to practice using their feelings as a point of investigating a text, students tend to generate more diverse observations in their metacognitive logs and ask more empathetic questions in doing partner work like think-write-pair-share.

FEEL-THE-TEXT STEPS

Feel-the-text can be done in both face-to-face and online learning environments, and the steps can be done either synchronously or asynchronously, which makes feel-the-text a great fit for a hybrid classroom.

1. *Introduce the feelings chart to students*—A feelings chart is an infographic that presents labels of different feelings from which students can choose. Some are color-coded, and some have the words arranged in a wheel, and some come with cartoon faces. There are many feelings charts online, many with a Creative Commons license. The infographic format is helpful because the visual organization encourages students to explore the chart rather than picking from a linear list in alphabetical or arbitrary order. It is important to give students a feelings chart instead of asking students to think of a word that describes their feeling because the chart can often remind students of more precise feeling labels that they know but do not frequently use.
2. Present the learning outcome with the sentence frame—A sentence frame is a formulaic sentence with fill-in-the-blank components that students can fill in to guide their response. For feel-the-text, the three components that students need to connect are (1) the quote, (2) the feeling, and (3) the rationale, so the prescribed sentence frame could be like this:

    I felt _____ (insert feeling word) when I read "_____ (insert quote)" because _____ (provide explanation).

    The sentence frame is an important part of this activity because it directs students' attention to the key actions in the learning outcome, which are choosing, connecting, and explaining. Having a sentence frame also eases anxiety for students as they would know what end product the teacher is expecting to see. It is helpful to ask students to generate multiple (three or four) annotations, one for each text-inspired emotional reaction, so that they can practice the annotation task several times.

    Although the sentence pattern seems self-explanatory, it is worth the time to clarify the purpose of each blank. First, emphasize to students that the point is not to identify what the author wants the reader to feel but to identify the authentic feeling that arises as they read the text, so the key is to find the feeling word on the chart that most precisely matches their feeling. Let them know that there is no right way to feel about a text. Authenticity is what matters. Second, remind students to keep the quote really short since long quotes make it difficult for themselves and others to see which part of the text created the emotional impact. Third, allow students to go beyond the blank for the explanation part. Let students know that the explanation part communicates their rationale,

which shows their critical thinking, so they are not limited to one sentence per emotional reaction. They can add more explanation for each reaction.
3. *Give students class time to read*—Time to read can happen in different ways depending on the course delivery mode. For online asynchronous learning or hybrid learning, the reading can be done as homework where students can take as much time as they need to generate and post their annotations before the group discusses them in person in class (hybrid) or comment on each other's post on the forum (asynchronous). For synchronous sessions, whether it's face to face or via video conferencing, it is helpful to give class time for reading even if students had already been asked to read the text for homework before attending class. Giving students 10 to 15 minutes in class to read and generate the annotations helps students who struggle with focus and time management to have a designated place and time to work through the text. It might feel awkward at first to have 10 to 15 minutes of silence during a Zoom session, but once the practice becomes normalized, the participants will begin to associate silent Zoom time as productive individual work time. To foster the quiet reading time, students in a face-to-face classroom can be asked to jot down their annotations on index cards from which they can read out later during group discussion, and students in a video conferencing classroom can be asked to type up what they want to share but not post them until discussion time begins.
4. *Invite students to share and discuss their annotations*—The prescribed sentence frame already asked students to explain why they paired a certain feeling with a particular quote, so the discussion prompt should be focused on *how* instead of *why*. The focus on *how* nudges students to further analyze the text, and it reminds the teacher to accept and validate the emotional connection that the student had already made and shared. These how-questions should always direct the conversation toward the text. The goal is to use the text-inspired reactions from individual participants as opportunities for the group to work toward understanding the text. Some examples of how-questions that students can ask each other follow:
- How did those words in the quote trigger that feeling?
- How did the feeling help you (or not help you) learn from the text?
- How would you explain in your own words the ideas that made you feel that way?

For synchronous discussions, (face to face or videoconferencing), students can be organized into small groups and encouraged to respond to each other by using some of the suggested how-questions. Remind students that the how-questions are conversation starters, so they need to listen carefully to each other and respond genuinely to help each other have a deeper understanding of the text.

For asynchronous discussions where students can respond to the forum at their own pace within a longer time frame, it helps to encourage students to notice diversity in the communal annotations. They can be asked to comment on posts where someone had a different feeling about the same quote or the same feeling about a different quote. They can also be asked to comment on a post where someone chose a quote they didn't notice before. To foster conversation on the forum, let students know that they should freestyle the first part of the comment (just explain why they chose to comment on the post!) and end the comment with a how-question to encourage the student who contributed the annotation to think more deeply about their annotation and respond with further insight.

When facilitating these discussions, there are two things to keep in mind. One, it's OK if the feeling a student has is based on a misinterpretation of the text! There is no need to immediately fix the interpretation. That feeling can still be used to help them examine the text. Follow-up how-questions can often help readers spot the misinterpretation, and the ensuing conversation would be a great opportunity to practice troubleshooting. Two, it's OK if the explanation part feels generic and irrelevant to the text. This happens sometimes because the student lacks the vocabulary to articulate the rationale and sometimes because they are struggling with the text. Either way, the feeling they had is still valid, and they can work with that to move forward. In SEL terms, when facilitating feel-the-text discussions, the teacher should approach the classroom with a belief-based energy. In "The Lure of Learning in Teaching," Dan Liston (2004) describes the approach as "an invitation that rests on an act of faith in, respect for, and an insistence that students can and will see, can and will appreciate what we, as teachers, have to offer" (p. 472). Put simply, teachers have to trust that the students are ready to learn.

5. Foreground the metacognition—While helping students to properly understand the text is the premise of all reading activity, the learning objective of feel-the-text is for students to, through practice, become aware of their text-inspired feelings as a tool for actively engaging with the text toward meaning and understanding. Therefore, it is crucial that the group has an opportunity to debrief on the experience of using feel-the-text as a strategy. This does not have to be a formal activity where students talk about metacognition. Reflection questions can be phrased as invitations for feedback, such as "How was this kind of annotation different from your usual type of writing in the margin?" or "How did seeing other people's emotional reaction to a text change the way you understand the text?" The teacher's role is to listen/read carefully and document the learning epiphanies in order to share them back to the whole group.

EVIDENCE OF LEARNING

When given the opportunity to reflect on their experience of learning to read, students often provide profound insights that help teachers learn. In SEL terms, this learning is not just about the teacher continuing to know more about the subject but also the teacher thriving in the teaching profession. In "'Spots of Time That Glow': Reverence, Epiphany, and the Teaching Life," Sam Intrator (2012) refers to the empowering and intensely energizing moments of teaching as "teaching epiphanies" (p. 63). Intrator explains the importance of recognizing these moments: "[teachers] cherish them because they involve being present when students come to their own moment of sudden insight, growth, or development" (p. 68). In other words, witnessing evidence of student learning fuels the teacher. Therefore, a teacher's growth needs to be fostered by making more of these learning moments visible and recognizable.

When I asked my students in a first-year university writing course to look back on the annotations and comments they posted throughout the semester and identify moments they are proud of, many chose to reflect on their feel-the-text annotation. There were 25 different learning activities they could choose from, and 44% of the students mentioned their contribution to the feel-the-text forum as one of their golden learning moments. One student wrote: "Looking back, I realized that I learn well when I can emotionally relate to something—that way I have a better understanding of what I am reading." This is a powerful statement because the student confidently dispels the myth that feelings are irrelevant in intellectual readings. Students are often told that feelings do not matter in academic reading because intellectual discussions should be about ideas. In fact, feelings drive understanding. When a student recognizes their emotions as one of many tools to access a text, they become more metacognitively aware of both reading strategies and learning strategies. In addition, by sharing text talk about feelings with their peers, students are sharing their reading processes and fostering a safe learning community where individual feelings are validated while the group collaborates on making sense of the text.

For the same end-of-semester reflection task, another student wrote: "Looking back, I realize that I learn well when I have to keep in touch with my emotions and how I am feeling as it can influence the paper that I write." This realization shows that the student had grasped a threshold concept in academic writing—writers are readers. When a student recognizes that their feelings about a text can influence their writing, they are recognizing the connection between what they are asked to read and what they are asked to write in the course. In other words, they are finding personal motivation in writing to explore and express what they want to say. In terms of the RA framework, they are developing skills in the cognitive dimension by setting reading purposes and adjusting reading processes.

EVIDENCE OF STRUGGLE

No learning activity works perfectly for every student, and some students do find feel-the-text to be a barrier rather than an aid. Sometimes, silence is a sign of struggle. While the participation rate for feel-the-text discussions tends to be higher than that of other learning activities because students who normally hesitate to comment on academic texts are willing to comment on their own feelings, there are also students who normally participate actively but choose to not share anything at all both online or in person. Often, these are students who are not necessarily shy but are very reserved. It is likely that they are not comfortable discussing their feelings with classmates and/or teachers with whom they have only a professional relationship. Yes, learning often involves stepping out of one's comfort zone. At the same time, their silence is a marker of personal boundary that must be respected. One way of responding to that silence while encouraging the student to participate is to privately offer the student the chance to do a private feel-the-text annotation with the next reading and/or the choice to earn the credit by writing a brief reflection on what they have learned through reading other people's feel-the-text annotations. Not all students will take the offer, but the invitation opens up the opportunity for further dialogue.

REFLECTING AS A TEACHER

Academic discourse is messy. It acts like a discipline that tries to encompass and unify many different academic disciplines. University students are told that every discipline requires them to know how to write an academic essay, but what they are asked to read in order to write the essay differs vastly depending on whether they are writing it for a literature course, a criminology course, or a biology course. Because the essay is the product that gets graded, students and teachers often fixate their attention on what a good essay looks like without paying attention to the reading and learning that comes before the essay writing. It is little wonder that many students resort to writing disengaged, regurgitative essays that feel like a patchwork of barely relevant references. They have not been taught all the steps that lead up to the essay-writing step.

To address this gap in teaching and learning, we can look to problem-solving approaches in the field of SEL where social emotional skills are often assumed by curriculum designers as background learning that happens by magic while teachers work on developing academic skills in students. Skill development does not happen by magic. It needs to be taught. In "The Need for Social and Emotional Learning," Elias and colleagues (1997) emphasize that "we must teach social and emotional skills, attitudes, and values with the same structure and attention that we devote to traditional subjects. And we must do so in a coordinated, integrated manner" (p. 9). The same can be said about the teaching of reading skills, attitudes, and values. The Reading Apprenticeship framework works well in helping educators in various capacities to design, coordinate, and integrate metacognitive reading strategies into established academic disciplines.

Teaching academic essay writing to first-year university students is scary. It's like trying to get someone excited about the season finale of a show they've never watched. We describe to them from experience the exhilaration of figuring out just exactly what we want to say as we try to nail that thesis statement in our essay, yet many of our students look at us blankly because they don't have anything they *want* to say. We need to help them find something they want to say. If the academic essay structure is meant to be a construction tool for refining their thoughts about the discipline-specific content and the academic writing conventions are meant to be a communication tool for sharing their refined thoughts in an audience-centered way, then the metacognitive reading strategies are the creative tool that help students generate thoughts as they interact with new content. In order to get original, insightful, and exciting essays out of students, we need to teach them how to use the creative tools.

Chapter 18

Using the Reading Apprenticeship Framework to Change College-Level Math Instruction

Christie Knighton

I work with future teachers at a midsize, suburban college in the state of Washington. I support students on their math journey; college-level math is a requirement for the AAS degree. At my institution in 2018, only 68% of students passed college-level math (Highline College, 2024). This statistic may be lower for students whose first language is not English. To address this challenge, I collaborated closely with the education and math departments to develop a supported math pathway specifically for Education students. The math department agreed to our proposed Math Prep course that used five units from the Curriculum for Accelerated Math (CAM) by TERC (Adult Numeracy Center, 2023). The agreement was to allow any student who completed these five units to go directly into Math 146, Introduction to Statistics, without taking the math placement exam. We decided to split these five units into two quarters: two units in summer (an 8-week term) and three units in fall (an 11-week term). Math 146 would be team-taught by myself and a math faculty member in winter term, and our first cohort began in summer term 2019.

DEVELOPING A SUPPORTED MATH PATHWAY

This all sounded lovely: I could teach students using a hands-on, conceptual approach to math instruction (the CAM curriculum); build a safe, inclusive classroom environment supported by the Reading Apprenticeship framework; and students wouldn't be required to take a standardized exam to get into college-level math. I learned pretty quickly that culture change in math teaching and learning is hard—both for students and teachers.

The students in this math pathway came from our language cohorts where students complete two state certificates in Early Childhood Education in a language other than English. The supported math pathway began in summer quarter, and students completed two quarters of math prep with me, an adult educator specialist with a math background. We began our time together creating an inclusive and safe community where students are able to explore their mathematical thinking, pose questions, and share their thoughts and ideas. One aspect of creating this environment involved setting norms. I asked students to think about a time that they successfully learned something new (in school or out). I encouraged students to consider what it was about that experience that helped them be successful in the new learning, and to share this with a partner. Partners then discussed with another partner group, and then lastly there was a whole-group share. This is how our class norms were created: students shared what they needed to be successful and feel comfortable in class and together we made a class list. Examples of norms were, "No judging when a question is asked" and "I need time to process with someone." We all agreed to follow these class norms, and also agreed that we could revisit them at any time and add to them if needed.

Another aspect of creating a safe and inclusive community was by having students reflect on their math background and share with one or two classmates. For homework on our first day, I asked students to answer one of these prompts: "Draw a picture, or write in words, or some other way communicate your answer this prompt: 'Math and I . . .'" or "Write a letter to math, starting with this prompt: 'Dear Math . . .'" During the next class, students shared with a partner what they were comfortable with about their reflection. I believe this built on our safe and inclusive community because students realized they had similar prior experience with math as other classmates. Many students in this cohort had negative experiences with past math classes, and through this sharing, they realized they were not alone. Both of these activities helped build support for the personal and social dimensions of the Reading Apprenticeship framework and resulted in a safe learning community for all.

Throughout the math prep courses, students continued to support each other by sharing their mathematical thinking. This happened in class with paired work at the beginning of each class period. I modeled my thinking for students and showed them I wanted to know the thought process that led them to their answer on their homework. Students were invited to share their thinking on the homework with a peer and to be open to their classmate's ideas. Each student received a "math talk and stems" bookmark to help guide their sharing. Questions on this bookmark included, "What made you decide to solve it like that?" and "What are you thinking now?" The math stems included sentence starters like, "I got different results because . . ." and "What I heard you say was. . . ." These tools helped students increase their own awareness of their thinking, along with providing the needed scaffolding for students to share their thinking with classmates. This routine helped continue to build a safe and supportive learning environment, increased students' metacognitive awareness of their mathematical thinking, and also built their cognitive and knowledge skills.

The CAM curriculum (Adult Numeracy Center, 2023) includes many opportunities for reflection. Examples of these questions included things like "How do you know?" and "Make a number line to show your reasoning" and "What did you notice each time you tried to combine unlike denominators?" In the beginning, students would often leave these questions blank. These questions were another tool to surface students' thinking and to expose the "why" of the math concept. At the start of each class, I asked students to share their thinking with a partner, and to focus specifically on these types of questions in the homework. Over time, students began to share their thinking in these questions and with each other.

None of this metacognitive awareness and sharing automatically happened with students. Despite repeatedly modeling my thinking, inevitably, when I first asked students to share their thinking, they simply told me their answer to the problem. Students seemed to appreciate hearing my thinking and seeing my processes, so when I asked again for students to share their thinking, I assumed I would gain all these insights by hearing their thinking. Many students still just told me their answer. I quickly learned that culture change in math instruction was hard for students. With repeated modeling, most students began to more automatically share their thinking and not just their answer.

TRANSITIONING TO COLLEGE-LEVEL MATH

College-level math began in the winter term, and by this time, the students and I had been together for six months. We created an active learning environment and students had increased their mathematical thinking, knowledge, and confidence. However, students were nervous about college-level math, but they trusted me, and I assured them they would be successful because of their hard work and their increased mathematical skills. This trust took time to build, but by the time we transitioned to college-level math in winter term, we had a strong community that supported each other in their work, and students had increased their metacognitive awareness around their mathematical thinking.

Behind the scenes, I began working with Trudy, a math professor, to build the curriculum for this college-level math course. This class was designed as an I-BEST course, which utilizes a team-teaching approach, where one faculty focuses on college-readiness skills and the other focuses on the specific content (SBCTC, 2024). I-BEST courses allow students to gain skills needed for their certificates or degrees at the same time as increasing their college-readiness skills. Together, Trudy and I built a curriculum that contextualized the content to education, children, or teaching.

This particular term, we had 26 students enrolled in this special college-level math class.

The workload of the class included weekly homework and quizzes, individual exams, and individual projects. Each exam was split into two: One-half was completed with a group, and one-half was completed individually. After the first exam, students completed a metacognitive reflection, both to help Trudy and me better understand students' thinking, and also to continue to build metacognitive awareness in students. Questions on this reflection asked students to share what they were confused about and what they did to reduce or eliminate their confusion. It also asked them to describe their process on a problem they did not correctly answer, and then they were asked to rework the problem. We found it was a bit of a challenge to get students to share their process. Instead, we found students simply worked on correcting their answers. This could possibly have been because we had not spent enough time building students' metacognitive awareness in this college-level math class, or it could have been because students were no longer feeling safe to share their thinking.

Toward the end of the quarter, students were struggling with a particular concept. Trudy had taught this course for many years and usually could anticipate where students would struggle. However, she didn't know how to help students with their understanding of a particular concept that we had revisited many times. After repeatedly reteaching this concept in class, we tried another approach. Students completed a version of a talk to the text. Each student was given an 11x17 paper with a bell curve and seven questions on the left side of the page, and this prompt on the right side of the page: "Write down your thinking/process as you work through this problem." Students had about 15 minutes of quiet work time to answer the questions and share their process. After this individual think time, students shared their thinking with a partner, and made any adjustments to their work before handing it in. Many students did not share their process and instead just wrote down how they solved the problem. However, enough students shared what they were thinking that Trudy and I had an "aha moment." We were able to see that students were confused about the greater than/equal to concept and how to apply this to reading a bell curve. This insight helped us design a new activity where we could redirect students' processes.

SUCCESS AND CONTINUING EVOLUTION

This class showed that with a cultural shift in teaching mathematics, students can be successful. We had a 100% pass rate for college-level math, which is far above the 71% college-wide pass rate for Introduction to Statistics the year prior, and above the overall 68% passing rate for all math courses in 2018 (Highline College, 2024). Multiple factors could have contributed to the success of this cohort. The first factor is this course was co-taught with a math instructor working collaboratively with an adult educator specialist. Another factor is that the activities, projects, and exams were contextualized into topics that relate to teaching, education, or children. Additionally, the Reading Apprenticeship framework was infused throughout the year-long cohort, and this contributed to the overall active, supportive, and safe learning environment. With this safe learning environment, students were likely more comfortable taking risks in their learning, especially when it came to sharing their thinking. Classroom routines were embedded to allow students to share their thinking. These opportunities not only helped students become more aware of their thinking; it also helped Trudy and me to better see how students were making connections. When there were misunderstandings, we could guide students with targeted questions to help them revise their thinking and understanding of mathematical concepts.

The supported math pathway we created has been successful in supporting students through college-level math, but not without tension and challenges. I expected some pushback from faculty, as most faculty, in general, teach how they were taught. This typically does not include creating an active learning environment or setting up an inquiry-based classroom. This experience to create a course that has metacognition at the center has allowed my co-teacher(s) and me ample opportunity to grow as instructors and to create a learning environment that is different from how we were taught.

What surprised me the most was that there was a lot of pushback from students. My view was rather Pollyannaish; I thought I would come into the classroom and build a strong community with students, and that they would be open and receptive to this new way of learning. All students in our first math cohort were not educated in the United States, and most of the students' prior learning experiences were with the teacher at the front of the classroom lecturing. I asked students to make themselves vulnerable by sharing their thinking and their confusions instead of simply asking for the answer, and this was vastly different from their prior learning experiences. We did get there, but it took a lot of repeated practice and ongoing maintenance of our safe learning environment. As Howard (2016) says, relationships precede learning, and this experience cemented this point. The success of this cohort with the infusion of the Reading Apprenticeship framework has led to a cultural shift in math instruction in our cohort math classes.

This supported pathway continues to evolve. We now teach Math 107, Math in Society, with a contextualized curriculum and the Reading Apprenticeship framework is embedded throughout the year-long cohort. We proudly boast that we have maintained a high pass rate, but it has dropped to 98%, which remains significantly higher than the current pass rate of 70% for the traditional Math 107 course in 2023 (Highline College, 2024).

Chapter 19

The Early Bird Special

Caren Kongshaug

I notice my adult class of 25 drops to 22. Somewhere between "Here are the four sentence types" and "Choose a topic that interests you," they quietly disappear. I take the usual measures to bring them back: Canvas messages, emails, phone calls. This approach can work, but not always, because there are many factors that make school a hardship for my students. I accept this, but it doesn't mean I don't feel a loss. It means I have to move on and think about who is left. What do they need? What keeps them coming back to the classroom? I wish I could offer a simple formula, but at the heart of teaching is a string of unpredictable moments. There is no one solution, yet when I am serving my students best, I am in *Reading Apprenticeship* mode. Kicking off the quarter with the major routines like think aloud and metacognitive inquiries invites engagement. Students experience learning as problem solving and making meaning collectively. Sure, some may feel resistant initially, but after some practice, it begins to work, and I can sense we are held together by a communal desire to learn. Last month I was asked if I could define *Reading Apprenticeship* in two words. I thought about it and came up with "courageous collaboration." I think that's apt. This chapter discusses my current thoughts about reading and offers a close-up of the first three weeks in my classroom where this essential courageous collaboration is established. My goal is to navigate our way into a safe and inclusive environment where students feel welcomed, want to come to class, and engage in learning. In simpler terms, every single student is important, and this is what I do to support their learning.

Before the quarter begins, I remind myself that reading takes practice, patience, and time. Even the most astute readers can read a text and not clock any information. Maybe they don't know much about the subject and the specialized language is over their heads, or maybe they were uninterested in the subject. Whatever the reasons (and there are many), they know, at that point, to start over and read it again with purpose, adjusting their level of attention. Other, less-experienced readers do not do this. Some give up on reading right then. When I hear my students say, "I read it, but I don't know what it means," I believe them, and I know why they don't get it: many students think they are reading when they are not actually reading. They make the classic mistake that looking, saying, and spending time with words equals reading. It is not so.

For this reason, the way we think about reading is important. In fact, *Reading Apprenticeship* distinguishes reading as an all-in game. We have to relate, bring ourselves forward, and expose ourselves little by little to the text. But how do we teach that to our students? When we read, we need to determine what we know and don't know—what we think, believe, and guess at. A good text will make us work for meaning, shaping something new for us. That is learning.

When we are in dialogue with a text, we can't help but forge a connection. This connection is a good starting point for deeper discussion.

Choosing appropriate texts for my class is also paramount. There are many considerations: level, content, accessibility, and copyright status. In general, I start out with a lower-level text than my course level and increase difficulty slowly throughout the quarter. I choose articles by theme, so students will build schema around a central idea. This quarter we are working on social justice issues; last quarter we read about climate change and the environment. Before that, it was Native American voices in contemporary society. Students are also asked to read from a blog of their choice; it could be an industry-related blog for their future program at the school, or a blog on specialized topics: American Sign Language, animal rights, gardening, mindfulness to name a few. Each week, students respond to a set of questions that mirror the lessons we are working on in class. Exposure to texts that are not leveled prepares them with real-world examples written for adults.

When I am with my students at the technical college, I disclose that they can read this material and pass this class even if their track record says otherwise. But I am not just a cheerleader. As *Reading Apprenticeship* makes clear, my students and I are in this together exchanging strategies, ideas, feelings, hunches, bad days and good ones—in short, doing whatever it takes to read in the moment. It would be a lot simpler to give the lecture and expect spit-back answers on the test. That, however, would leave all the thinking to me and the memorizing to the students. This is not what we are after.

"You tell me what it means," I say. At first, students are hesitant—excellent at one-word replies or teasing silences. I take it all in: each shrug, lost look, and attempt at an answer. I let them in on a secret: We are just talking to each other. That's it. Slowly and tentatively, ideas are expressed about the reading and their lived experiences: there's no way to get it wrong. I may have to ask two or three times for their take, but that is okay. I model patience. Soon, the pressure is softened and heart rates calm. This is how I experience the first week with my students. But what are we really doing?

As a reading teacher and English instructor, I heavily emphasize previewing the text. Early on, I teach how to preview the text by spending at least 30–45 minutes exploring what this means. One of my lessons asks students to preview the text and talk about what they notice. At first, most students are simply skimming the text as fast as they can, firm in their belief that faster is better like the bus route to school, or a hamburger bagged at the window. They are not really sure what you are supposed to do. I haven't explained it other than "It means to look at the text before reading." After five minutes or so, I ask them what they noticed. Honestly, there's not much reporting, but I listen, make note of the brave few that name the topic. So I say, "Let's do it again. But first, notice the text features. Do they offer clues to the "who, where, why, when and how"?

If "text features" draws a blank stare, we take a time-out from our preview and do a mini-lesson on text features. I use a one-page chart that has many of the common features: title, author bio, headings, photographs, charts, graphs, illustrations, captions, sidebars, table of contents, italicized vocabulary, and bolded words. Each text feature has an accompanying visual and space where students define the term. They do this work in small groups, and we check and compare surfacing questions or previous knowledge. Then, I repeat we are ready to preview while noting text features and asking questions.

They start over, and this time when asked to share with their table mates, the noise level increases. I see students more or less eagerly sharing—pointing to photos, headings, and bolded words. Again, their ideas are articulated on the whiteboard. Almost always, students miss the publication date. Or, if they do identify this, they do not express any accompanying thoughts. When I ask them to preview for the third time, some students chuckle, some roll their eyes feigning friendly exhaustion, and then, there's always a few who now see this activity as a game to win. It usually takes this third time, with a little prompting on my part, to get students to say, "This was written ten years ago, so it may not be true anymore" or "This was written ten years ago and still is true." Thus, a new discussion begins with the term relevancy.

Now, it may seem like this lesson is prescriptive, and that I do it the same way each time. That would be inaccurate. I let my students dictate how the lesson flows and what terms come to the forefront first. I have a general idea that I want to teach preview, text features, asking questions, and making predictions. How this actually unfolds is determined in the moment while I witness my students unpack the text.

After this lesson, when I say, "Let's preview the text," we take 5 to 7 minutes and share what took over 30 minutes the first time. I listen to students free associate, reveal what they already know, ask interesting questions, and identify what might be confusing for them. These preview conversations set the stage for active engagement when they read it alone. In addition, students report interest in finding out what the article will say, learning about the topic, and seeing if they "get it." When they come back to class, we dig deeply into the HOW of reading. What do they do when they read? What are other possible ways of making sense of the reading?

Using reading strategies and routines helps deconstruct a challenging text. Some students choose color coding their texts, making stars and numerating the paragraphs. I usually model making notes in the margins. If the reading is digital, we use ready-made notetaking charts, or digital mark-up text tools. Talking to each other helps sort out the questions and express what inspires. In any of my classes, the routines we use to make sense of text become common talking points. We make lists for all to try. Then we read. Using strategies is not the end of the story, though. No strategy is helpful if you aren't thinking and engaging while using the strategy; for example, note the person who highlights every line in the text. Where is the thinking there? Subsequently, modeling how I read (a cornerstone of the Reading Apprenticeship framework) is essential, so students can see what I do. I usually begin by reading a page or two out of an HVAC manual. If you know me, you know this is not my expertise by a long shot. I am not knowledgeable about heating and refrigeration, so my model usually elicits a lot of sympathy as I stumble through the specialized language and illustrations. Often, there is someone who does know about this subject, and they will always interrupt and offer their insight and experience. (I just love when that happens.) It illustrates a key aspect of reading, which is we can relate, engage, and comprehend information we already have some previous knowledge about. Secondly, in the classroom, we want to help each other problem solve.

Modeling how to handle and persist through the hard times of reading is critical because it gives direction to the lock-step panic so often felt by students. By the third week of class, the idea that we can problem solve this text together becomes a common and eager practice. For me, when I note this happening, I recognize that we are building our learning community. Although I start with my HVAC model, I do move on to other subjects I am versed in. However, starting this way allows the students to see that I don't always have a good grasp on the material. "That's okay; that's a given," I tell them. It also levels the playing field in the classroom: the instructor doesn't know how to read this, either.

Learning can often feel messy. It's common to mislead ourselves with one mud-pie idea after another. For instance, sometimes students are not aware that there are gaps in their learning affecting their conclusions, and they wonder why they continue to make mistakes on short answer questions or math word problems. Other examples include the fallout from poor critical thinking skills and dubious logic. Undoubtedly, adult learning can be rough, a head-knocker, and compounded by doubt and self-judgment. However, what is the alternative? Tell students what to think? Stop asking them to read? Hope they get it by osmosis? Obviously not. When I think about reading and learning, I am reminded of a lesser-known alchemical secret: A muddied idea becomes golden when it is shared, asked enough questions, and reshaped by many. In my classroom, the early bird special (weeks 1–3), includes a practice on working together, so students can figure out what they think about what they already know and, equally important, what they think about the new ideas and applications. Learning is equated with friendly faces, familiar routines, and firsthand AHAs even when the work is seemingly too hard. This approach isn't always perfect, but it works. When I slice it open to evaluate it, deconstruct the classroom spaces and the people within, I find learning is always about courage—courage to connect and courage to continue. Knowing this softens my heart. Not all students are ready to learn when they enter the room, so creating a space where we learn how to learn is imperative. It's as if on day one they hear me say, "Time to leap off the high dive!" Their eyes go wide, but what I am really saying is "You can do this; I know you can." It's that kind of courage.

Chapter 20

Building Semester-Long Groups to Support the Social Dimension of Learning and Problem Solving in the Large Biology Classroom

Erin Stanfield

Throughout my 10 years teaching lower-division biology courses, I have consistently run up against a major obstacle for supporting both effective and equity-driven instruction—an underlying mismatch between student *expectations* and the *reality* of reading and writing in STEM. Often, my students report a low interest in and lack of appreciation for the relevance of reading comprehension and writing proficiency in their STEM major and future careers. Furthermore, they often report that their very discomfort with reading and writing is one of their reasons for majoring in STEM as opposed to social science or humanities. Of course, as all STEM professionals can attest, skillful reading and writing are essential to understanding and communicating science with peers and the general public alike. Additionally, these cognitive skills are also key for absorbing research methods and application.

Frustratingly, as both a STEM professional and instructor, I plainly recognize that the underlying mental processes involved in effective reading and writing mirror the same problem-solving and critical thinking skills that form the backbone of science as a way of understanding the world. Furthermore, these reading and writing abilities allow students to take their scientific knowledge outside of the classroom and apply it to understanding and solving real-world problems. At the same time, supporting a large group of students in the lecture hall in this important skill development seems daunting.

My solution: Focusing and leveraging the social dimension of learning in the large biology classroom to support more focus on reading as problem solving.

Fortunately, I have found an approach to implement Reading Apprenticeship (RA) design principles for supporting reading- and writing-focused activities in a large-enrollment (more than 80 students) biology lecture course: semester-long student groups. In my experience, students are largely successful (and indeed flourish) in following along with regular RA-focused practice so long as they are practiced regularly and with clear instructions. These Reading Apprenticeship strategies form a foundational element for my large STEM courses and are supported by harnessing the *social dimension* of learning through semester-long groups as a mode for effective in-class activities and tackling complex reading.

Because the classroom is fundamentally a social space, implementing the semester-long group model capitalizes on the social nature of learning to foster a conducive environment to maximize knowledge attainment. The social dimension is evident as the students engage with the material alongside their peers, the instructor, the various authors that they encounter. Additionally, knowledge is more likely to "stick" and persist beyond the course when it is interrogated, deconstructed, analyzed, and reassembled with peers in a collaborative and supportive environment (Deslauriers et al., 2019). Through dialogue, exposition, hypothesis-testing, explanation, interpretation, and compromise within their groups, students are better able to integrate new information and processes using the advantages of existing knowledge and skills (Yager, 1991). By supporting students practicing these moves during class time, students are making more meaningful changes in the ways they understand content and apply concepts to novel applications (Wood et al., 2014).

In order to fully access and leverage the social context for learning in the large classroom, I decided to create semester-long groups as a solid foundation to build upon and reinforce the conditions for strong social engagement. Over the semesters, I have learned that students will much more likely engage with their peers when they are comfortable and have the opportunity to interact in an authentic manner, reinforcing relationships built on trust. When implemented regularly and with clear structure (so folks know what to do and *why* they're doing it), my students report a higher sense of inclusion, feeling of belonging, and that there is a space for them to have a voice. In addition, both the better and lesser prepared or content-familiar students benefit from the group activities. Those with more advanced preparation and familiarity benefit from the opportunity to explain and instruct as well as more time for those at a more introductory level to practice and build knowledge.

At first, effectively supporting the social dimension in the large classroom setting seemed daunting, as, by design, instruction hinges on students operating as a unified mass of individuals focused on the amplified figure of the instructor. Due to the sheer number of students, it seems there must be a compromise between making connections with and among students and overall teaching efficiency. Consequently, I felt the need to create a path for students to meaningfully connect with and support each other and work against the tendency for students to "disappear" into the crowd. Because larger class sizes are increasingly becoming a major mode of instruction to widen the pipeline for students into STEM, I needed to find a way to support the social dimension and increase equity by supporting the success of students who might not otherwise be retained. Designing the course around regular small-group activities seemed the perfect fit for promoting the social context for learning while also leveraging students for more peer-to-peer learning.

BUILDING SEMESTER-LONG GROUPS

To leverage the social context and support equity in regular in-class group activities, I decided to also implement a *complex instruction* (CI) model (Cohen & Lotan, 2014). The CI model supports equity and prevents unequal participation by providing rotating roles for each class session. For every class, the roles of facilitator, recorder, and reporter are rotated among the group members. Also, because the groups have assigned seating areas, the transitions to and from group activities during class are efficient. This swift transition has been particularly helpful during two-stage exams, when students reengage with a portion of the exam in their designated groups after completing their individual exam (Gilley & Clarkston, 2014).

Additionally, the semester-long group helps students form long-term relationships, builds rapport, and facilitates learning *together* while creating a sense of community. Because the groups are not self-selected, students are able to form new relationships with classmates and there is less likelihood of clique-based dynamics of inclusion/exclusion. To assess the group allocation, I survey students midway into the semester about their satisfaction with their groups and the group activities. The vast majority of students report high to very high satisfaction with their group mates and the flow of group activities. In the rare cases of students reporting significant conflict or challenge, I successfully rearranged groups; however, less than 1% of students have requested such an intervention over the 10 semesters I have been teaching with this model. Likewise, students report appreciating the semester-long groups and associated activities when queried at the end of semester:

"The semester-long groups helped me improve my studying skills, I found that working together in groups with other people helped me become better at studying."

"Time was spent on what we could think of collectively. More minds mean more collective insight."

"Working with my group was always helpful in experiencing new perspectives and seeing what I needed help with. I can stand to learn a lot from the people I'm surrounded by, which can be unfortunately easy for me to forget sometimes, but having those class activities to get us bouncing off one another was always really helpful and exciting when we got to see how we did as a collective."

To organize these groups, I query the students (via an assigned survey) about

- where they prefer to sit in a lecture hall (toward the back, middle, or front);
- the role they tend to play in group learning (more extrovert, ambivert, or introvert);
- their general/professional interests and major; and
- their goals for the semester.

Each of the questions helps structure the groups. Because the groups have a specific seating location, it is key that students identify the general area of the lecture hall (in the back, middle, or closer to the front) that they prefer. Communicating the role that they tend to play in group learning (more of an extrovert vs. middle vs. introvert) helps avoid forming groups with lone introverted students surrounded by multiple extroverted students. To further support more equitable engagement per the CI model, students are assigned varying roles for each day, to avoid particular students consistently monopolizing leadership roles. Finally, student-reported major, professional interests, and goals allow me to create groups based on similar affinities to connect like-minded students and increase the potential of forming deeper connections for learning outside of the classroom.

Once groups are formed, each group is designated a number, arranged into a larger color-coded table, and organized by student first name and last initial. I also provide a seating chart highlighting the locations of groups in the classroom. To facilitate the CI model, each student is designated a letter A–D to facilitate rotating between group roles (Cohan & Lotan, 2014). To ensure students know their groups and seating areas, both the group designations table and seating map are shown at the beginning of class for the first few weeks. Rotating role designations are likewise shared during each in-class group activity.

SEMESTER-LONG GROUP WORK ROUTINES

Understanding the importance of the social dimension for learning and supporting social bonds among the students, I aim to establish the semester-long groups very early in the semester (by the beginning of the second week of class). When implemented with corresponding class time divided into multiple group activity segments interspersed by short lecture periods, students adapt to the collaborative nature of the classroom and overcome any initial hesitancy. When I first began the semester-long group model, I didn't always assign groups by the second week of class and tended to implement group activities more sporadically. In each of these semesters, students were much more resistant to the group format, and reported significantly lower satisfaction with and gains from group learning.

Following the CI model, students are assigned rotating roles for daily activities of facilitator, reporter, recorder, and questioner (Cohen & Lotan, 2014). The assigned roles are communicated to the students, based on their group letter designations, via lecture notes, and on group activity materials.

In the first three weeks of class, group activities are closely tied to building trust, and sharing experiences and strategies for attempting the readings. On the first day, I task students with attempting a new strategy for the assigned reading. Beginning on the second day, students are invited to respond to a Google Form activity asking them to list their teammates' names and answer the following questions:

- Describe at least one reading strategy that you noticed using to make sense of the reading. Where in the text did you do that?
- Where/how did you learn to use this strategy?
- Comparing your strategy with your teammate today, what did you notice? What similarities or differences?
- What background knowledge did your team draw on to make sense of this text?
- Where did you learn this background knowledge?
- What one strategy described by a classmate are you willing to try out for the upcoming homework?

As the semester progresses, students continue reflecting and sharing their experiences with the pre-class readings. In addition, group activities are focused on specific text excerpts and/or figure(s) and several inquiry questions, including guiding questions about *how* they determined their answers and *why* it was chosen. I review these completed group activities to track attendance and participation. I provide feedback on responses that widely miss the intended mark by email or notes on their worksheet/other materials. Later I post a key of ideal responses on Canvas. To ensure participation in group activities, I assign them 15% of the overall course grade.

SHOWCASE OF THE GROUP-BASED LEARNING: DEVELOPING EFFICACY AT UNPACKING COMPLEX TEXTS (*EVOLUTION IN ACTION*)

A major challenge that students face in my class is unpacking/distinguishing information relevant to the reading at hand and relating this information to the big underlying ideas of the course. To effectively engage in this deep reading, students are required to identify a reading purpose, self-monitor their reading process, assess the provided information, and evaluate whether it relates to the focus/purpose of the reading. One of the most important incarnations of this deep reading is encompassed by distinguishing between the four major mechanisms of evolution described by real-world scenarios (in text, figural, or video format). Deciphering the real-world evolution scenarios is also the nexus of several sub-tasks:

1. Recalling the various mechanisms of evolution and their distinguishing features
2. Identifying evidence from the text to support one mechanism over others
3. Building a claim that supports the most-likely mechanism at work based on evidence from the text
4. Explaining their reasoning

Deciphering the real-world evolution scenarios functions as a threshold concept. Prior to gaining a developing or mastery level of interpreting these types of problems, students generally do not focus on the central relevant information and instead grasp at and apply misconceptions based on an incomplete understanding of the mechanisms underlying biological processes. However, once this problem solving is developed, students generally report that they are unable to "not see" the underlying mechanism at work—that they are so very obvious that they cannot believe they ever were not able to clearly see the driving mechanisms at work.

For beginners, distinguishing between the mechanisms of evolution in real-world scenarios requires both cognitive and knowledge-based challenges including

- unfamiliar vocabulary with specific disciplinary meanings and
- long, complex information-dense text.

The regular group-based activities provide in-class practice in parallel with additional opportunities offered in homework and discussion course contexts. Regular group participation also helps prepare students for working efficiently together on the collaborative section of exams throughout the semester.

Problem 1: Challenging and Unfamiliar Vocabulary

Throughout Introductory Biology, students encounter a significant amount of new vocabulary and existing vocabulary with new precise and technical meanings. It is through tackling the real-world evolution problems that students are actually compelled to grapple with and make sense of this vocabulary. Because this problem solving requires students to identify and work though vocabulary embedded in real-world scenarios, misinterpreting even a single part of the meaning can result in missing major clues about the mechanisms in action. Again, the CI group structure supports and reinforces students' vocabulary development, providing resources to help make sense of more challenging terms and concepts. Groups provide an opportunity for collaboration in breaking down and identifying root words, recalling vocabulary introduced in the pre-class homework, sharing strategies for recalling these words, and working together through activities to help distinguish between key evolution vocabulary terms and what other phenomena are indicated by the terms. The vocabulary-focused activities are often framed as warm-up activities to help orient the students to new content or as a way to segue to a more challenging activity applying their reasoning in a real-world scenario.

Problem 2: Long and Complex Information-Dense Text

Throughout the semester, students develop expertise in working with long and complex information-dense text. Through collaboration with teammates, students are supported in practicing and developing strategic approaches to assimilating these texts. The main strategies include identifying/recalling the reading purpose, practicing *reading resilience* (sustaining reading effort), active reflection while reading, and applying information into an evolution scenario problem-solving *decision tree*. Each of these skills are strengthened through specific group-based activities that help build students' resilience and confidence in their abilities.

When approaching the real-world evolution scenarios, students focus on information provided in the prompt to identify and recall the reading purpose while working through the text. This focus on purpose is further supported by the CI groups by the rotating *student questioner* role. The questioner's role is to keep the group focused on the reading purpose by drawing teammates' attention to the prompt and redirecting their attention based on the question that they need to answer. Because the roles rotate, each teammate has the opportunity to take on the questioner role regularly (at least every other week) and, through practice, gain mastery of this skill for reading complex texts.

Students also have regular opportunities to build *reading resilience* (sustained reading effort) by sharing the experiences and strategies they used for completing the pre-class reading, as well as how they applied their thinking to the challenge questions. I generally position this reflection closer to the beginning of class time as an opportunity to warm up to the content and reconnect with teammates before embarking on new content-driven activities of the day.

Additionally, group activities catalyze the practice of *active reflection* while reading, seeking connections with overall purpose and/or previous knowledge, and annotating texts in response to questions. The groups embark on several *talk to the text* and annotation practice sessions while logging notes about textual clues. Groups also work through readings and complex figures, tracking where key, as well as ancillary/connected information is located.

I have found CI groups to be an effective mode to review the problem-solving steps required in approaching real-world evolution scenarios, and to work through the *decision tree* for identifying the mechanisms of evolution at work. Students work together to recall/review the steps of the decision tree and then collaborate in applying the tree to evaluate evolution in action. At the end of working through the decision tree, students are led through a key learning outcome of providing evidence and explanation for their claims.

CONCLUSION

Through the semester-long groups, students report building deeper relationships, having a support network to take risks, being more engaged, and having lessons become ingrained rather than lost from class to class. In my course, students do not describe a passive learning environment; indeed, regular group activities are described by students as helping make learning "energizing," "dynamic," and "memorable" as repeatedly described by students in course evaluations. While the rotation of the student roles within the group can seem an extra hurdle at the beginning of the semester, students report appreciating "not always having to play the same role" and "having clear expectations for what each student is supposed to be doing." Students report feeling both supported and responsible for supporting their group members, providing stronger purpose and reason to prepare for and attend class:

"I found that I really enjoy working with others and helping plan our approaches to the different questions . . . when my groupmates showed their appreciation to my consistency and diligence."

"I got along very well with all my group members and when I was facilitator, I made sure all of us were on-topic and turned in the best work we possibly could. I also would forward completed activities to my group members if they were absent, so that they'd be a little less lost the next time we had lecture."

As the instructor, I appreciate the collaborative atmosphere for learning, and not feeling that I have to answer all the questions that arise for students. Ever since I have implemented the semester-long group activities with the CI group roles, I often overhear students' boisterous discussions and polite debates over class topics that didn't take place with previous course models. These interactions leave memorable impressions of how the topics fit into the course schema and to the wide world beyond.

Chapter 21

Restorative Pedagogy in Online Courses: Capitalizing on Relationships through Reading Apprenticeship Routines

Andréa Pantoja Garvey

In June of 2020, as we remained in lockdown and I attempted to recover from a disorienting end of the semester, I found myself reading the book *Braiding Sweetgrass* by Robin Wall Kimmerer (2013). In reading her moving account of how to approach restoration of the land from a traditional indigenous perspective, which focuses on relationships (i.e., humans' relationships with the land, relationships among the various organisms in the ecosystem), I was reminded of my classroom approach as a relational space for student restoration, for restoration of educators as co-creators in the process of learning, a space where students can reclaim their sense of agency as learning is taking place through reciprocal relationships in the classroom. I was also reminded of Paulo Freire's critical pedagogy in which transformative education occurs as the learners empower themselves as active critical thinkers, an approach that decenters the power of the educator by placing them as the "animator" of dialogues or "coordinator of debates." From this perspective, learning co-emerges through dialogical circles, or what Freire referred to as "cultural circles," with participants (learners and educators) mutually respecting one another as active participants (Freire, 1963). Accordingly, as the educator continues to facilitate critical reflection as the "coordinator of debates," students are encouraged to position themselves as authors of their learning, affirming their lived experiences as a powerful resource (Freire, 1963; 1981).

Relationships, I must note from the start, capture the variety of dialogues students enter into throughout their educational journey: interpersonal dialogues (current and prior ones) with their instructors, counselors, support staff, and fellow classmates, as well as the more private, intrapersonal dialogues with discipline-specific texts and themselves as learners. In this chapter, I share a few online classroom routines that capitalize on relationships that are aimed at creating opportunities for students to deepen their learning while also restoring their sense of self as empowered and inquisitive scholars, thereby illustrating what I am referring to as **restorative pedagogy**. I first present how the notion of restorative pedagogy revealed itself as I reflected on my own online classroom practice, especially during the uncertain and challenging times we experienced at the beginning of the Covid-19 pandemic. Then, I share some qualitative data in the form of excerpts from my asynchronous online courses in which students in my psychology courses are engaged in metacognitive dialogues with themselves and with others (such as fellow classmates and myself as the instructor), mediated by discipline-specific texts that were carefully curated for the courses. Finally, I close the chapter reaffirming the power of relationships as we reposition ourselves in the classroom as co-participants of the learning, as the "coordinator of debates" (borrowing Paulo Freire's terminology), supporting students and their growth as empowered inquisitive scholars.

HOW RESTORATIVE PEDAGOGY REVEALED ITSELF

With the abrupt disruption of life as we knew it prior to March 2020, along with college campuses and K–12 schools suddenly closing, students attempted to hold mental space for learning while also grappling with global uncertainties, readjusting their daily routines, and grieving the loss of loved ones due to Covid-19. At the same time, educators were rapidly adapting their classroom practices without being able to rely on a variety of routines and strategies they had carefully developed over their years of teaching. For me, these abrupt and involuntary changes precipitated by the Covid-19 pandemic further intensified my self-reflections about my own classroom experiences—both as an educator and as a former student. Amid the overwhelming unpredictability we all faced, many community college students reminded me of the challenging life circumstances they were experiencing such as having to share devices, work space areas, and slow internet (when available); serving as teachers for their young children or siblings who were also in remote learning; helping their aging parents or grandparents move to safer locations; experiencing house and food insecurity due to loss of their part-time jobs that supplemented their family income; among other disruptions. It appeared to me that I needed to make it more visible that the classroom was a space not only to foster discipline-specific learning but also students' process of reclaiming their positions as empowered inquisitive scholars. Reimagining education, including the position of educators in the classroom and the role of college courses in students' lives, was further reaffirmed. As many educators may recall, as early as the summer of 2020, a variety of webinars, reports, and publications centered on holistic approaches for recruiting, retaining, and supporting college students was observed. To illustrate, by 2022, the *Chronicle of Higher Education* reported that the Covid-19 pandemic has made more visible the often invisible need for colleges to embrace a more student-centered approach to success that goes "beyond academic markers of progress" (par. 10). But how to implement in an online asynchronous classroom a restorative pedagogy that is holistic, centered on relationships and that supports discipline-specific learning? Reemphasizing the Reading Apprenticeship model in my online classroom practice and reconnecting with Paulo Freire's dialogical, process-oriented approach were particularly fruitful, as described next.

HOW RELATIONSHIPS SUPPORT A RESTORATIVE PEDAGOGY

As a classroom faculty, I found myself frequently revisiting Paulo Freire's core principles centered on dialogue and empowerment as well as the Reading Apprenticeship model's focus on fostering students' metacognitive awareness. An important part of this awareness is an awareness of themselves as inquisitive learners as well as an awareness of the learning process itself. Capitalizing on relationships and approaching the classroom as a relational community of continuously changing members are central in the restorative pedagogy proposed herein. For the restorative pedagogy to become visible to both students and ourselves as classroom practitioners, frequent relational opportunities centered on the learners' experiences needed to occur. Mediated by discipline-specific texts, the Reading Apprenticeship routines used in my asynchronous online courses did exactly that: they fostered students' metacognitive dialogues with themselves, fellow classmates, and/or myself in the role of instructor. In my more than 25 years of teaching and from talking to experienced educators from various disciplines, it has become increasingly more visible to me that student educational growth and empowerment emerge through the apparently trivial relational situations students experience in their classrooms and in the college campus at large.

The following excerpts, taken from a self-reflective project students submit at the end of the term, illustrate the variety of ways online students can asynchronously engage in metacognitive dialogues with themselves as they *talk to the text*—discipline-specific texts. These excerpts also illustrate students positioning themselves as empowered authors of their educational/professional journey (emphasis added).

> "While reading that about 700 women in the United States die from complications related to pregnancy each year, **I was very surprised**. The fact that 60% of these deaths could have been prevented **does not sit right with me** and, **whenever I become a nurse, I would like to change that**."

As shown above, the newly learned fact about pregnancy complications in the United States (i.e., "*I was very surprised*") seemed to trigger discomfort in the student (i.e., "*does not sit right with me*"), an important experience to facilitate a potential transformation in the student position as an empowered author of change (i.e., "*whenever I become a nurse, I would like to change that*"). The student career choice is thus reaffirmed as a path for social change: a nurse who "*would like to change that* [preventable maternal mortality]." In the next example, extracted from another student self-reflective project, the student focuses on the concept of compassion fatigue (emphasis added).

> "I'm reflecting back on the video 'Compassion fatigue: What it is and do you have it?' This video **stood out to me because** almost everything asked at the beginning of the video is **exactly how I felt for a long time**. . . . Compassion fatigue is a real thing but I didn't even know it existed until I watched it. **Now that I know why** I've been feeling this way, I need to learn to **put myself first**."

In the above excerpt, as the student learns about compassion fatigue, they are empowered with an understanding of their own experience of compassion fatigue (i.e., "*exactly how I felt for a long time*"). This increased awareness places the student in a metacognitive space in which they realize the importance of making a personal commitment toward better self-care (i.e., "*Now that I know why . . . I need to learn to put myself first*").

In the context of student-to-student asynchronous discussions, the excerpts below illustrate the students' movement toward a deeper and more meaningful understanding of a topic (i.e., conception of age) while also facilitating an increased metacognitive awareness of themselves in relation to others around them (emphasis added).

> **Student 1**: "I think the conception of age **was one of the most intriguing topics** to learn about. . . . This construct **allowed me to dig deeper into how societal evolution** has directly influenced not just how we view ourselves, but the way we see one another. . . . **It's a critical component of ensuring** that we're using an adequate **level of discernment while speaking with** and studying **folks from diverse backgrounds**. I wouldn't engage with someone who has a chronological age of 30 and a psychological age of 12 in the same way that I would engage with someone who had both chronological and psychological ages of 30. **It would require a different means of communication and awareness**."

Student 2 reaffirms student 1's reflections, while sharing their own example: *"What a wonderful analysis of the topic! . . . **I can tell by an example of my brother**, who, when he was 30, already considered himself old, and talked about it all the time. **His perception of himself** was much older than he was, it **led him to a prolonged depression**, he did not find himself in life, could not fulfill himself, his marriage cannot be called happy either, and now at 45, he looks much older than his biological age."*

Student 1 replies back, concluding: *"Thank you for both the compliment and for sharing your connection to the subject with me. It's fascinating how much the brain can yield such a cognitive impact on our corporeality. . . . The conception of age shows us how **there's always something more to understand**."*

Of particular note, the above asynchronous exchange between these two students makes more visible the thinking process students engage in as they reflect about their anticipated lived experiences with individuals with diverse psychological abilities (i.e., "*It would require a different means of communication and awareness*"). With a deeper understanding of the concept of psychological age, these students not only express greater compassion toward others but also illustrate their position as more self-aware inquisitive scholars (i.e., "*there's always something more to understand*").

The examples above reveal how changes emerge in the student's understanding of discipline-specific texts as well as themselves through brief "aha moments" of self-reflective engagement. By facilitating frequent opportunities for students to position themselves as reflective scholars, they not only deepen their understanding of discipline-specific content, but they also move toward a metacognitive space of meaningful and sustainable learning. Additional examples from my lifespan development psychology course are highlighted below to further illustrate how some "small," low-stakes assignments have the potential to facilitate transformative changes in the students' positionality in their educational journey.

RESTORING STUDENT AGENCY THROUGH METACOGNITIVE DIALOGUES

In the past semesters, around that point of the term when students start showing signs of feeling overwhelmed, mentally checked out, or even starting to consider withdrawing from their courses, I share the book recommendation, *Laziness Does Not Exist*, written by social psychologist Devon Price (2021). When presenting my recommendation through a course announcement, I mention that the author invites us to reframe our feelings of "laziness," encouraging us to start looking at these feelings as indicative that we need to slow down, that we need to reflect on how we are measuring success and what changes we can make to support our success. As part of my announcement, I also highlight an excerpt from the book (shown below), using discipline-specific texts as a tool to reframe one's experiences of productivity and potentially trigger one's restorative process of self-awareness as competent and inquisitive scholars:

> *the laziness lie* [is] *a belief system that says hard work is morally superior to relaxation, that people who aren't productive have less innate value than people who are productive. It's an unspoken yet commonly held set of ideas and values. It affects how we work, how we set limits in our relationships, our views on what life is supposed to be about. The Laziness Lie has three main tenets.*

1. *Your worth is your productivity.*
2. *You cannot trust your own feelings and limits.*
3. *There is always more you could be doing.* (Price, 2021, p. 15)

After sharing the above excerpt, I model *selective vulnerability*—a powerful culturally responsive practice that facilitates student engagement (Hammond, 2015). Equally important, I would like to add, selective vulnerability supports the decentering of the power assigned to the instructor, placing them as co-participants of the learning process positioned as "coordinator of debates." More specifically, I share with my students that I struggle with the third tenet of the laziness lie (i.e., *"there is always more you could be doing"*), often resulting in intense migraines and excessive pressure on myself to do more! Mindful of potential time constraints, I direct students to Price's 2018 shorter article, *Laziness Does Not Exist—But Unseen Barriers Do*, as well as to their 17-minute interview, *"You aren't lazy. You just need to slow down."* I then ask students to privately email me their thoughts and reactions within two weeks of my announcement.

Below are some excerpts from these private student submissions illustrating how apparently "sidetracked" dialogues can serve to support students' restorative process of their positions as inquisitive and empowered scholars in their academic journey. Of particular note, the portions in bold emphasize the student process of reframing their own experience away from a deficit lens (e.g., *"Instead of dropping off . . . ,"* *"struggled with procrastination and it is NOT laziness,"* *"I always have this sense of guilt . . ."*) toward a more appreciative stance of their life circumstances and self-empowerment (e.g., *"I reached out and we are working together to finish out the semester strong,"* *"Awareness and acceptance is the antidote,"* *"I know I have definitely had situational factors that have affected my school and work life"*):

> *"As we have discussed,* **self compassion is hard and is something I am actively working on.** *. . . A bit ago you reached out when giving me extra credit for taking RAD* [reading program at our college campus]. *You noticed my interaction with the class had fallen off a bit and asked what was going on/ if everything was okay. Instead of coming from a place of judgment, you presented with curiosity and concern. . . . It worked.* **Instead of dropping off the face of the Earth, I let you know what was going on, I reached out to my RAD teacher and we are working together to finish out the semester strong.**"

> *"I have definitely* **struggled with procrastination and it is NOT laziness.** *. . . It is the way we view ourselves and our capabilities and all this is subconscious, we are not even aware, so if one is struggling it is like a ball of yarn we don't even know where to start to unwind, so why even start.* **Awareness and acceptance is the antidote.** *It would be nice if those around can provide some of that same grace."*

> *"I come from an immigrant family where the work ethic that has been drilled into us is all about productivity. . . . Coming from that scenario,* **I always have this sense of guilt** *when I'm not doing anything productive. . . .* **It feels refreshing to be able to look at people with a sense of empathy**, *rather than from the lens of judgment that the hegemonic culture so often pushes."*

> *"I fully agree with all of Price's thoughts regarding laziness and procrastination.* **I know I have definitely had situational factors that have affected my school and work life.** *. . . Although I've done fairly well in my classes, I am constantly feeling lazy and beating myself up for not doing extra credit and not studying more."*

Another opportunity that has facilitated changes in students' process of restoring their sense of agency has been through metacognitive reflections about what has worked well and what has not worked well when they prepare for a "high-stakes" multiple-choice exam. Upon completion of the exam, students gain access to a discussion board titled *My Studying Habits*, and are encouraged to share their tips for success and what kinds of adjustments (if any) they plan to make moving forward. Below are some examples of such exchanges. Note how students demonstrate their increased metacognitive awareness as they monitor their own thinking process, taking ownership of their learning (e.g., "*I noticed . . . ,*" "*I'm someone who struggles with . . . ,*" and "*if your focus ability allows, . . .* "):

> "*I found it very useful to first listen to the chapter narrations created by Dr. Garvey and then create my study guide while looking at the printed textbook. I **noticed that the auditory and visual combination really helped me** absorb the information better. As far as things I wish I had done differently, I didn't take many notes on the videos and articles for these chapters so that is something I will definitely be doing in the future.*"

> "***I'm someone who struggles with** remembering things; **hence I make phrases** out of parts of the chapters of the text. . . . And even in everyday life, it's personally important to make time for yourself and find a routine that helps me not get easily overwhelmed.*"

> "*I too take advantage of the chapter narration because it keeps me focused on the reading. **If in the chapter narration I come across key terms and concepts, I pause the video and have a notebook** that I write down those key terms and concepts. When it got close to the exam time (like a week before), I translated that information into flashcards. Flashcards **work best with me because** I can take them wherever I go and quickly run through them . . . **if your focus ability allows,** I speed up the playback speed for the readings and videos. Definitely be cautious with that one because it can turn quickly into just sound real fast if you aren't focused.*"

Another set of routines encouraged in my asynchronous online courses is for students to carefully analyze confusion about specific exam questions. More specifically, students are asked to provide the exact wording of the question, their reasoning for selecting the incorrect answer, and their current understanding of the correct answer. I explicitly emphasize that the key in this process is to explain their reasoning. When these metacognitive reflections occur in a public discussion board, I remain actively present by posing scaffolding questions to help students *think about their thinking*, serving as a "coordinator of debates." This is yet another classroom moment in which *making the invisible visible* (in this case, their own ability to correct an inaccurate understanding) constitutes a powerful tool for restoring and reaffirming their sense of self as inquisitive and self-perpetuating learners (i.e., gaining insight about discipline-specific content but also about themselves as learners). The "correct" reasoning does not come from me (this constitutes another opportunity to decentralize the "professor" power). Instead, the "correct" reasoning co-emerges as students engage in these metacognitive dialogues with one another, with themselves, and with me.

These asynchronous online discussions of "exam errors" normalize confusion and fill the online learning environment with provocative conversations as students collaboratively resolve conceptual inaccuracies and engage in metacognitive dialogues about their reading and problem-solving routines. Bit-by-bit, students co-create "aha moments" and share their academic struggles, collaboratively identifying possible solutions, as they engage in metacognitive conversations about challenging questions from a multiple-choice exam. The asynchronous exchange below illustrates a student engaging in *think aloud* in a public discussion board as they share their reading of the exam question and their thinking process when selecting the incorrect answer. Note how the student clarifies their own thinking as they are describing their thinking process (highlighted in bold below). This illustrates the emergence of the student metacognitive awareness about a discipline-specific concept through a self-dialogue framed for a public discussion.

> **Student 1** reflects: *For me, question 6 was not clear and I debated with myself quite a while before choosing an answer; **but I really did not think c.** [correct answer] would be the right answer. I feel that the textbook did not provide enough information on the topic. For example, let's look at how passive genotype-environment correlation is explained; it happens when children passively inherit the genes and the environments their families provide (p. 41).* **Thinking more about question 6, I can see how c. is the correct answer.** *Evocative genotype-environment correlation is accomplished when the social environment reacts to individuals based on their inherited characteristics. But, it seems to me that these two types of correlations are pretty easy to mix; I feel that in both types, the parents are responsible and do create the environment they think is best suited for their child's interests. Is the passive correlation happening when parents do not necessarily and actively modify their environments (the environment they provide just happens to be the right one for promoting the child's abilities) versus the evocative correlation which happens when parents do modify their environments?*
>
> **Instructor** responds: *Thank you for sharing in great detail your thinking process. It is always challenging to differentiate nuanced concepts like these. You got it. . . . A key distinction between Passive and Evocative is to look at* **how the environment** *is influencing the* **developing person**. *In the example of* **question 6**, *the "secret ingredient" was in the parents modifying the environment in response to. . . . So, the developing person is* **evoking** *a response from the environment. You nailed it!* B)

When opportunities such as the one illustrated above are created in the online classroom, "aha moments" can occur through guided self-dialogues, student-instructor asynchronous dialogues, and/or student-to-student asynchronous dialogues. Mindful that a variety of invisible factors may hinder student engagement in these public opportunities for metacognitive dialogue (e.g., feeling uncomfortable and/or feeling too vulnerable to share their confusion), I also individually reach out to students whose grades are below 69% (or who have recently experienced at least a 11% decline in their course grade) to offer them a private opportunity to review their exam using the Reading Apprenticeship knowledge-building routine called *tracking concept development* (TCD; for a more detailed description of the TCD, see Schoenbach et al., 2012, p. 249). More specifically, my email communication follows:

> Greetings, [*insert student name here*]:
>
> Is everything okay with you? I am reaching out because I noticed you didn't do too well on the exam. I'd like to encourage you to review your exam using a tool called tracking concept development (TCD) and possibly earn some points back on your exam. The goal of the TCD is to help you examine your current understanding of specific concepts, encouraging you to revise them and reflect on how this new understanding was achieved. In doing so, you not only clarify areas of confusion, but you also develop more effective reading/problem-solving habits for future studying. Lastly, I would like for you to peek through the *My Studying Habits* discussion board where many of your colleagues are sharing their struggles with the exam and suggestions for future exams.
>
> Are you up for engaging in this metacognitive exercise?

Here's how the TCD works:

- Select 1–4 questions from your exam that you got incorrectly and/or that you considered difficult.
- Review your selected questions following the **four steps listed** below.
- Submit your TCD to me via email by [*insert 2-week date here*] for a possible manual regrading of those exam questions you analyzed.
    1. **Selected question.** Write down the exam question and the possible answers, providing the question number as it appears on your exam.
    2. **My previous understanding.** Describe your understanding of that topic **before** you saw the correct answer. Why did you select that incorrect option? Do not rush through this process! The point of this exercise is to encourage you to slow down and **think about your thinking**.
    3. **My revised understanding.** Describe your new understanding of the topic that supports the correct answer. Why do you think the correct answer is the best answer for that question? If needed, go back to your textbook/class notes, assigned videos and revisit any relevant material that supports your insights.
    4. **How I arrived at this new understanding.** Describe **how** you arrived at the new, more accurate understanding of the topic. What have you learned about how you studied for this exam? What are you considering doing differently as you move forward in this class and prepare for your next exams? Is there anything you are considering doing differently next time you take your exam? Explain.

Below are excerpts from students describing their process of increased metacognitive awareness during step 4 of their exam review (emphasis added).

*"This was actually really helpful and helped me learn how to go through these chapters and what to really focus on. . . . I can see a lot of it is **me rushing through** the exam and **not taking my time with the questions**."*

*"I don't think I did anything wrong with my studying. **I think I just took a (somewhat) personal experience and didn't think any harder than that before giving my answer**. . . . What I'm taking away from this opportunity you've given us to go over our answers is that I **need to take my time**, not rush or panic and take that extra 30 seconds to double-check my answer. I think I spent quite enough time studying, that's never the issue because I actually really enjoy the reading materials. **It's the test-panic** I have with all subjects and **rushing through**. I'll work on that and I hope that my next exam will reflect that."*

*"It became clearer to me to **study for knowledge, long-lasting knowledge**, and not just rush to memorize information without an understanding so you can pass an exam. I also learned to **be more careful** and not overconfident, to check the questions a second time and be sure the desired answers are highlighted. . . . I figured out early that **reading and note-taking depend on the same skills**. When I read and write at the same time, I link both sounds and constructive words at the same time. Most of the time, I **use the abbreviations** I understand and **diagrams** I can translate while taking notes. This method is faster and helps me to recall accurately in time of review or when needed. Good note-taking helps me to **record, organize my ideas, think critically about what I read**, and record my thoughts about them while they are fresh. It also enables me to be aware of areas I need to further develop for deeper knowledge and understanding. Thank you so much for the privilege to review my exam."*

*"When reflecting on this exam, I can see numerous things that went wrong. My study habits in the beginning of the semester **were not as structured as I have it down now** and it shows when I look*

back at my notes from chapter 1 to now. I barely had written anything (not sure where my brain was), **I did not read the** [online] **discussions, which after I went through and read all of them I see how beneficial being engaged** in that would have been to further my comprehension on the subjects, or even going to the Student Lounge [an open-ended discussion board] **and ask for help.** When I was taking the exam, I didn't isolate myself from my kids. A **quiet space is very crucial to being able to hear yourself read the questions out loud to understand fully.** Lastly, I left a lot of time on the exam that I could have gone through the questions a couple times and through my notes [exam is open-notes] to confirm. Now, seeing where I went wrong and **what needs to be changed for future exams, not just for this class but in general.** . . . Hopefully, with my new realizations, I can excel in my courses and get better grades and understanding of what I'm learning."

When asked to pause and reflect on specific points of conceptual confusion, the excerpts above illustrate how the students engaged in more careful cognitive monitoring, detecting inaccuracies in their thinking and ways to avoid them in the future. In other words, when our course assessments serve the dual purpose of assessing learning and scaffolding of further learning, students not only improve their knowledge base for the discipline but they also learn how to activate metacognitive dialogues about themselves as empowered learners. By using a variety of classroom routines (e.g., a public group discussion about the exam versus a private review via the TCD, or sharing a provocative reading on academic engagement along with my own self reflections about it), a supportive culture of inquiry is created, which in turn contributes to student engagement in metacognitive dialogues about their own learning processes and themselves as learners.

CONCLUDING REMARKS: RELATIONSHIPS AS CENTRAL IN A RESTORATIVE PEDAGOGY

Intentionally emphasizing the Reading Apprenticeship model and reconnecting with Paulo Freire's dialogical approach further reaffirmed my philosophy of using the classroom as a relational space to foster both learning and opportunities for students to reclaim and/or restore their sense of self as inquisitive and empowered learners. Based on anonymous student surveys at the end of my courses, students have been responding positively to these classroom practices, feeling welcomed, cared for, and cultivated as inquisitive scholars. As a student wrote in a public discussion board in one of my psychology courses (emphasis added):

"As expected, my journey with this class has been an exceptional one. ***Not only was I able to walk out of this class with more knowledge than I came into it, but I was also able to come away with so many skill sets that I will be applying in order to improve all of my relationships over time.*** *I was able to identify certain behaviors about myself that contribute to healthy and unhealthy habits, coping mechanisms etc."*

I would like to emphasize once again an important pillar of the restorative pedagogy: **relationships.** As Kimmerer (2013) mentioned; *"restoring land without restoring relationships is an empty exercise"* (p. 338). Similarly, attempting to foster learning by adopting "trendy" instructional strategies and technologies without restoring our relationships with our students as inquisitive learners, without framing reading of discipline-specific texts as another type of relationship, without recognizing our classrooms as relational spaces where both learning and healing can occur for all of us, becomes an empty exercise.

In their 2020 book, *Relationship-Rich Education: How Human Connections Drive Success in College*, Felten and Lambert also capitalize on the power of relationships—in their case, interpersonal relationships—in the context of undergraduate education. Analyzing a total of 385 interviews of students, faculty, student life staff, and administrators from community colleges, research universities, liberal arts college, technical colleges, and large online universities in the United States, the authors propose relationship-based principles with rich examples to illustrate and inspire. In their own words, "relationships are a flexible and adaptable approach to meeting the needs of diverse students" (Felten & Lambert, 2020, p. 12), and thus relationships need to be at the core of the institution's practices and policies. I also would add that relationships are a powerful restorative technology for all classroom participants: students and instructors.

In this chapter, I provide examples of how relationships permeate the classroom experience, capitalizing on both inter- and intrapersonal dialogues mediated by discipline-specific texts that empower and foster students' metacognitive awareness while also situating myself as a participant learner and facilitator—or, using Paulo Freire's terminology, "coordinator of debates" or "animator" of dialogue. It is my contention that the restorative pedagogy described herein not only serves as one of the most powerful "technologies" to foster academic success, but it also serves as an opportunity for students to engage in self-restoration, while also restoring our position as a guiding "animator" of learning. I have found these relational practices particularly empowering and restorative when working with students from marginalized backgrounds who might walk into our classrooms unsure if they belong and, perhaps, feeling unseen or even resentful at our educational system. I know what that feels like based on my experience as an immigrant woman who moved from Brazil to the United States in 1994 to attend an academically rigorous graduate program. At that time, I was unsure if I belonged and sometimes questioned my decision of moving from South America (Brazil) to North America (United States). It was through small and frequent moments of relational connection with discipline-specific texts, meaningful peer collaboration, nurturing and individualized scaffolding from my professors that I gradually restored my sense of self as an inquisitive and empowered learner who was driven to further pursue my education. In doing so, I restored my sense of belonging while also reaffirming my desire to become an educator who could offer the same kind of restorative pedagogical moments to my students as it was done for me.

Chapter 22

Readers Wanna Read: Developing Self-Regulated Readers in the Online Classroom

Julie Gamberg

The first time I heard "Reading Apprenticeship," I thought—and I believe said aloud—*That's a terrible name!* My new colleague, Tiffany, with her kindly listening face and a near-term-pregnancy glow, nodded and told me more. I asserted—a little proud, maybe a little defensive—that as an equity-minded community college composition instructor, *I was already doing* the *Reading Apprenticeship Framework*, and more! *Community building*? Check. *Annotation teaching*? In multitudes! *Active learning, collaborative projects, and layers of reflection and revision?* That was my daily bread.

Now, many years later, I have come to know Tiffany's meet-them-where-they-are face well, and I have come to appreciate her gentle, probing questions, the complexity of this framework, and the way in which we support one another with stories of implementation, data, analysis, and collective reflection. This is mine.

Shortly after our first conversation, Tiffany managed to bring many of her new colleagues, including me, to a Reading Apprenticeship conference where I spent real time with the framework and, on second view, it was more like a candy-striped lifeline in the sea of student data that I knew was telling me I wa*s not quite there*. While students did well when we worked together, they were not leaving with the skills and confidence I wanted them to have. I was also *not* making the progress I wanted to on closing equity gaps. I was inventing, modifying, remixing, and reusing strategies constantly; my classroom, my syllabi, my lesson plans were a choppy sea where I could never relax.

The Reading Apprenticeship framework put many disparate practices that many of us were trying to do in our classes into an interconnected web of concrete, holistic routines and strategies that worked not just because they had clever names, like "talking to the text," but because they were thoughtfully scaffolded; because they recognized the importance of things like building schema or "tolerating ambiguity" when working with new or complex topics; and, because they did not isolate the personal, social, and cognitive dimensions of learning with entirely different strategies, theories, or frameworks. Also, most importantly, because they made explicit that which was hidden even to me—the multilayered process of becoming a disciplinary expert that, by the very nature of what Reading Apprenticeship calls our "expert blind spot" we are often not able to adequately break down for our students, thus creating a "sink or swim" learning environment even when we think we are thoughtfully scaffolding learning. Despite the immense amount of work I spent supporting my students, they were not *receiving* much of that support. I am not the only comp instructor who has recognized that in spite of spending my weekends giving careful feedback on student writing, those comments often went unread or read but not implemented. "I used to work so hard for my students," I remember Tiffany telling me. "But I was doing the work *for* them. Now I help them learn how to do the work." It took me many years to implement the Reading Apprenticeship framework in such a way that I began to see these promised shifts.

And then I started teaching online.

When I made the shift to fully online teaching—several years before the pandemic—I was sad to see that the Reading Apprenticeship metacognitive routines I had carefully implemented in my face-to-face courses didn't fully make the journey with me. Yet, my online classes went well. I had engaged in rigorous distance education training and eventually earned a role teaching faculty all over California to teach humanized, equitized online courses. I had a new set of necessary skills and, although I wasn't using the Reading Apprenticeship framework as overtly as I had in my face-to-face classes, the interconnectedness of the framework dimensions was already somewhat "baked into" the way I did things in my course, lesson, and assessment designs and practices, so I did not see a sharp drop in success rates. Yet, during the crisis of the pandemic—with students falling through the cracks because of overwork, illness, depression, and unmanageable stress—success rates did begin to drop, and students began to seem more disconnected, an experience I know that many of us share. As I recognized the need for bigger changes in my online courses, I began experimenting with how to use the Reading Apprenticeship framework and strategies more robustly in asynchronous online courses. The most pivotal change I made was in refining a strategy for the modeling and practice of the metacognitive think aloud, which layers and incorporates the four dimensions of the Reading Apprenticeship framework: social, personal, cognitive and (disciplinary) knowledge-building. With student input, we landed on a formula that has increased students' academic reading skills, their confidence, and their regular use of metacognitive routines. One student, in her end-of-course reflection, writes, "I believe that I have grown as a learner in this course because I have seriously learned different strategies in this class which I didn't come across before in my past school years such as metacognitive think aloud and RRJ (Reading Response Journal). I see much value in these skills because I have already started to use them in my other classes." It was exciting to see that students were leaving the class with skills they felt were transferable, as well as reporting a real shift in their relationship to academic reading.

From student response data spanning three classes, 95% of students reported being able to read metacognitively at a 4 or 5 on a 0–5 scale, as in the bar graph in figure 22.1.

All of this came not a moment too soon!

No sooner had I spent a semester floating on a calm sea than large language models (LLMs) and generative AI came to upend my discipline *and* online education. Yet, the pedagogical shifts that I had spent a couple of years working on—which also included implementing linguistic equity and upgrading practices—provided a comparatively soft landing for my students and me. The metacognitive routines we established were a bit of a bulwark, shielding us from the worst of unacknowledged LLM use in online work. Do my students use ChatGPT and other LLMs on various assignments—no matter how well scaffolded, individualized, linguistically dynamic, inclusive, and relational our work is? Yep! A bit. And like many of my colleagues, I am working now, once again, on another pedagogical shift—an ethical AI framework. But had it not been for the use of the Reading Apprenticeship framework in my online classes, layered with other powerful and complementary practices, I am sure I would have been in a very

I can metacognitively read to notice what I am thinking about the text as I read it.
56 responses

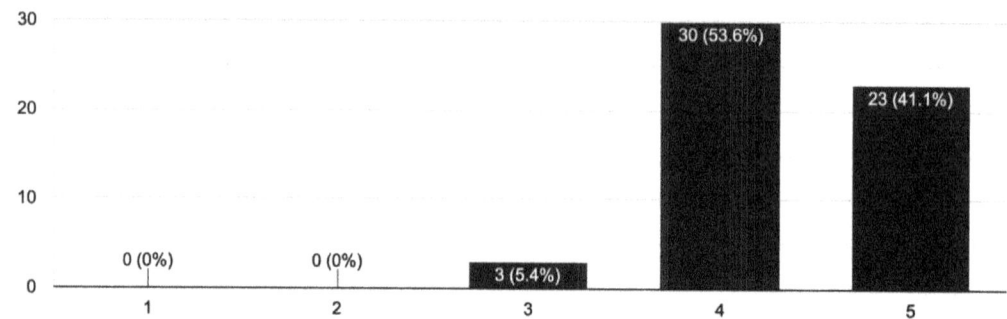

Figure 22.1. Student Self-Reports on Metacognitive Reading
Julie Gamberg

different boat, on a very different sea. Several of my colleagues have reported that the majority of work they received this past year was AI generated. Yet, with metacognitive routines embedded in online classes, with a framework that holistically incorporates personal, social, cognitive, and discipline-based learning, my students and I have been able to ride these waves and continue learning and growing together.

Metacognition was a central element to students' sense of their own growth in our class, as reported by more end-of-course feedback:

> *I have grown so much both as a learner and a writer. I learned how to navigate through the assignments and understand their main requests. I learned how to properly read and reflect on numerous texts like an expert.*

> *Metacognitive thinking helped me grow a lot as a learner. Before, when I would not understand something, I would just ignore it. . . . Now, when I don't understand something, I use metacognitive thinking to help me understand and learn. I do feel more confident in both my academic reading and my writing, the things I learned in this class helped me a lot in feeling that way.*

Because my students were responsive to metacognitive practices, and regularly engaged in reflection, it was my hope that they might benefit so much from the layering of the personal and social dimensions along with the cognitive and knowledge-building dimensions of those practices that they would move toward *choosing* to employ successful reading strategies beyond when there were explicit assignments or requests to do so. We often talk about revision in writing, but what I was hoping to see was revision *in reading*. Just as it's important for students to be aware of the need for revision in their writing and to—ideally—internalize the concept of revision as part of writing, could they also internalize awareness of the moments in reading where they were becoming confused, lost, less curious, less connected? Through a pair of lessons that focus on the think aloud strategy as a primary lens for practicing metacognitive conversation as well as build on and merge with the other Reading Apprenticeship practices and activities we do in the course, we made great gains in *reading revision*. What follows is an explanation of an interactive video assignment and a small-group discussion assignment in an asynchronous online English 101 course.

LESSON ONE: INTERACTIVE VIDEO THINK ALOUD

Decisions: Text and Medium

For this assignment, I model a think aloud of a text from Michelle Gonzales and Kisha Quesada Turner's linguistic equity work at Las Positas College about positionality. Because positionality can be a complex concept, yet it is one that we will return to throughout the course, this think aloud grounds us not only in strategies that help us better understand and respond to complex readings, but also in language that helps us bring the personal and social into academia, which is exactly what positionality is about!

The medium of the think aloud in the online course is equally important. Because the Reading Apprenticeship framework has so many relational components, and because we co-create with our students—building, scaffolding, interconnecting—it is vital to use a humanized model of online teaching as framework for the asynchronous class. Video is one important part of humanizing the online environment. Humanizing researcher Michelle Pacansky-Brock (n.d.) asserts that "Video is a powerful medium for cultivating your warm human presence online, as well as creating accessible, byte-sized learning chunks that support your students' learning rhythms. Unlike classroom instruction, video puts students in the driver seat, allowing them the option to watch and rewind as much as they need without the shame of raising one's hand and asking, 'Um, could you say that again?'"

Video not only humanizes our connection with students in general, but in Reading Apprenticeship, it allows us instructors to engage the cognitive and knowledge-building dimensions of the framework by modeling for students how to scan and break down a text, to notice our thinking while reading, to approach and solve reading issues or problems, and to engage in disciplinary discourse. Additionally, interactive video, a type of video that pauses at key points for reflection, quizzes (which can be ungraded) surveys, discussions, writing prompts, and so on, further helps students to stay engaged and to respond throughout the video, bringing their curiosity and shifting academic identity into "the conversation" of the video.

Reinforcing Metacognition and Modeling the Think Aloud

In the video I created, I used graphics, text, images, and floating language on the screen while I retained the humanizing element by appearing in the corner of the screen and narrating. I added interactivity with pauses that ranged from quick knowledge checks to ungraded quizzes using words and images, as well as deeper reflection on personal, social, and cultural experiences with metacognition and reading. I began the video by reintroducing metacognition—something we touched on in an earlier video, building on—and deepening—prior knowledge.

I then introduced the concept of the think aloud and shared ideas about the connection between metacognition, thinking aloud about reading a text, and our ability to grow as readers. Again, I had several pause points for knowledge checks, reflection, and contemplation. Finally, I demonstrated the think aloud, reading the text about positionality, which was also on the screen with me—the reader—on the screen too! This is where interactivity really shines. I might even argue—radically—that the combination of dynamic video (words, images, sound, instructor face) with well-timed pauses and interactions, allows students to fully engage with the process of watching an instructor grapple with a text and reflect on that grappling—even more than doing this activity face to face!

In the video, I was able to focus the pause points so students could reflect on the "moves" I was using as a reader. When I misread a word and thus misunderstood a sentence, I was able to take a poll and ask students what went wrong and what I should do. I was able to switch seamlessly between a think aloud and metacognition *about doing a think aloud* by scrolling text across the screen explaining *Now I am doing the think aloud* and *Now I am talking to you about the think aloud and why and how to do it*, and I was able to offer reflection points for students to offer ideas about how I was building or presenting my own reader identity. Finally, I was able to offer a critical pause point, one in which students were invited to practice their own think aloud, with their short video going directly to me for instructor feedback.

LESSON TWO: GENTLY SCAFFOLDED PEER OBSERVATION AND FEEDBACK

The Assignment

The following week, students are given a *metacognitive think aloud* assignment—set up as an asynchronous discussion—in small groups in which they have previously established norms and engaged in activities aimed at increasing community and fostering a sense of belonging.

For the assignment, students record a five-minute video of themselves (they can be off-camera if they would like by recording a screencast of the text, or having the camera point at something else; about half of the students choose to show their face) reading the text that they have just been assigned, bell hooks's (1994b) essay, "Seeing and Making Culture: Representing the Poor" (which they will interact with again in future assignments).

Students then post their videos in the small-group discussion board, and respond to another student, answering questions about the metacognitive strategies they observed their peer using in their think aloud video.

Supported Autonomy

For this discussion, unlike our prior discussions in which I only respond to student posts in the form of private, individual responses, I respond publicly to the discussion board, interweaving my responses with peer responses.

I am sometimes first to respond to one student, but last to respond to another. My responses are modulated to further model the practice of observing and articulating a metacognitive process and listing reading strategies that were noticed. By intertwining my responses with the small-group peer responses, I can gently push students further when needed, or expand dialogue, yet also let students take the lead or take back the lead, as they are practicing these skills.

The workflow I've described resulted in many exciting and interesting impacts on our class.

1. Many students—the majority—responded to two or more students, even though the assignment only requires one response.
2. Students were able to focus on listing and noticing reading strategies before discussing the text. This resulted in more layered meaning-making, and a more explicit connection between reading strategies and textual analysis.
3. Beyond students explicitly noticing the way a peer's strategy may have connected to a result, such as an insight or a misunderstanding, students also engaged directly with one another's analysis of the text and responded to and made connections with one another's personal and cultural connections to the text. They were able to scaffold themselves to a

more difficult level of analysis without skipping the steps of engaging in the metacognitive conversation.
4. Students pointed out to one another when their peer's video was simply a read-aloud and did not employ metacognitive strategies.
5. Students supported one another in suggesting additional reading strategies or ways to get started.
6. Students deepened their connection, sense of community with one another, and sense of individual and community academic identity.

In addition to those results, perhaps the true power of this assignment sequence is that it is the assignment in which students began to identify a need or desire for *reading revision* independently of my request for revision. This looked like noticing when they are and aren't understanding or connecting to a text, developing strategies to increase understanding and connection, and, more importantly, *choosing* to reconnect. Students regularly commented—the majority of students commented along the lines of "next time, I'll . . ."; "I want to work on/get better at . . ." (often paired with an appreciation for another student's "moves"); and "I'm going to try this in . . ." (another context).

Sometimes these observations would happen after receiving peer feedback and reflecting on the assignment, but it also happened during and after *giving* peer feedback. Students gained not only intrinsic motivation to revise their reading strategies, and sometimes even their definition of themselves as a reader—but they also gained the metacognitive skills to engage in a self-led ongoing cycle of reflection and growth.

Research from Wentao Li and Fuhui Zhang (2021) demonstrates that the combination of instructor and peer feedback, paired with revision goals, leads students to the holy grail of *self-regulated revision*, where students continue to engage in the process of revision, and more importantly, in the *idea* of revision, beyond any submission or resubmission requirement. This is exactly what was happening in our class!

One premise of Reading Apprenticeship is that "reading in community can lead to improved meaning-making," and this workflow—which pairs the personal and social dimensions of reading in an online course with instructor and peer feedback—created a profound shift in, riffing off of Li and Zhang's term, *self-regulated reading revision*.

In a fully online environment, with asynchronous contact, students increasingly became metacognitive readers who could fluidly monitor their own comprehension, analyze and engage with textual ideas, theorize about a text, create intra-textual meaning (including the "text" of their personal, social, and cultural knowledge), and critically respond. The workflow we came up with is doable in an online class and was transformative for my students. As one student put it, when asked in a final reflection what surprised her about the course, "I would say the metacognitive is what surprised me. I was very surprised that it stuck to me throughout the end of this course." Or as another said, "I have definitely grown as a learner in this course. I feel as if learning about metacognitive thinking and other reading strategies has helped me a ton, both in this class and in the future."

Chapter 23

Social Annotation as a Transdisciplinary Strategy for Engaging Diverse Learners

Jonelle Strickland

Remarkably, humans have been *annotating*—adding commentary to explain or extract meaning from a text—and *socially annotating*—reading and thinking collaboratively—for tens of centuries, marking both forms of annotation well-established pedagogical tools for deepening our understanding of various texts. In the East, we see Pei Songzhi annotating scrolls from the Three Kingdoms as early as the fourth century ("Records of Three Kingdoms," n.d.), while in the fifth-century-BCE West, we have evidence of live audience participation in the construction of Homeric epic (Muellner, 2015). Since the rise of digital platforms, we also see acts of social annotation occurring across a wide variety of academic and nonacademic disciplines, including marginalia on rap lyrics and blogs (see Kalir, 2022, p. 9). In today's digital era, there are several tools to help instructors facilitate social annotation as a strategy for engaging diverse learners' cognitive and noncognitive needs.

SUPPORTING STUDENT WRITERS DURING THE GENERATIONAL STAGE

Many teachers of writing are likely already familiar with the use of live documents (e.g., Google docs, Microsoft Office, Jamboard, etc.) as a form of peer review. However, these applications can be equally valuable to support developing student writers, especially when coupled with explicit reading goals and strategies during the generational stage of writing. Consider the following sample prompts for an English class (1) and a Criminal Justice class (2):

1. Picturing *is the practice of creating mental images as if one were watching a movie. As you read, draw/select a minimum of three images to reveal what argument the author could be making (or contesting). Post your three images and three quotes. Then reply to each of your groupmate's posts by explaining why you think they have selected their combinations of image and text.*
2. *A case brief is a summary of a published judicial opinion. As you read, note where information can be found to support the following sections: facts, procedure, issue, holding, rationale, and concurrence/dissent. If there is a word or an idea that you do not yet understand, write a question mark in the margin. If you see a question mark and you*

know the answer, write it down next to the question mark. Remember, during this preliminary stage of reading, there can be more than one possible answer.

Notice how each of these social annotation assignments steer students toward critical thinking. In the first prompt (suitable for a humanities classroom), students are practicing a preliminary version of direct quote analysis. By creating original pairings of image and text and by attempting to explain each other's pairings, students are charged with thinking more deeply about a particular passage and its relationship to the primary argument of the text (and sometimes even identifying the primary argument of the text). In the second prompt (suitable for a social sciences classroom), students are collectively breaking down a complex text into six key elements that will help them to summarize a judicial opinion. In each scenario, students are spared the liability of performing a single *dissection* and can instead process multiple *cross-sections* of meaning, an iterative process leading to more critical, nuanced thinking. With each new cross-section (student interpretation) comes unique insider disciplinary knowledge. Consider the diverse connections (and interpretations of a text) offered by students majoring in math, physics, psychology, Spanish, journalism, or ethnic studies. Now consider the aggregate effect that each of these insights might have on a single student reader, especially how these plural modes of thinking might help this student to see beyond their initial impressions or even to notice that *all* thinking is contingent upon our unique experiences and social networks. To put this another way, because "reading practices are the processes and cultural assumptions which readers use to make sense of a text" (Moon, 1999, *Reading Practices*, p. 137), these kinds of diverse readings offer students more than just cognitive exploration, but also entry points into differing cultural/disciplinary landscapes. Now picture this kind of democratized, iterative collaboration throughout the generational process. Social annotation is not only a cognitive tool for writing about texts; it is an equity and metacognitive tool for examining diverse interpretations of stories and data.

THE NEED FOR SOCIAL ANNOTATION IN CROSS-DISCIPLINARY SETTINGS

As an educator teaching in *two* counties—Orange and Los Angeles—across *two* disciplines—English and Criminal Justice—and within *two* institutional settings—at a medium-sized community college in the suburbs and a large Cal State University in the city—my understanding of what reading, writing, or research *should* look like in the classroom is akin to picking the right lane of traffic on a Southern California freeway: *what works at four o'clock on a Tuesday is not always what works at four o'clock on a Tuesday*. This quandary having been acknowledged, I also find myself grateful for the frequent opportunity to change lanes: the fact that I am learning from and interacting with so many different students, colleagues, and, yes, even citation manuals, can be an asset insomuch as these interactions force me to avoid "entrenchment" and become "rhetorically flexible" in more than one academic discourse (Anson, 2016, pp. 77–78). As a teacher participating in two disciplines, I am acutely aware of the need to adapt and explore different modes of teaching to effectively reach different student populations with distinct disciplinary needs. Similarly, when exposing our students to the practice of social annotation, we are helping them to develop their own "rhetorical dexterity" (Anson, 2016, p. 78) in the form of metacognition or *thinking about thinking*. Through social annotation, students are learning that there is more than one way to respond to a text. Furthermore, students are learning that some of their most critical reflections arise when they are able to synthesize a variety of responses, including their own. Like cross-disciplinary instruction, social annotation prompts learners to reflect on their "habituated ways of thinking" (Anson, 2016) as they consider and adapt to new writing situations through new cultural/disciplinary lenses promising a wider network of shared reading/writing experiences.

WHAT (SOME) STUDENTS ARE SAYING ABOUT SOCIAL ANNOTATION

Before discussing how to leverage social annotation as a pedagogical tool, I would like to share a couple of student perspectives:

> I really enjoyed the collaborative learning in this course because it helped me share my opinion and for others to give me advice for example on my essays. I enjoyed the discussion the most because everyone was able to share their thoughts and their work.

> Unit 4 [social annotation] has introduced to me a new beacon of hope. I struggled in previous course units due to keeping silent and, even though I did all the work, I really regret not putting myself out there. I've learned to use active voice in both speech and literature, and I've met some interesting peers as a result of coming out of my shell. I feel more purposeful and hopeful overall.

In both student remarks, we can see evidence of cognitive change taking place. While the first student is revising an essay (engaging in the writing process), the second student is developing their use of a new rhetorical skill ("I've learned to use active voice"). Meanwhile, each student's social-emotional capital is also being activated as evidenced by their use of words such as "enjoyed," "interesting," "more purposeful," and "hopeful." If these remarks haven't yet convinced you to invest in social annotation, then you might consider the epistrophe in this student's reaction: "Everything in this class has a *purpose*, and it is a very important *purpose*." Through these end-of-the-semester reflections, a majority of students are revealing how a classroom experience embedded with social annotation is helping them to joyfully persist.

Of course, the reality is that not every writer experiences social annotation positively. Take, for example, the following student's comment about feeling disconnected from a group whose members were routinely absent on days when social annotation took place during class: "Do not rely on your classmates, they will not always help you." While anyone who has assigned (or been assigned) group work is likely to have encountered a version of the above, this does not mean that one should abandon social annotation as a strategy for engaging and connecting students. As a collaborative pedagogy, social annotation works best in a dynamic teaching environment in which the teacher is willing and able to change alongside the needs of her students. Thus, when we invest in this kind of collaborative classroom, we are committing ourselves to learning from the past. For example, I could have been more proactive about communicating with groups mid-project and, when beneficial, helping some groups to reconfigure either by absorbing new members or by creating asynchronous break-off groups to accommodate long-term absences. If mid-semester adaptation is difficult (as I predict it might be in, say, a large or accelerated section), then this may indicate the need for a different classroom strategy. However, for those of us who have the means to monitor and facilitate a dynamic, collaborative environment, some of the fruits of our labor of love (in students' own words) can be the achievement of "joy," "hope," and "purpose." Starting with small, low-stakes assignments, practicing instructor modeling, and periodically reading the classroom can all help to make the adoption of social annotation a more equitable student experience.

LOW-STAKES "PRACTICE" ANNOTATION SESSIONS

Not all learners may be ready or comfortable engaging in social annotation. Some students may be critical of their knowledge of the topic: *What if my idea is wrong?* Or of their level of academic fluency: *What if I don't sound smart enough?* To alleviate some of these jitters, I ask students to engage in practice annotations by co-exploring the course syllabus. Using a live document, I might first highlight a phrase from the text (e.g., "Student Hours"), and then type in the margin, "What are these?" Another student will answer, "Student hours are . . . " or highlight the answer in the text. Besides generating procedural questions, I like to model a few reactions, too, as in "Dang, I never knew you could get free books, and I've been here two years!" After seeing that their language need not be formal, students quickly assimilate to the process of sharing some of their own values and feelings about academia and campus life. For this reason, I prefer not to grade these early-in-the-semester annotations, or if I must attach a grade, I do so based on completion. More importantly, I make sure that students know their voices are being read. Through a series of low-stakes, formative assignments, I can also gauge how I might build sustainable metacognitive relationships with students as the class transitions to more difficult academic content.

READING GROUPS AS OPPORTUNITIES FOR COLLABORATION

After completing these practice annotation sessions, students are ready to apply their social annotation skills to some more challenging course content. To assist students in their understanding of what many of them perceive as challenging texts, I activate Canvas Groups as spaces where they can upload their annotations (as file attachments, as marked-up screen shots, as audio comments, as discussion posts, etc.) and then compare these initial ways of thinking to those of their classmates. I use this platform (including a link to the Canvas Student Guides to improve functionality) in both my face-to-face and online modalities of teaching. This is done to engage different types of learners. For the most part, students are encouraged to utilize their group platforms as they see fit. If Canvas isn't working for them and they all want to use Zoom or Snapchat or annotate on paper napkins at a local campus eatery (yes, this has happened), I am comfortable with this kind of flexibility—as long as students are documenting their work and as long as this adaptation works for the whole group; otherwise, we default to Canvas. Some more introverted groups may need a little more support to get started. In F2F settings, I use circle groups to facilitate direct eye contact and frequently seat myself alongside my students while also mirroring my energy, tone, and body language with that of the group. Scaffolding student reading within a collaborative pedagogy not only assists with motivation and perseverance, but it also has the potential to deepen student-to-text connections and student-to-peer connections that might not have developed independently. It's not always easy to convince students their interpretations are valid or, once shared, that their peers' differing interpretations may also be valid, but with persistence, lots of icebreakers, and early scaffolding exercises, this process does become more manageable.

OPEN SOURCE OR LMS?

One advantage of using familiar tools such as Microsoft Teams or the Google Suite is that these tools reduce our cognitive loads, freeing up the space for instructors to develop (and students to explore) content. A second advantage is that many of these familiar applications tend to be open source or already funded through our school or district budgets. On the other hand, developing software devoted to helping users streamline the annotation experience—Diigo, Hypothes.is, Kami, Perusall—is also available. Most of these applications allow users to annotate web pages and PDFs directly and organize and share mark-ups as tags, groups, or files. Some of these applications can be integrated within a learning management system (LMS), a plus when it comes to protecting student privacy, studying student engagement patterns, and automatically populating the gradebook. Based on my own experiences, I prefer to use Diigo as a more "traditional" outlining tool and Hypothes.is as a media-rich tool. I have yet to experiment with either Kami or Perusall, but these are among some of the applications that my colleagues are using in their classrooms. Whether adapting an open-source or LMS-supported software, one important consideration is comfortability. *What is the look and feel that empowers you as an instructor? What is the functionality that engages your students? Does this response vary based on your discipline?* Remember, choosing a tool to implement social annotation is not the same as choosing whether to implement social annotation. If one tool doesn't work for a particular assignment, try another, and perhaps another, until you find the one that unlocks students' "joyful persistence."

AS LONG AS YOU DO NOT STOP

What I have found particularly challenging (and ultimately rewarding) about my experiences teaching social annotation is the deeply varied responses from students. While several students demonstrate strong connections between annotations and the written deliverables that follow—often written with more poignancy, accuracy, and textually rich language—other students (in fact, more than I might wish to acknowledge) are still not submitting final projects. Sigh. (At least they are submitting their annotations. Smile.) In follow-up reflection assignments, these non-completing students most frequently cite "a lack of time" as the primary reason for their nonparticipation, a trend more clearly noticeable in my asynchronous online sections, prompting me to reflect on which student demographics each modality typically serves. *Two* counties, *two* disciplines, *two* institutional models, and now, *two* user modalities. Although social annotation is not revolutionizing submission rates (at least not yet in my own classrooms), I remain convinced that transformative learning is still at play. Consider, for example, the learner who acknowledges personal responsibility for their end-of-the-semester performance: "I did not end the unit as well as I would have liked. . . . This revealed that as a college student I need to be more serious and not procrastinate. I should ask for help when I need it and not push it away." Or consider those who remind us that their learning may not always be visible in the gradebook: "I did really enjoy the readings from the book. . . . I think all the preparation did help me prepare for this essay that although I did not actually write I most definitely wrote in my head"; and "This class although I failed, taught me a lot and in fact, we did learn about how failing is *not* always a bad thing if you learn from your mistakes and use those experiences to try again." In each of these end-of-the-semester responses (taken from students who did *not* earn a passing grade but who did in fact participate in social annotation) is evidence of learning in progress. Finally, coming from a student with perfect attendance (including participation in social annotation) who nevertheless did not submit a single mastery assignment: "This class was honestly one of the few reasons I had to get up and out of bed in the mornings and put in the effort to get out of my pajamas . . . without it I had no other reason to leave my home." One cannot understate the value of using social annotation as an important social-emotional learning and metacognitive tool to engage some of our most vulnerable student learners.

Chapter 24

The We and the Me: The Social and Personal Dimensions

Lora Bagwell

If nothing else, the events of 2020–2021 taught us that all humans have their own unique experiences. Even when we share a skin tone, political or religious affiliation, or citizenship, our experiences are not the same. We all have our own stories and bring our own background knowledge or schema to everything we do, including reading. These experiences build the neural pathways in our brains. When our brains read information that can be connected to an established neural pathway, the brain has a better chance of remembering that information. Have you recognized yourself in a character in a novel? I have. Have you read a math textbook and recognized a use for algebra in your real life? I still need help from my math friends for that, but I can make connections between a textbook discussion of cell reproduction and cancer because I have lived the experience. As we recognize our connections to texts and our approaches to reading texts, we are developing the personal dimension or the "me." This metacognitive awareness allows us, instructors and students, to bring information to the discussions in the classroom. If we bring our collective experiences together, we double, triple, or quadruple the background knowledge we bring to the texts being read and the strategies used to read those texts. Developing the social dimension or the "we" in our classroom provides the opportunity for students to share their experiences and connections as well as acquire new knowledge. Isn't this why we ask our students to read and write in the first place? When teachers develop learning environments that foster feelings of safety and belonging, students are comfortable exploring and building their personal reading identities. Because of the we, students strengthen their me.

I am an associate professor of reading and assistant dean of English at Pellissippi State Community College (PSCC) in Knoxville, Tennessee. I teach corequisite reading and college success courses for students in their first semester at PSCC. The corequisite courses were designed using the Reading Apprenticeship framework and heavily influenced by growth mindset and intelligent practice. I use Reading Apprenticeship routines in my courses to create a sense of belonging and a safe environment in which students work to improve their reading abilities and acquire the skills needed to successfully transition to higher education. While I plan lessons to move students through as many of the dimensions as possible, I feel my strengths are building the social and personal dimensions in the classroom. The following pages are a discussion of what I find important in developing the social and personal dimensions as well as the Reading Apprenticeship routines I find helpful in the process. My courses also emphasize the importance of a growth mindset and particularly intelligent practice. Additionally, I sprinkle a few stories from my classroom to illustrate the positive effects of Reading Apprenticeship and intelligent practice.

When a colleague found and shared the Reading Apprenticeship framework with me, I immediately fell in love. Finally, I had validation for my teaching style and philosophy. No longer was the importance of building community and creating relationships only a personal gut feeling. The positive effects of relationship building were research-based. Reading Apprenticeship places the social dimension on equal footing with the personal, cognitive, and knowledge-building dimensions. The metacognitive conversations weaving in and out of each of the dimensions allow students and teachers to identify their strengths and challenges when reading for understanding. The social dimension provides the space to discuss these strengths and challenges. During these discussions, students and teachers make their invisible thinking processes and strategies visible. Everyone walks away from the discussions with new strategies and skills to improve their performance in the other dimensions and ultimately their reading comprehension. For instance, as readers participate in conversations with other readers, they begin to develop in the personal dimension as well. The we builds the me. Their metacognitive skills improve, so they recognize their strengths and weaknesses. Readers acknowledge their purpose is not always the same, and with that knowledge, they understand the strategies needed to read the text successfully are not always the same. They learn to set reading goals for themselves and identify the strategies needed to meet those goals. With more confidence in their personal abilities, their overall reading ability improves, and they are more likely to share in discussions with other readers. In this case, the me builds the we. Do you see a pattern here? Improvement in one dimension leads to improvement in other dimensions. In my classroom, I use the social dimension as the launching pad.

Of course, students must trust the process to find success, so before I begin building the social dimension in my corequisite reading and first-year seminar courses, I introduce my students to the growth mindset work of Carol Dweck and the concept of intelligent practice. Intelligent practice is a combination of effort, good strategies, and help from others (Dweck, 2012). In 2014, Mary-Jo Apigo and Miguel Powers presented intelligent practice in formula form in their Growth Mindset Curriculum (Powers & Apigo, n.d.). Their formula was expressed as Effort + Good Strategies + Help from Others = Intelligent Practice. I adjusted the formula slightly for my students and present the formula as Effort x Good Strategies x Help from Others = Intelligent Practice (Success). The multiplication signs are key to the formula because all three parts of the formula are vital for success. When one of the factors is missing, we are basically multiplying by zero, so the product of the formula is zero. All the effort in the world will not lead to success if a student is not also using good strategies and receiving help from others. Success is limited if any of three components are missing. Students learn strategies from instructors and other students when reading in the classroom is social. The help comes from other students, instructors, tutors, librarians, friends, etc. As an instructor, one of the most difficult things I tackle each semester is convincing students that getting help from others is not a sign of weakness but the exact opposite. Building the social dimension in the classroom encourages a positive attitude toward receiving help from others and provides a safe environment for students to share good strategies. Also, active students are expending effort. Students have a difficult time being passive when participating in the routines of the Reading Apprenticeship classroom. Students taking an active role in their learning identify their personal strengths and weaknesses and how they can help others. The we builds the me, and the me builds the we. Designing instruction that encourages intelligent practice and builds the social and personal dimensions is another formula for success.

STORYTIME

A great example of this comes from one of my classes in the spring of 2022. I begin each class by greeting each student and asking them how they are that day. Most of the time, I get "good" or "great" as a response usually followed by, "and how are you?" The greeting is a fantastic way for everyone to feel connected each session as well as seen and heard. Occasionally, a student shares more. In this case, Maria replied "NERVOUS!" I asked why. Maria said that her citizenship test was next week. The conversations started. Other students expressed their best wishes and provided words of encouragement. Later, this led to a conversation about celebrating. As it turns out, the traditional naturalization ceremonies had been canceled due to ongoing public health protocols related to the Covid-19 pandemic. In response, my class organized their own ceremony for Maria. Most students had never taken part in a naturalization ceremony and knew little about the citizenship process. These conversations led to some uncomfortable discussions that allowed students to surface personal experiences and share those experiences with others, and everyone's personal knowledge increased. One conversation led to Maria stating that not all people who speak Spanish are from Mexico. (She is from Colombia.) Other students began to feel more comfortable talking about personal experiences, which broke down many barriers to honest conversations. Students felt comfortable in their learning environment. Throughout the semester, my students' discussions around their readings were honest, productive, and enriched because students felt safe sharing their personal knowledge in a social setting. Another student shared that in his native country the schools posted all students' rankings by name for everyone to see. The rankings brought prestige or shame to their families in the town. Of course, this brought gasps from around the room and many questions. The students continued to learn from one another, and their awareness of individual experiences expanded. All these personal stories enriched our conversations and our connections to the novels, essays, and even the journal articles that the students read. The students began to develop their identity as readers or their personal dimension. Stories from other students appeared as connections in the journals and reading logs during the semester. When we discussed the reading logs, students shared their comments, questions, feelings, and connections. As a group, we looked for answers to their questions and identified connections to all the feelings and connections shared. Students realized that they could learn from each other. Many times, expertise surfaced during the discussions, and study groups formed—the we built the me once again.

Once students are primed to accept new strategies and help from others, how do instructors create an environment where the social dimension can thrive? Expecting students to share their personal thoughts on the first day of class is not reasonable. Instructors must establish a community where students feel safe to share. Icebreakers help, as do norm-setting or community agreement sessions. My students and I set classroom community agreements twice each semester. The first session occurs on the first or second day of class as a modified think-pair-share. The process begins by giving students five to six questions to "think" about for a few minutes. The questions ask the students to identify what helps them learn. What do they, their instructor, and their classmates need to do to create an environment conducive to learning? After thinking, the students form two lines facing each other. They use those "thinking" questions to academic speed date. One line of students moves with each question while the other line of students remains in place. When the speed dates are over, students have talked to at least five other students and discussed important behaviors needed for success in the course. The seeds for a safe learning environment are planted. The session ends in a class-wide share session where students determine the community agreements for the course. We repeat the sessions at midterm or a bit earlier if the class is not engaging with their instructor or their classmates. Many times, until the students have a few weeks of experience, they do not know what they need from the instructor and each other. The community agreements give students ownership in the class and their learning. After the activity, I ask students to connect the results of the community agreement session to the ideas of growth mindset and intelligent practice. Metacognitive conversations never end in a Reading Apprenticeship classroom.

With agreements in place to establish roles and expected behaviors and uncover any hidden rules, students are ready to begin sharing on a more personal level. The personal reading history assignment provides a great opportunity to do just that while also aiding the students in discovering their reader identities and starting yet another metacognitive conversation. Typically, the assignment begins with the instructors sharing their reading history as an example for the students and to demonstrate the instructors' willingness to be vulnerable themselves. The assignment then follows a think-pair-share routine. The prompts ask students to reflect on their experiences with reading such as . . .

A. What are your earliest memories of reading?
B. Who/what supported your reading development?
C. Provide an example of a time when you felt confident in your reading.
D. Provide an example of a time when you felt challenged as a reader.

Students consider these questions and share with a partner. The pair-share is followed by a class share-out. During this discussion, students look for connections between their histories and their classmates' histories. I ask my students to look back to the classroom agreements to determine if adjustments need to be made to the community agreements based on the students' histories. Over the years, I have also introduced students to other reading histories through texts written by Jeannette Walls and Sherman Alexie, and a video history featuring college and pro football player Malcolm Mitchell. Walls and Alexie both learned to read well early in life, but Malcolm Mitchell did not feel comfortable with his reading ability until well into college. All three have authored successful books, though. Their personal reading histories were unique, which gave them all very different paths to their writing careers. Their experiences always bring the success graphic (Martin, 2011) to mind. The picture shows two arrows. One arrow's shaft is straight, indicating a linear and straightforward path to success. The second arrow's shaft is a jumbled mess, indicating many detours, setbacks, and revisions on the path to success. The jumbled mess is the correct illustration for most successful pathways.

STORYTIME

When students share their personal histories, I always have a student say thank you for the assignment. The comment is usually something like "I thought I was the only person in the room who felt this way about reading," or "now I know I am not the only one who faces reading challenges." They can see themselves in each other, and the histories of Jeannette Walls, Sherman Alexie, and Malcolm Mitchell. A few years ago, one student was particularly affected by the assignment. Lucy came to me after class in tears—good tears. Lucy thanked me for the experience. Lucy grew up in a home where everyone liked to read but her. She had lived years with an undiagnosed reading disability. Even after her diagnosis, she felt like a reading outsider in her own home. Lucy said, "This is the first time I have ever felt like an insider when it comes to reading." She had appropriated the term *insider* from the reading history assignment. She felt safe and like she belonged. The sharing was working. Thank goodness for the we!

When students feel like they belong, they attempt the deeper reading and metacognitive work that in the past felt daunting. This feeling of belonging allows students to be vulnerable in their academic conversations with other students and provides the confidence needed to explore the strategies required to improve their engagement with text and to evaluate their ability to use the strategies and monitor their comprehension. After students feel comfortable in the classroom, talking to the text and think alouds are great ways to bring the social and personal dimensions of reading together. I describe talking to the text to my students as annotations on steroids. Talking to the text is more than the occasional comment or highlight. When talking to the text, readers develop their metacognitive skills. They make connections and ask questions of themselves, the text, and the author. Readers may stop occasionally and summarize in the margins to check their understanding. They are building and evaluating their background knowledge and monitoring their comprehension. When this conversation with the text becomes a routine, readers begin to recognize their strengths and weaknesses and the strategies that work well for them and the ones that do not. This work is building their identities as readers or the me. If they share these pumped-up annotations in the form of a think aloud or on a social learning platform, the activity enters the social dimension. A think aloud is not a read aloud. The readers are reading the text, but they are also revealing their thought processes and strategies as they go. In the same manner as talking to the text, the reader is asking questions, making connections, and making their personal thoughts and strategies visible to others. While listening to a think aloud, the listeners are making notes of the questions, connections, and strategies. The purpose is to increase the background knowledge of the listener, help both the reader and the listener to form strong neural pathways for the information, and for the listener to appropriate strategies from the reader. This brings all parts of the intelligent practice formula together. The readers are demonstrating effort, sharing their good strategies, and acting as help from others all at the same time. The listeners are also demonstrating effort and receiving help from others. Now, the metacognitive conversations are getting serious, thanks to the we!

STORYTIME

Think alouds are one of the most effective activities for teachers across all disciplines to use to apprentice their students into reading as a mathematician, physical scientist, social scientist, artist, or any other discipline expert. I have worked for years to encourage professors across my college to include literacy support in their classrooms. Many times, teachers in professional development sessions completed think alouds with one another, but most sounded like read alouds. Finally, a few years ago, a group of professors representing our ten high enrollment courses completed think alouds in pairs with a text from an introduction to music class, and this group got it! When dealing with a text outside their discipline, I believe their expert blind spots were removed. In the past, I encouraged faculty to bring texts from their disciplines with them to use in the think aloud. This was a mistake. When readers have a tremendous amount of background knowledge in a subject area, difficult areas in the text are not as obvious to them. The comments with the text outside their discipline included statements like "Wow, is this what it is like for my students to read my texts?" "I don't feel comfortable with some of my assumptions." "No wonder my students do not read the textbook assignments I give." While all these individuals are highly educated, they were not music history experts. This social activity brought them personal revelations. The we revealed the me. Thankfully, this activity led to many instructors developing plans to support their students' reading needs in their courses. Many instructors were developing the social dimension in their classrooms, but now they included the Reading Apprenticeship routines in their classrooms. After the professors implemented the routines in their courses, instructors and students responded to anonymous surveys. The results were overwhelmingly positive (General Education Strategy Team, 2021). The students and the instructors got it!

When we create a safe environment for our students to share experiences, strategies, and skills, the students are free to focus their efforts on intelligent practice and to grow personally as readers. Our reading experiences cannot be separated from our personal experiences. We are what we read, and we read what we are. Think about that for a minute. Much of our background knowledge comes from what we read, and the meaning we bring to our reading comes from earlier reading and other personal experiences. There is no escaping it! When we take our personal experiences into a social setting, we are sharing all those experiences with others as well as making the experiences of others our own. We are better readers when the sharing happens—the we helps the me, and the me helps the we.

Chapter 25

It's Time to Eighty-Six the Old Menu

Aimee Beckstrom Escalante

When I first learned about Reading Apprenticeship (RA) it was a natural extension of what had been modeled my entire childhood by my mother, Carol. How do you teach readers to move from feeling like an outsider with a text to finding and using tools to help them peek, and maybe live, inside it? While my experiences with Reading Apprenticeship have primarily focused on teaching texts for an education course, any text can make a reader feel like an outsider. Even a sticky plastic diner menu.

Carol was the best teacher I have ever known. She owned a learning center that specialized in teaching children and adults with dyslexia and comprehension issues. With her gentle and focused guidance, you learned with the impression that you had discovered it on your own. She was modeling and guiding you to "find" tools you didn't even know you possessed or required. If she sensed you needed help, you were immediately swept under her wing and steered toward a solution. While on a family vacation in the rural Idaho panhandle, my mother discovered that her friend's 13-year-old son, Mike, read at a 1st-grade level. She acted quickly and arranged with his parents to have him receive intensive reading (encoding and decoding) support while living with us in California for the summer. It was that summer that I had my first insight into the idea of how texts can make someone feel like an outsider. "I'll have a hamburger," Mike said as soon as he sat in the booth. The menu lay unopened on the table.

When he got up to wash his hands, my mother discreetly noted that Mike used tools to help him compensate for his reading challenges. If the menu didn't have pictures, he'd order something that was likely to be on the menu such as a hamburger or eggs. Mike had tools to help him navigate some menus, but they were inconsistent and failed him with a pictureless text. The tools he would be building with my mom went beyond making him more of an insider with standardized tests and textbook. He had the opportunity to shed his outsider status with decoding and comprehension in day-to-day activities.

From an early age, I felt like an insider with reading. I can't remember a time that I was not surrounded by books. If my sisters or I showed the slightest interest in a book or a subject, we were whisked off to the library or the bookstore so we could explore that author or subject further. Reading was presented as a bonding and pleasurable experience. If a text was challenging or dared to make us feel like an outsider, we had a guide to teach or remind us of the tools to unlock the text. My mother read aloud to me as a child. When we gathered for family vacations, this practice continued even after I graduated from college and had moved away. I still have the book we were in the middle of reading when she passed 22 years ago.

A natural extension of this experience was working at my mother's learning center. I began teaching reading—decoding, encoding, and comprehension—when I was 14 and continued working there in some capacity until I started teaching at the collegiate level. Occasionally I worked with adults and observed how they relied on compensatory techniques (e.g., contextual clues, redirection, distraction, etc.) that were more unreliable and limiting at higher reading levels. When I learned about Reading Apprenticeship in my current role as a lecturer at California State University, Monterey Bay, my understanding of reading privilege expanded beyond dyslexia and basic comprehension.

Since 2014, I have been teaching future teachers in a liberal studies class focused on issues in education. Over the years, a disturbing pattern of a class equity gap emerged. Latinx, particularly male, students were not performing as well as white students. Reading Apprenticeship helped me analyze and address why some of my students were feeling like outsiders with the reading and writing in my classes, which contributed to this equity gap. A survey of my class found that Latinx students were more likely to connect a lack of success with ability and were less likely to feel they belonged in the class—a much different perspective than I had as a student.

I had created a class culture and curriculum that didn't match the experience of some of my students. How many of my students felt like Mike in my class? They may not have needed someone to read a menu to them, but how many of the texts made them feel like insiders? Was I providing the same tools my mom did to help them confidently move from outsiders to insiders?

Implementing Reading Apprenticeship practices was a natural extension of my experience with Carol's modeling and culture at the learning center. I wanted to shift the class by helping students feel like insiders in the texts that we were using in class, not only by giving them the tools to "decode" them, but also by reinforcing and reminding them of all the texts and material in which they were already insiders—the decoding skills they already had. Students needed the opportunity to read and write in different genres that reinforced and enabled them to explore their own experiences and insider status. Students would begin by exploring who they were as students before they tackled subjects related to education as a whole. First, they created a non-linguistic representation of their cultural journey including the important influences that had taught them the core values they still carry with them as students (ESCALA, 2020). This assignment allowed for nonverbal communication and freedom of expression, and emphasized who they are and where they've come from. Since it was posted on a discussion forum, students were able to compare and contrast their experiences with those of their peers. By finding commonalities in their experiences and cultural journey, they helped build community and create a culture of learning and exploration. They could see the areas in which some of them were insiders, while others were outsiders. The following is a student sample and responses:

Student: O.

😊👨+👩💬❤️👨 💭(3)😊(me) (3)👶.

We 👨💭💬 in 2009 🏠. I 🙋 →⬆️ SOON TOP.

I 🎵💻🍽️✨⭕.

🎓🐎 and 🐈. 😊⋮. 🐾. →SOON 🏠

Continue... ✏️📘🥡→📱

I am describing when my family and I immigrated to the United States from Mexico back in 2009. I needed to adapt and learn the new language, English. I describe that I like to listen to music, watching TV, working out, going for walks, and playing soccer. I graduated King City High School and Hartnell College. I am now attending CSUMB and majoring in Liberal Studies.

Reply
What I see in your picture is how important your background is. Something we have in common is listening to music.

Reply
Hi O! What I see in your image is learning to adapt to a new place. It reminded me how I was when I came here to the U.S. in 2007. I did not know the language or anything at that time and I felt so left out. Adapting to a new country was not easy for me but I was able to get through the rough path of learning the new language.

Reply
Hi O, I see we have a lot of things in common. I myself and my family as well migrated here and I too had to adapt to a new environment as well as to learn a new language. I too like soccer, well more like LOVE soccer but you get the idea. What position do you play?

Reply
What I see in your cultural journey is that you had to face adversity at a young age. From having to learn the language of English at around 9 years old. What we have in common is we both have a cat and dog as pets. Great stuff, O go Barcelona!

After exploring who we were as students, we explored who we were as a class. Students also took the personal reading history (Schoenbach et al., 2012, p. 79) and shared their results with each other and with me. We were able to see how some of us grew up surrounded by books, while others had fewer than 10 books at home. About 50% of the students had parents who read in Spanish and 50% had parents who read in English. We used this data to explore and discuss how we could teach children in our future classrooms. We considered how our own personal reading history may influence what kinds of assignments and assessments we could create in our classrooms and how we might use our own cultural journeys to influence our curricula. We established class norms and analyzed behaviors (within and among ourselves, peers, and the teacher) that would help lead to success. All of us agreed and reinforced that communication with each other would help improve our chances of success.

Once we established our own status as insiders, we used that perspective to explore issues in education that make students feel like outsiders and how we as teachers can affect that. I changed the syllabus to include more diverse writers and texts including Hammond (2015) and Pierson (2013) in addition to the previous text I had used by Ritchhart (2015). We continued to read peer-reviewed texts, but I also added opinion pieces (Love, 2020), Tweets (Shalaby, 2022), Ted Talks (Ferrera, 2019), and comics (Inman, 2020). One of the assignments included writing a dialogue poem based on the assigned reading by Anderson-Zavala and colleagues (2017). Students had the opportunity to embrace the identity of an insider/outsider as it related to the different perspectives of the authors and theories. Some students chose to write one of the sides of dialogue in Spanish. It was the first time I had given the students an opportunity to write in a language other than English.

Student poem inspired by: "Fierce Urgency of Now: Building Movements to End the Prison Industrial Complex in Our Schools"

Title: Sin nombre

Quiero ser maestra cuando sea grande
    You can't because you're poor
Mi sueño es ir ala universidad para ayudar
    You can't because you're poor
Puedo hablar dos lenguages
    You can't because you're poor
Soy inteligente
You can't because you're poor

Student Poem inspired by "A Fierce Urgency of Now: Building Movements to End the Prison Industrial Complex in Our Schools"

But . . .
Mom can we pick up my chromebook today?
    Mijo, trabajo todo el día.
But I need it for class tomorrow . . .
    Entonces vas a perder un día de clase.
But that counts as an absence.
    Lo siento mijo.
But my teacher is going to give me a detention.
    No puedo faltar un día de trabajo.
But I am going to be behind on my classes.
    Nosotros necesitamos comer.
But Mom . . .
    Lo siento mijo . . .

Student poem inspired by "Fierce Urgency of Now: Building Movements to End the Prison Industrial Complex in Our Schools"

I am a hero
I look for hope
    There is no hope
I look for those to save
    I can not be saved
I seek to bring joy
    I only see fear
I won't give up
    You will waste your time
I won't abandon you
    You will forget me
People can change
    I don't know how
I can teach you
    But will I learn
With hope, we all will

The changes in the readings, assignments, and class community building were designed to reinforce that all of my students had insider strengths that they could use when texts or material made them feel like outsiders. Once we had spent a few weeks focusing on our status as insiders, we began the scaffolding for the research paper. Once we had spent a few weeks focusing on our status as insiders, we began the scaffolding for the research paper. In the past, the research paper for the class had been a gatekeeper. If students didn't pass the paper, they didn't pass the class. In the past, approximately 20% of students failed the paper and the class. It was incredibly high stakes and stressful for the students and me. The paper required that students read complex peer-reviewed articles that often served to reinforce a students' outsider status and the fail rate reflected that. My hope was that the emphasis on changing students' perceptions of their insider/outsider status would positively impact what tools they used and how they used them when approaching difficult texts. But how do you measure and assess these tools? When Mike completed his intensive summer tutoring, his reading assessments showed that his reading had improved a number of grade levels. He no longer needed someone to read the menu to him and he could enter high school as a more confident reader. He may have still felt like an outsider at times, but he had measurable tools. There isn't a similar assessment for insider/outsider perceptions. I am unable to assess whether or not students feel like insiders when reading the academic educational texts at the end of the semester. I have noted the changes in their writing as a whole and can measure the increasing improvement in the equity gap. However, grades are only one measure and can be impacted by many external factors, such as illness, housing, and finances. Sometimes success can be measured by the positive change of energy in a room, an "aha moment," or a subtle smile. Success can be measured by the excitement a teacher feels after class and the need to share when and how you see a student make a connection. Success can also be measured in how students reflect on their growth and movement from outsiders to insiders:

The writing assignment I am most proud of is the literature review. This was the first time I had to do one. At first, I was nervous and did not want to complete it. But, after attending virtual classes and having it explained, it was easy to write. . . . I believe that my writing skills have improved and the way I organize the information around my topic has improved. Since I am better able to research my topic, this has enabled me to organize my thoughts into coherent paragraphs. My writing has a better flow and makes better sense. . . . Thanks to the LS300 class, I was able to transfer the skills learned to other classes. These classes also required me to analyze, evaluate, and synthesize complex information. I was able to meet the requirements. One of my classes also required that I complete one literature review, and I was able to complete that assignment and gain a very good grade.—Student A

I enjoyed your class. It was not hard, but it allowed me to challenge myself to better things and gain confidence in speaking up about my thoughts. I liked the structure of the class and I enjoyed working in groups.—Student B

Some of my most treasured conversations with my mother were when she shared new ideas about teaching or talked through how to solve a challenge or experiment with a new technique. My mother would have embraced Reading Apprenticeship. She would have immediately seen the impact it can make for a student and how it can potentially foster a love, or at least lukewarm like, for reading. I long to tell her about the growth that my students have made and how I can feel the change in energy in the room when a student has an "aha moment." I feel that I am passing on her wisdom when I teach the next generation of teachers. Her legacy continues with them and their future students.

Afterword

In the opening of their article, "Threshold Concepts and Troublesome Knowledge: Linkages to Ways of Thinking and Practicing within the Disciplines," Meyer and Land (2003) write of threshold concepts that a threshold concept "represents a transformed way of understanding, or interpreting, or viewing something without which the learner cannot progress" (p. 1). In the context of this project, the learners—both the authors of this collection and many of the readers—are educators. Our transformed understandings relate to our students, our disciplines, the nature of reading, the nature of teaching, and the relationships among those participants in our classrooms.

We have proposed in this collection three conceptual thresholds that faculty must cross to use reading effectively in their courses:

- Reading is a problem-solving process.
- Students must be entrusted with the work of making sense of texts.
- Reading is social and personal.

As you read in the introductions to these sections in this book, each of these concepts is multidimensional. As you read in the chapters, there are many ways of enacting these understandings in learning situations. One of the themes that arises repeatedly in these chapters is the courage needed to do so, especially in light of the tensions of academic apprenticeship that underlie all of these threshold concepts. It is a risky business to share one's thinking. We might make an academic or a social mistake; we might reveal aspects of our worldview that we usually keep close to the vest. Learners and educators alike can expect to be challenged when we put our ideas next to one another in a reciprocal metacognitive conversation. And yet, in today's world of endlessly generating "content," building capacity for these negotiations—making sense of things while holding space for the wisdom of established expertise and the potential brilliance of new perspectives—is critical for both academic progress and personal and professional empowerment.

We hope that readers will take inspiration from the work done by the authors in this collection, that their bravery, commitment, and hard work will encourage you to take your own risks—sharing your own meaning-making processes and stumbles, really welcoming students' perspectives into the classroom, creating opportunities for metacognitive conversation. There will be oscillations in your practice when you try to enact these routines, activities, and understandings. Trust that stumbles forward still represent progress, and that will help you make it through.

We hope that your students will begin to see themselves more in your classrooms and disciplines and create their own places within those spaces. As students practice thinking about their strategies for problem solving, we expect they will take greater control of their learning and invest more effort in their learning from and with texts. Seeing themselves as scholars, we hope that your students will take more risks in your classrooms and beyond.

A few tips synthesized from these chapters:

- Take time and intention to build a strong learning community.
- Take time and intention to *maintain* a strong learning community.
- Model thinking, reading, and problem solving—briefly and often—especially with new genres or tasks.
- Provide opportunities for students to engage in guided practice, trying on reading, thinking, and problem-solving strategies modeled by others.
- Design your work to require and enable students to learn from and with texts.
- Design your work to require and enable students to learn from and with each other.
- Show students you value confusion and discomfort in your learning spaces—negotiate with them how much you all can tolerate.
- Embrace, model, and maintain an inquiry mindset. In other words, stay teachable!
- Build your own community to share stumbles, strategies, innovations, and inspirations. This work is more fun and enlightening together!

References

Abbot, W. M., & Nantz, K. (2017). Utilizing interdisciplinary insights to build effective reading skills. In A. S. Horning, D. L. Gollnitz, & C. R. Haller (Eds.), *What is college reading?* (pp. 139–160). The WAC Clearinghouse; University Press of Colorado. https://doi.org/10.37514/ATD-B.2017.0001

Accardo, A. L., & Finnegan, E. G. (2019). Teaching reading comprehension to learners with autism spectrum disorder: Discrepancies between teacher and research-recommended practices. *Autism: The International Journal of Research and Practice*, *23*(1), 236–246. https://doi.org/10.1177/1362361317730744

Adams, B., & Wilson, N. (2020). Building community in asynchronous online higher education courses through collaborative annotation. *Journal of Educational Technology*, *49*(2), 250–261. https://doi.org/10.1177/0047239520946422

Adams, N. E. (2015). Bloom's taxonomy of cognitive learning objectives. *Journal of the Medical Library Association*, *103*(3), 152–153. https://doi.org/10.3163/1536-5050.103.3.010

Adler-Kassner, L., & Wardle, E. (Eds.). (2015). *Naming what we know: Threshold concepts of writing studies*. Utah State University Press.

Adler-Kassner, L., & Wardle, E. (2020). Recognizing the limits of threshold concepts theory. In L. Adler-Kassner & E. Wardle (Eds.), *(Re)Considering what we know: Learning thresholds in writing, composition, rhetoric, and literacy* (1st ed.) (pp. 15–35). Utah State University Press. https://doi.org/10.7330/9781607329329

Adult Numeracy Center—TERC. (2023). Projects and research. https://www.terc.edu/projects/adult-numeracy-center/

ALA's Literacy Clearing House. (2023). Information Literacy. American Library Association. https://literacy.ala.org/information-literacy/

Ali, D. (2017). Safe spaces and brave spaces: Historical context and recommendations for student affairs professionals. *NASPA Policy and Practice Series*, *2*, 1–13. https://naspa.org/images/uploads/main/Policy_and_Practice_No_2_Safe_Brave_Spaces.pdf

American Association of School Librarians. (2022). *AASL Standards for the 21st-Century Learner*. American Library Association. https://standards.aasl.org/

Anderson, L. W., & Krathwohl, D. R. (2001). *A taxonomy for learning, teaching and assessing: A revision of Bloom's Taxonomy of educational objectives*. Longman.

Anderson-Zavala, C., Krueger-Henney, P., Meiners, E., & Pour-Khorshid, F. (2017). Fierce urgency of now: Building movements to end the prison industrial complex in our schools. *Multicultural Perspectives*, *19*(3), 151–154. https://doi.org/10.1080/15210960.2017.1331743

Andreassen, R., Jensen, M. S., & Bråten, I. (2017). Investigating self-regulated study strategies among postsecondary students with and without dyslexia: A diary method study. *Reading & Writing*, *30*(9), 1891–1916. https://doi.org/10.1007/s11145-017-9758-9

Anson, C. M. (2016). Habituated practice can lead to entrenchment. In L. Adler-Kassner & E. Wardle (Eds.), *Naming what we know: Threshold concepts of writing studies* (pp. 77–78). Utah State University Press.

Anson, C. M. (2017). Writing to read, revisited. In A. S. Horning, D. L. Gollnitz, & C. R. Haller (Eds.), *What is college reading?* The WAC Clearinghouse; University Press of Colorado. https://doi.org/10.37514/ATD-B.2017.0001

Aschenbach, C., Blake, T., Gavaskar, V., Sanchez, R., & Whetzel, T. (2021). *The role of faculty in tutoring and learning centers in the community college*. Academic Senate for California Community Colleges.

Association for Undergraduate Education at Research Universities (UERU). (2022). *The equity/excellence imperative: A 2030 blueprint for undergraduate education at U.S. research universities.* https://wac.colostate.edu/docs/books/boyer2030/report.pdf

Association of College & Research Libraries. (2015). *ACRL Framework for Information Literacy for Higher Education*. American Library Association. https://www.ala.org/acrl/standards/ilframework

Baron, N. (2021). *How we read now: Strategic choices for print, screen, and audio*. Oxford University Press.

Barradell, S. (2013). The identification of threshold concepts: A review of theoretical complexities and methodological challenges. *Higher Education, 65*(2), 265–276. https://doi.org/10.1007/s10734-012-9542-3

Bathgate, M. E., Aragón, O. R., Cavanagh, A. J., Frederick, J., & Graham, M. J. (2019). Supports: A key factor in faculty implementation of evidence-based teaching. *CBE—Life Sciences Education, 18*(2), 1–9. https://doi.org/10.1187/cbe.17-12-0272

Behrens, S. J. (1994). A conceptual analysis and historical overview of information literacy. *College & Research Libraries, 55*(4), 309–322. https://doi.org/10.5860/crl_55_04_309

Bergey, B. W., Deacon, S. H., & Parrila, R. K. (2017). Metacognitive reading and study strategies and academic achievement of university students with and without a history of reading difficulties. *Journal of Learning Disabilities, 50*(1), 81–94. https://doi.org/10.1177/0022219415597020

Bloom, B. S. (1956). *Taxonomy of educational objectives, handbook 1: The cognitive domain*. David McKay.

Blummer, B., & Kenton, J. M. (2014). *Improving student information search: A metacognitive approach.* Chandos Publishing. https://doi.org/10.1016/C2013-0-18367-5

Bourdieu, P., Passeron, J. C., & de Saint-Martin, M. (1994). *Academic discourse*. Stanford University Press.

Bowler, L. (2010). A taxonomy of adolescent metacognitive knowledge during the information search process. *Library & Information Science Research, 32*(1), 27–42. https://doi.org/10.1016/j.lisr.2009.09.005

Bransford, J. D., Brown, A. L., & Cocking, R. R. (Eds.). (1999). *How people learn: Brain, mind, experience, and school*. National Academies Press.

Britt, M.A., Rouet, J. F., & Durik, A. M. (2018). *Literacy beyond comprehension*. Routledge.

Broz, W. J. (2011). Not reading: The 800-pound mockingbird in the classroom. *English Journal, 100*(5), 15–20.

Bryk, A. S., & Schneider, B. (2003). Trust in schools: A core resource for school reform. *Educational leadership, 60*(6), 40–45.

Bunn, M. (2013). Motivation and connection: Teaching reading (and writing) in the composition classroom. *College Composition and Communication, 64*(3), 496–516.

California Community Colleges' Success Network. (2023). *Communities of practice*. https://3csn.org/communities-of-practice

California Community Colleges' Success Network. (2024, February 24). *The story of 3CSN*. https://3csn.org/story-of-3csn

Campaign for College Opportunity. (2017). *Spotlight Practice: Reading Apprenticeship Community College STEM Network.*

Cantor, N. (2020). Transforming the academy: The urgency of recommitting higher education to the public good. *Liberal Education, 106*(1–2), 48–55.

Carillo, E. C. (2015). *Securing a place for reading in composition: The importance of teaching for transfer*. Utah State University Press.

Carillo, E. C., & Horning, A. S. (2021). *Teaching critical reading and writing in the era of fake news.* Peter Lang.

Carter, M. (2007). Ways of knowing, doing, and writing in the disciplines. *College Composition and Communication, 58*(3), 385–418.

CAST. (2018). Universal Design for Learning Guidelines version 2.2. http://udlguidelines.cast.org

Chevalier, T. M., Parrila, R., Ritchie, K. C., & Deacon, S. H. (2017). The role of metacognitive reading strategies, metacognitive study and learning strategies, and behavioral study and learning strategies in predicting academic success in students with and without a history of reading difficulties. *Journal of Learning Disabilities, 50*(1), 34–48. https://doi.org/10.1177/0022219415588850

Chronicle of Higher Education (2022). The student-success challenges ahead. https://www.chronicle.com/featured/student-success/challenges-ahead?cid=gen_sign_in

Clinton-Lisell, V., Taylor, T., Carlson, S. E., Davison, M. L., & Seipel, B. (2022). Performance on reading comprehension assessments and college achievement: A meta-analysis. *Journal of College Reading and Learning, 52*(3), 191–211, https://doi.org/10.1080/10790195.2022.2062626

Cohen, E. G., & Lotan, R. A. (2014). *Designing groupwork: Strategies for the heterogeneous classroom* (3rd ed.). Teachers College Press.

College of San Mateo. (2013). *Reading Apprenticeship Faculty Inquiry Group.* Unpublished raw data.

Cook, L. K., & Mayer, R. E. (1988). Teaching readers about the structure of scientific text. *Journal of Educational Psychology, 80*(4), 448–456. https://doi.org/10.1037/0022-0663.80.4.448

Cook-Sather, A., & Alter, Z. (2011). What is and what can be: How a liminal position can change learning and teaching in higher education. *Anthropology and Education Quarterly, 42*(2011), 37–53. https://doi.org/10.1111/j.1548-1492.2010.01109.x

Corrin, W., Somers, M. A., Kemple, J., Nelson, E., & Sepanik, S. (2008). *The Enhanced Reading Opportunities Study: Findings from The Second Year of Implementation.* National Center for Education Evaluation and Regional Assistance, U.S. Department of Education.

Costino, K. A. (2018). Equity-minded faculty development: An intersectional identity-conscious community of practice model for faculty learning. *Metropolitan Universities, 29*(1). https://doi.org/10.18060/22170

Cousin, G. (2009). *Researching learning in higher education.* Routledge.

Croce, K., & K. McCormick, M. (2020). Developing disciplinary literacy in mathematics: Learning from professionals who use mathematics in their jobs. *Journal of Adolescent & Adult Literacy, 63*(4), 415–423. https://doi.org/10.1002/jaal.1013

Davies, L. J. (2017). Getting to the root of the problem: Teaching reading as a process in the sciences. In A. S. Horning, D. L. Gollnitz, & C. R. Haller (Eds.), *What is college reading?* (pp. 161–182). The WAC Clearinghouse; University Press of Colorado. https://doi.org/10.37514/ATD-B.2017.0001

Deacon, S., Cook, K., & Parrila, R. (2012). Identifying high functioning dyslexics: Is self-report of early reading problems enough? *Annals of Dyslexia, 62*(2), 120–134. http://doi.org/10.1007/s11881-012-0068-2

Delpit, L. D. (1992). Acquisition of literate discourse: Bowing before the master? *Theory Into Practice, 31*(4), 296–302. https://doi.org/10.1080/00405849209543556

Deslauriers, L., McCarty, L. S., Miller, K., & Kestin, G. (2019). Measuring actual learning versus feeling of learning in response to being actively engaged in the classroom. *Proceedings of the National Academy of Sciences (PNAS), 116*(39), 19251–19257. https://doi.org/10.1073/pnas.1821936116

DeTemple, J., & Sarrouf, J. (2020, April 21). Questions for connection and purpose. *Inside Higher Ed.*

DiGiacomo, D. K., Usher, E. L., Han, J., Abney, J. M., Cole, A. E., & Patterson, J. T. (2023). The benefits of belonging: Students' perceptions of their online learning experiences. *Distance Education, 44*(1), 24–39. https://doi.org/10.1080/01587919.2022.2155615

Donaldson, J. P., & Allen-Handy, A. (2020). The nature and power of conceptualizations of learning. *Educational Psychology Review, 32*(2), 545–570. https://doi.org/10.1007/s10648-019-09503-2

Downs, D. (2021). Critical reading in a screen paradigm: From deficit to default. *Pedagogy, 21*(2), 205–224. https://www.muse.jhu.edu/article/793508

Durisen, R. H., & Pilachowski, C. A. (2004). Decoding astronomical concepts. In D. Pace (Series Ed.) & J. Middendorf (Vol. Ed.), Decoding the disciplines: Helping students learn disciplinary ways of thinking: Number 98. *New directions for teaching and learning* (1st ed., pp. 33–43). Jossey-Bass.

Dweck, C. S. (2006). *Mindset: The new psychology of success.* Random House Publishing.

Dweck, C. S. (2012). *Mindset: How you can fulfill your potential.* Robinson Publishing.

Edmunds, K. (2017, December). Weaving more effective teaching and learning practices in mathematics and beyond: Adopting reading apprenticeship at Pasadena City College. STEM Active Learning Vignette Series. Equal Measure. http://www.equalmeasure.org/wp-content/uploads/2017/12/PCC-WestEd-Vignette_FINAL_011018_updated-with-date-on-cover.pdf

Elias, M., Zins, J., Weissberg, R. P., Frey, K. S., Greenberg, M. T., & Haynes, N. M. (1997). The need for social and emotional learning. In *Promoting Social and Emotional Learning.* Association for Supervision & Curriculum Development.

Erickson, B. L., Peters, C. B., & Strommer, D. W. (2006). *Teaching first-year college students.* (Rev. and expanded ed.). Jossey-Bass.

ESCALA Educational Services. (2020). Create a cultural journey. *The Certificate of College Teaching and Learning in Hispanic Serving Institutions.* https://www.escalaeducation.com/our-offerings/courses-programs-webinars/certificate-in-college-teaching-learning-in-hsis

Fang, Z., & Chapman, S. (2020). Disciplinary literacy in mathematics: One mathematician's reading practices. *Journal of Mathematical Behavior, 59,* 1–15. https://doi.org/10.1016/j.jmathb.2020.100799

Feldman, J. (2018). *Grading for equity: What it is, why it matters, and how it can transform schools and classrooms.* Corwin.

Felten, P., & Lambert, L. M. (2020). *Relationship-rich education: How human connections drive success in college.* Johns Hopkins University Press.

Ferrera, A. (2019, April). My identity is a superpower—not an obstacle [Video]. Ted Talk. https://www.ted.com/talks/america_ferrera_my_identity_is_a_superpower_not_an_obstacle.

Folse, K. S. (2004). *Vocabulary myths: Applying second language research to classroom teaching.* University of Michigan Press.

Freire, P. (1963). Conscientização e alfabetização: Uma nova visão do processo. *Estudos Universitários: Revista de Cultura da Universidade do Recife, 4,* 5–23.

Freire, P. (1981). Criando métodos de pesquisa alternativa: Aprendendo a fazê-la melhor através da ação. In C. R. Brandão (Ed.), *Pesquisa Participante* (pp. 34–41). Editora Brasiliense.

Garcia, G. A. (2019). *Becoming Hispanic serving institutions: Opportunities for colleges and universities.* Johns Hopkins University Press.

Garrison, D. R., Anderson, T., & Archer, W. (1999). Critical inquiry in a text-based environment: Computer conferencing in higher education. *The Internet and Higher Education, 2*(2), 87–105. https://doi.org/10.1016/S1096-7516(00)00016-6

Garrison, R. (2019). Online collaboration principles. *Online Learning, 10*(1), 25–34. https://doi.org/10.24059/olj.v10i1.1768

Gay, G. (2018). *Culturally responsive teaching: Theory, research, and practice* (3rd ed.). Teachers College Press.

Gee, J. Paul. (2004). *Situated language and learning: A critique of traditional schooling.* Routledge.

General Education Strategy Team. (2021). Implementation of reading strategies in the classroom at Pellissippi State Community College. Unpublished raw data.

Gilley, B. H., & Clarkston, B. (2014). Collaborative testing: Evidence of learning in a controlled in-class study of undergraduate students. *Journal of College Science Teaching, 43*(3), 83–91.

Gogan, B. (2017). Reading as transformation. In A. S. Horning, D. L. Gollnitz, & C. R. Haller (Eds.), *What is college reading?* (pp. 41–56). STET WAC Clearinghouse, University Press of Colorado. https://doi.org/10.37514/ATD-B.2017.0001

Goldman, S. R., Britt, M. A., Brown, W., Cribb, G., George, M., Greenleaf, C., Lee, C. D., Shanahan, C., & Project READI. (2016). Disciplinary literacies and learning to read for understanding: A conceptual framework for disciplinary literacy. *Educational Psychologist, 51*(2), 219–246. https://doi.org/10.1080/00461520.2016.1168741

Graff, N., Kersnar, R., Shapiro, D., & Leuzinger, R. (2022). Understandings of reading: Insights from faculty development with Reading Apprenticeship. In K. Manarin (Ed.), *Reading across the disciplines* (pp. 44–63). Indiana University Press.

Greenleaf, C., Hanson, T., Herman, J., Litman, C., Rosen, R., Schneider, S., & Silver, D. (2011a). *A study of the efficacy of Reading Apprenticeship professional development for high school history and science teaching and learning.* Final report to Institute for Education Sciences.

Greenleaf, C., Litman, C., Hanson, T. L., Rosen, R., Boscardin, C. K., Herman, J., Jones, B. (2011b). Integrating literacy and science in biology: Teaching and learning impacts of Reading Apprenticeship professional development. *American Educational Research Journal, 48*(3), 647–717. https://doi.org/10.3102/0002831210384839

Greenleaf, C., Schoenbach, R., Friedrich, L., Murphy, L., & Hogan, N. (2023). *Reading for understanding: How Reading Apprenticeship improves disciplinary learning in secondary and college classrooms* (3rd ed.). Jossey-Bass.

Greenleaf, C., & Valencia, S. W. (2017). Missing in action: Learning from texts in subject-matter classrooms. In K. A. Hinchman & D. A. Appleman (Eds.), *Adolescent literacies: A handbook of practice-based research* (pp. 235–256). Guilford Press.

Grim, V., Pace, D., & Shopkow, L. (2004). Learning to use evidence in the study of history. In D. Pace (Series Ed.), & J. Middendorf (Vol. Ed.), Decoding the disciplines: Helping students learn disciplinary ways of thinking: Number 98. *New directions for teaching and learning* (1st ed., pp. 57–66). Jossey-Bass.

Gyuris, E., & Castell, L. (2013). Tell them or show them? How to improve science students' skills of critical reading. *International Journal of Innovation in Science and Mathematics Education, 21*(1), 70–80.

Hammond, Z. (2015). *Culturally responsive teaching and the brain: Promoting authentic engagement and rigor among culturally and linguistically diverse students.* Corwin/Sage.

Highline College. (2024). *Pass rates table (mathematics).* https://www.highline.edu/

Hogan, N., Magruder, E., and McCormick, S. (2023). Texts, tasks, and talk: A social learning pathway to STEM literacy, engagement and belonging. In M. D. Cox and J. McDonald (Eds.), Leading, facilitating, and convening educational social learning spaces: Theory and practice [Special issue]. *Journal on Excellence in College Teaching, 34*(4).

Hogan, N., & Rose, S. (2018). This is what we came here to do: Literacy at the heart of institutional culture change. *Journal of Adolescent & Adult Literacy, 62*(3), 337–341.

hooks, b. (1994a). Seeing and making culture: Representing the poor. In *Outlaw culture: Resisting representations.* Routledge.

hooks, b. (1994b). *Teaching to transgress: Education as the practice of freedom.* Routledge.

Horning, A. S. (2013). Elephants, pornography and safe sex: Understanding and addressing students' reading problems across the curriculum. In A. S. Horning (Ed.), Reading and writing across the curriculum [Special issue]. *Across the Disciplines, 10*(4). https://wac.colostate.edu/atd/special/reading/

Horning, A., & Becker, A. (2006). *Revision: History, theory, and practice.* Parlor Press; The WAC Clearinghouse. https://wac.colostate.edu/books/referenceguides/horning-revision/

Horning, A. S., Gollnitz, D. L., & Haller, C. R. (Eds.). (2017). *What is college reading?* The WAC Clearinghouse; University Press of Colorado. https://doi.org/10.37514/ATD-B.2017.0001

Houtman, E. (2015). "Mind-blowing": Fostering self-regulated learning in information literacy instruction. *Communications in Information Literacy, 9*(1), 6–18. https://doi.org/10.15760/comminfolit.2015.9.1.178

Howard, G. R. (2016). *We can't teach what we don't know: White teachers, multiracial schools* (3rd ed.). Multicultural Education Series.

Hua, Y., Hendrickson, J. M., Therrien, W. J., Woods-Groves, S., Ries, P. S., & Shaw, J. J. (2012). Effects of combined reading and question generation on reading fluency and comprehension of three young adults with autism and intellectual disability. *Focus on Autism and Other Developmental Disabilities, 27*(3), 135–146. https://doi.org/10.1177/1088357612448421

Hurley, T. A., and Fekrazad, A. (2020). E-textbooks, inclusive access, and academic performance. In T. A. Hurley (Ed.), *Inclusive access and open educational resources e-text programs in higher education* (pp. 177–184). Springer.

Immordino-Yang, M. H., Darling-Hammond, L., & Krone, C. (2019). Nurturing nature: How brain development is inherently social and emotional, and what this means for education. *Educational Psychologist, 54*(3), 2019, 185–204. https://doi.org/10.1080/00461520.2019.1633924

Inman, M. (2020). *You're not going to believe what I'm about to tell you.* The Oatmeal. https://theoatmeal.com/comics/believe

Inoue, A. B. (2019). How do we language so people stop killing each other, or what do we do about white language supremacy? *College Composition and Communication, 71*(2), 352–369.

Inoue, A. B. (2020). Teaching antiracist reading. *Journal of College Reading and Learning, 50*(3), 134–156. https://doi.org/10.1080/10790195.2020.1787079

Intrator, S. M. (2012). "Spots of time that glow": Reverence, epiphany, and the teaching life. In A. G. Rud & J. Garrison (Eds.), *Teaching with reverence*. Palgrave Macmillan. https://doi.org/10.1057/9781137012166_5

Jamieson, S. (2013). Reading and engaging sources: What students' use of sources reveals about advanced reading skills. In A. S. Horning (Ed.), Reading and writing across the curriculum [Special issue]. *Across the Disciplines, 10*(4). https://wac.colostate.edu/atd/special/reading/

Jensen, M. N., & Scharff, L. F. V. (2019). Improving critical reading with e-texts: A controlled study in a collegiate philosophy course. *Journal of the Scholarship of Teaching and Learning, 19*(3), 49–64. https://doi.org/10.14434/josotl.v19i2.23868

Jeong, J. Y., & Gweon, G. (2021). Advantages of print reading over screen reading: A comparison of visual patterns, reading performance, and reading attitudes across paper, computers, and tablets. *International Journal of Human–Computer Interaction, 37*(17), 1674–1684. https://doi.org/10.1080/10447318.2021.1908668

Kahlert, S. (2021). *The persistent writer: How to thrive in your college writing class.* Perdisco Press.

Kalir, J. (2022). *The value of social annotation for teaching and learning: Promoting comprehension, collaboration and critical thinking with Hypothesis* [White Paper]. Hypothesis. https://web.hypothes.is/research-white-paper/

Kezar, A. (2014). *How colleges change: Understanding, leading, and enacting change.* Routledge.

Killingsworth, M. J. (2005). *Appeals in modern rhetoric: An ordinary language approach.* Southern Illinois University Press.

Kimmerer, R. W. (2013). *Braiding sweetgrass: Indigenous wisdom, scientific knowledge, and the teachings of plants.* Milkweed Editions.

Knight, V. F., & Sartini, E. (2015). A comprehensive literature review of comprehension strategies in core content areas for students with autism spectrum disorder. *Journal of Autism and Developmental Disorders, 45*(5), 1213–1229. https://doi.org/10.1007/s10803-014-2280-x

Krashen, S. (2013). *Second language acquisition: Theory, applications, and some conjectures.* Cambridge University Press.

Land, R., Rattray, J., & Vivian, P. (2014). Learning in the liminal space: A semiotic approach to threshold concepts. *Higher Education, 67*, 199–217. https://doi.org/10.1007/s10734-013-9705-x

Lekas, H. M., Pahl, K., & Fuller, L. C. (2020). Rethinking cultural competence: Shifting to cultural humility. *Health Service Insights, 13*, 1–4. https://doi.org/10.1177/1178632920970580

Li, M., & Li, J. (2023). Using Perusall to motivate students' curriculum-based academic reading. *Journal of Computers in Education (the Official Journal of the Global Chinese Society for Computers in Education), 10*(2), 377–401. https://doi.org/10.1007/s40692-022-00234-y

Li, W., & Zhang, F. (2021). Tracing the path toward self-regulated revision: An interplay of instructor feedback, peer feedback, and revision goals. *Frontiers in Psychology, 11*(2020). https://doi.org/10.3389/fpsyg.2020.612088

Liston, D. P. (2004). The lure of learning in teaching. *Teachers College Record, 106*(3), 459–486. https://doi.org/10.1111/j.1467-9620.2004.00347

Lochhead, J., & Whimbey, A. (1987). Teaching analytical reasoning through thinking aloud pair problem solving. In J. E. Stice (Ed.), Developing critical thinking and problem-solving abilities. *New Directions for Teaching and Learning, 1987*(30).

Lockhart, T., & Soliday, M. (2016). The critical place of reading in writing transfer (and beyond): A report of student experiences. *Pedagogy, 16*(1), 23–37. https://doi.org/10.1215/15314200-3158589

Lombardi, A., Murray, C., & Kowitt, J. (2016). Social support and academic success for college students with disabilities: Do relationship types matter? *Journal of Vocational Rehabilitation, 44*, 1–13. https://doi.org/10.3233/JVR-150776

Love, B. (2020, June 20). An essay for teachers who understand racism is real. *Education Week*. https://www.edweek.org/leadership/opinion-an-essay-for-teachers-who-understand-racism-is-real/2020/06

Lunsford, A. (2016). Writing is performative. In L. Adler-Kassner & E. Wardle (Eds.), *Naming what we know: Threshold concepts of writing studies* (classroom ed., pp. 43–44). Utah State University Press.

MacGregor, J. (1990). Collaborative learning: Shared inquiry as a process of reform. In M. D. Svinicki (Ed.), The changing face of college teaching (pp. 19–30), *New Directions for Teaching and Learning, 1990*(42). https://doi.org/10.1002/tl.37219904204

Manarin, K., Carey, M., Rathburn, M., & Ryland, G. (2015). *Critical reading in higher education: Academic goals and social engagement*. Indiana University Press.

Manzano-Sanchez, H., Outley, C., Gonzalez, J. E., & Matarrita-Cascante, D. (2018). The influence of self-efficacy beliefs in the academic performance of Latina/o students in the United States: A systematic literature review. *Hispanic Journal of Behavioral Sciences, 40*(2), 176–209. https://doi.org/10.1177/0739986318761323

Martin, D. (2011). *This is a book*. Grand Central Publishing.

McKinney, J. P., McKinney, K. G., Franiuk, R., & Schweitzer, J. (2006). The college classroom as a community: Impact on student attitudes and learning. *College Teaching, 54*(3), 281–284. https://doi.org/10.3200/CTCH.54.3.281-284

McLeod, Pauline, & Huddleston, Michael (illustrator). (1994). *Aboriginal art & stories*. Intechnics Pty Ltd.

McNair, T. B., Albertine, S., Cooper, M. A., McDonald, N., & Major, T. (2016). *Becoming a student-ready college: A new culture of leadership for student success*. Jossey-Bass.

Meyer, A., Rose, D. H., & Gordon, D. (2014). *Universal design for learning: Theory and Practice*. CAST Professional Publishing.

Meyer, J., & Land, R. (2003). Threshold concepts and troublesome knowledge: Linkages to ways of thinking and practicing within the disciplines. In C. Rust (Ed.), *Improving student learning: Theory and practice—Ten years on*. OCSLD, Oxford.

Meyer, J. H. F., and Land, R. (2005). Threshold concepts and troublesome knowledge (2): Epistemological considerations and a conceptual framework for teaching and learning. *Higher Education, 49*(3), 373–388. https://doi.org/10.1007/s10734-004-6779-5

Miller, C. R. (1984). Genre as social action. *Quarterly Journal of Speech, 70*(2), 151–167. https://doi.org/10.1080/00335638409383686

Miller, R. E. (2016). On digital reading. *Pedagogy, 16*(1), 153–164.

Moje, E. B. (2015). Doing and teaching disciplinary literacy with adolescent learners: A social and cultural enterprise. *Harvard Educational Review, 85*(2), 254–278.

Moll, L. C. (2019). Elaborating funds of knowledge: Community-oriented practices in international contexts. *Literacy Research, 68*(1), 130–138. https://doi.org/10.1177/2381336919870805

Moon, B., Ed. (1999). Literary terms: A practical glossary. *National Council of Teachers of English*, NCTE Chalkface Series, pp. 127–134.

Muellner, L. (2015). Annotations and the ancient Greek hero: Past, present, and future. *Comunicar, 44*(22), 45–53. http://dx.doi.org/10.3916/C44-2015-05

Murdoch, D., English, A. R., Hintz, A., & Tyson, K. (2020). Feeling heard: Inclusive education, transformative learning, and productive struggle. *Educational Theory, 70*(5), 653–679. https://doi.org/10.1111/edth.12449

Murillo, L. A., & Schall, J. M. (2016). "They didn't teach us well": Mexican-origin students speak out about their readiness for college literacy. *Journal of Adolescent & Adult Literacy, 60*(3), 315–323. https://doi.org/10.1002/jaal.581

Nasir, N. I. S., & Hand, V. (2008). From the court to the classroom: Opportunities for engagement, learning, and identity in basketball and classroom mathematics. *Journal of the Learning Sciences, 17*(2), 143–179. https://doi.org/10.1080/10508400801986108

National Academies of Sciences, Engineering, and Medicine. (2018). *How people learn II: Learners, contexts, and cultures*. National Academies Press. https://doi.org/10.17226/24783

New Teacher Project. (2018). *The opportunity myth: What students can show us about how school is letting them down—and how to fix it*. https://tntp.org/publications/view/the-opportunity-myth

Nguyen, K. M. (2021). Limiting labels: Opportunities to learn and college readiness among English language learners. *Sociology Compass, 15*(2). https://doi.org/10.1111/soc4.12848

Nilson, L. B. (2013). *Creating self-regulated learners: Strategies to strengthen students' self-awareness and learning skills*. Stylus Publishing.

Noah, T. (2020). *Born a crime: Stories from a South African childhood*. Cornelsen.

Odom, M. L. (2013). Not just for writing anymore: What WAC can teach us About reading to learn. In A. S. Horning (Ed.), Reading and writing across the curriculum [Special issue]. *Across the Disciplines, 10*(4). https://wac.colostate.edu/atd/special/reading/

Pacansky-Brock, M. (n.d.). Advancing Professional Development as equity infrastructure. *Bumper Videos & Microlectures*. https://brocansky.com/humanizing/bumper-microlectures

Pace, D. (2004). Decoding the reading of history: An example of the process. In D. Pace (Series Ed.) & J. Middendorf (Vol. Ed.), Decoding the disciplines: Helping students learn disciplinary ways of thinking: Number 98. *New directions for teaching and learning* (1st ed., pp. 13–22). Jossey-Bass.

Pace, D. (Series Ed.), & Middendorf, J. (Vol. Ed.). (2004). Decoding the disciplines: Helping students learn disciplinary ways of thinking: Number 98. *New directions for teaching and learning* (1st ed.). Jossey-Bass.

Panadero, E. (2017). A review of self-regulated learning: six models and four directions for research. *Frontiers in Psychology, 8*, 422. https://doi.org/10.3389/fpsyg.2017.00422

Paulson, E. J. (2012). A discourse mismatch theory of college learning. In R. Hodges & K. Agee (Eds.), *Handbook for training peer tutors and mentors* (pp. 7–10). College Reading and Learning Association.

Pearlman, S. J. (2013). It's not that they can't *read*; It's that they *can't* read: Can we create "citizen experts" through interactive assessment? In A. S. Horning (Ed.), Reading and writing across the curriculum [Special Issue]. *Across the Disciplines, 10*(4). https://wac.colostate.edu/atd/special/reading/

Pearson, P. D., Palincsar, A., Biancarosa G., et al. (2020). *Reaping the rewards of the reading for understanding initiative*. National Academy of Education.

Pedersen, H. F., Fusaroli, R., Lauridsen, L. L., & Parrila, R. (2016). Reading processes of university students with dyslexia—An examination of the relationship between oral reading and reading comprehension. *Dyslexia (Chichester, England), 22*(4), 305–321. https://doi.org/10.1002/dys.1542

Pichette, F. (2005). Time spent on reading and reading comprehension in second language learning. *Canadian Modern Language Review/La revue canadienne des langues vivantes, 62*(2), 243–262. https://doi.org/10.1353/cml.2006.0008.

Pierson, R. (2013). Every kid needs a champion [Video]. *TED Talks Education*. https://www.ted.com/talks/rita_pierson_every_kid_needs_a_champion?language=en

Polman, J. (2009). Mastery and appropriation as means to understand the interplay of history learning and identity trajectories. *Journal of the Learning Sciences, 15*(2), 221–259. https://doi.org/10.1207/s15327809jls1502_3

Polya, G. (1945). *How to solve it: A new aspect of mathematical method*. Princeton University Press.

Porter, G. W. (2022). Collaborative online annotation: Pedagogy, assessment and platform comparisons. *Frontiers in Education (Lausanne), 7*, Article 852849. https://doi.org/10.3389/feduc.2022.852849

Powers, M., and Apigo, M. J. (n.d.). *The growth mindset academy*. https://www.thegrowthmindsetacademy.com/

Pretzlaff, E. (2017). Seeing the differences: Writing in history (and elsewhere). In P. Sullivan, H. Tinberg, & S. Blau (Eds.), *Deep reading: Teaching reading in the writing classroom* (pp. 109–118). National Council of Teachers of English.

Price, D. (2018). *Laziness does not exist, but unseen barriers do.* https://humanparts.medium.com/laziness-does-not-exist-3af27e312d01

Price, D. (2021). *Laziness does not exist.* Atria Books.

"Records of Three Kingdoms." (n.d.). In *New world encyclopedia.* https://www.newworldencyclopedia.org/entry/Records_of_Three_Kingdoms

Reed, M. G., Godmaire, H., Abernethy, P., & Guertin, M. A. (2014). Building a community of practice for sustainability: Strengthening learning and collective action of Canadian biosphere reserves through a national partnership. *Journal of Environmental Management, 145,* 230–239. https://doi.org/10.1016/j.jenvman.2014.06.030

Renton Technical College. (2011). *Reading Apprenticeship course data.* Unpublished raw data.

Ritchey, K. A., & List, A. (2022). Task-oriented reading: A framework for improving college students' reading compliance and comprehension. *College Teaching, 70*(3), 280–295. https://doi.org/10.1080/87567555.2021.1924607

Ritchhart, R. (2015). *Creating cultures of thinking: The 8 forces we must master to truly transform our schools.* Wiley.

Ritchhart, R., & Church, M. (2020). *The power of making thinking visible: Practices to engage and empower all learners.* Wiley.

Ritchhart, R., Church, M., & Morrison, K. (2011). *Making thinking visible: How to promote engagement, understanding, and independence for all learners.* Jossey-Bass.

Rodrigue, T. K. (2017a). The digital reader, the alphabetic writer, and the space between: A study in digital reading and source-based writing. *Computers and Composition, 46,* 4–20. https://doi.org/10.1016/j.compcom.2017.09.005

Rodrigue, T. K. (2017b). Digital reading: Genre awareness as a tool for reading comprehension. *Pedagogy: Critical Approaches to Teaching Literature, Language, Culture, and Composition, 17*(2), 235–257. https://doi.org/10.1215/15314200-3770133

Roosevelt, T. (1910). "Citizenship in a Republic," Speech at the Sorbonne, Paris, https://www.presidency.ucsb.edu/documents/address-the-sorbonne-paris-france-citizenship-republic

Rose, M. (1980). Rigid rules, inflexible plans, and the stifling of language: A cognitivist analysis of writer's block. *College Composition and Communication, 31*(4), 389–401.

Ruban, L. M., McCoach, D. B., McGuire, J. M., & Reis, S. M. (2003). The differential impact of academic self-regulatory methods on academic achievement among university students with and without learning disabilities. *Journal of Learning Disabilities, 36*(3), 270–286. https://doi.org/10.1177/002221940303600306

Sartini, E., Knight, V. F., Spriggs, A. D., & Allday, R. A. (2018). Generalization strategies to promote text comprehension skills by students with ASD in core content areas. *Focus on Autism and Other Developmental Disabilities, 33*(3), 150–159. https://doi.org/10.1177/1088357617735815

SBCTC. (2024, January 30). *Integrated Basic Education Skills and Training (I-BEST).* https://www.sbctc.edu/colleges-staff/programs-services/i-best/

Schoenbach, R., Greenleaf, C., & Murphy, L. (2012). *Reading for understanding: How reading apprenticeship improves disciplinary learning in secondary and college classrooms* (2nd ed.). Jossey-Bass.

Schoenbach, R., Greenleaf, C., & Murphy, L. (2017). *Leading for literacy.* Wiley.

Schotka, R., Bennet-Bealer, N., Sheets, R., Stedje-Larsen, L., & Van Loon, P. (2014). *Standards, outcomes, and possible assessments for ITTPC certification.* https://www.crla.net/images/ITTPC/ITTPC_Standards_Outcomes_Assessments_Level_1.pdf

Shalaby, C. [@CarlaShalaby]. (2022, August 7). *This is a time of year when educators are busy writing and revising rules and policies for the new year. Offering 8 questions here that we might use as filters for our decisions. How we "manage" a space can be a chance to practice freedom instead of modeling control.* [Tweet]. X. https://twitter.com/CarlaShalaby/status/1556306626281443328?s=20&t=rIFbNECgx5fpm0FzNIkISg

Shanahan, T., & Shanahan, C. (2008). Teaching disciplinary literacy to adolescents: Rethinking content-area literacy. *Harvard Educational Review, 78*(1), 40–59. https://doi.org/10.17763/haer.78.1.v62444321p602101

Slavin, R. E. (1995). *Cooperative learning: Theory, research, and practice* (2nd ed.). Allyn & Bacon.

Smagorinsky, P., Cook, S., and Johnson, T. S. (2003). The twisting path of concept development in learning to teach. *Teachers College Record, 105*(8), 1399–1436. https://doi.org/10.1111/1467-9620.00296

Soliday, M. (2011). *Everyday genres: Writing assignments across the disciplines.* Southern Illinois University Press.

Strano, B. (2023). Untitled poem by Beth Strano. *Facing History and Ourselves.* www.facinghistory.org/resource-library/untitled-poem-beth-strano

Sullivan, P. (2019). The world confronts us with uncertainty: Deep reading as a threshold concept. In L. Adler-Kassner & E. Wardle (Eds.), *(Re)considering what we know: Learning thresholds in writing, composition, rhetoric, and literacy.* Utah State University Press.

Sullivan, P., Tinberg, H. B., & Blau, S. D. (2017). *Deep reading: Teaching reading in the writing classroom.* National Council of Teachers of English.

Tang, K.-S., Lin, S.-W., & Kaur, B. (2022). Mapping and extending the theoretical perspectives of reading in science and mathematics education research. *International Journal of Science and Mathematics Education, 20*(Suppl 1), 1–15. https://doi.org/10.1007/s10763-022-10322-1

Tinberg, H. (2017). When writers encounter reading in a community college first-year composition course. In P. Sullivan, H. B. Tinberg, & S. D. Blau (Eds.), *Deep reading: Teaching reading in the writing classroom.* National Council of Teachers of English.

Tørrissen, Bjørn Christian. Venus of Willendorf figurine. (2020, January 13). CC-BY-SA-4.0 Retrieved from https://commons.wikimedia.org/wiki/File:Venus_of_Willendorf_-_All_sides.jpg

Townsend, L., Hofer, A. R., Hanick, S. L., & Brunetti, K. (2016). Identifying threshold concepts for information literacy: A Delphi study. *Communications in Information Literacy, 10*(1), 23–49. https://doi.org/10.15760/comminfolit.2016.10.1.13

Trainin, G., & Swanson, H. (2005). Cognition, metacognition, and achievement of college students with learning disabilities. *Learning Disability Quarterly, 28*(4), 261–272.

UCLA Social Research Methodology Evaluation Group. (2015). PCC pathways student success study. https://pasadena.edu/academics/support/pathways/docs/Pathways_Student_Success_Study_ucla.pdf

University of Louisville. College of Education & Human Development. (2022). *Modeling.* https://louisville.edu/education/abri/primarylevel/modeling

University of Missouri, Kansas City. (n.d.). *Supplemental instruction. Academic support and mentoring.* https://www.umkc.edu/asm/supplemental-instruction/index.html#

Urbanek, M. T., Moritz, B., & Moon, A. (2023). Exploring students' dominant approaches to handling epistemic uncertainty when engaging in argument from evidence. *Chemistry Education Research and Practice, 24*(4), 1142–1152. https://doi.org/10.1039/d3rp00035d

Villanueva, V. (1993). *Bootstraps: From an American academic of color.* National Council of Teachers of English.

Walton, K., Allen, J., Box, M., Murano, D., & Burrus, J. (2023). Social and emotional skills predict postsecondary enrollment and retention. *Journal of Intelligence, 11*(10), 186. https://doi.org/10.3390/jintelligence11100186

Wang, N., Wilhite, S. C., Wyatt, J., Young, T., Bloemker, G., & Wilhite, E. (2012). Impact of a college freshman social and emotional learning curriculum on student learning outcomes: An exploratory study. *Journal of University Teaching & Learning Practice, 9*(2), 120–140. https://doi.org/10.53761/1.9.2.8

Wenger, E. (2000). *Communities of practice: Learning, meaning, and identity.* Cambridge University Press.

Wexler, N. (2018, April 13). Why American students haven't gotten better at reading in 20 years. *The Atlantic.* https://www.theatlantic.com/education/archive/2018/04/-american-students-reading/557915/

Willingham, D. T. (2017) *The reading mind: A cognitive approach to understanding how the mind reads.* Jossey-Bass.

Windschitl, M. (2019). Disciplinary literacy versus doing school. *Journal of Adolescent & Adult Literacy*, *63*(1), 7–13. https://doi.org/10.1002/jaal.964

Wineburg, S. S., Martin, D., & Monte-Sano, Chauncey. (2013). *Reading like a historian: Teaching literacy in middle and high school history classrooms.* Teachers College Press.

Wolf, M. (2018). *Reader, come home: The reading brain in a digital world.* Harper, an imprint of HarperCollins Publishers.

Wood, A. K., Ross, K. G., Hardy, J., & Sinclair, C. M. (2014). Analyzing learning during peer instruction dialogues: A resource activation framework. *Physical Review Physics Education Research*, *10*(2), Article 020107. https://doi.org/10.1103/PhysRevSTPER.10.020107

Wortham, S. (2004). The interdependence of social identification and learning. *American Educational Research Journal*, *41*(3), 715–750. https://doi.org/10.3102/00028312041003715

Yager, R. E. (1991). The constructivist learning model. *The Science Teacher*, *58*(6), 52–57.

Yancey, K. B., Craig, J. W., Davis, M., and Spooner, M. (2017). Device. Display. Read: The design of reading and writing and the difference display makes. In P. Sullivan, H. Tinberg, & S. Blau (Eds.), *Deep reading: Teaching reading in the writing classroom* (pp. 33–56). National Council of Teachers of English.

Yeager, D. S., Purdie-Vaughns, V., Garcia, J., Apfel, N., Brzustoski, P., Master, A., Hessert, W. T., Williams, M. E., & Cohen, G. L. (2014). Breaking the cycle of mistrust: Wise interventions to provide critical feedback across the racial divide. *Journal of Experimental Psychology: General*, *143*(2), 804–824. https://doi.org/10.1037/a0033906

Young, J. A., & Potter, C. R. (2012). The problem of academic discourse: Assessing the role of academic literacies in reading across the K–16 continuum. In A. S. Horning (Ed.), Reading and writing across the curriculum [Special issue]. *Across the Disciplines*, *10*(4). https://wac.colostate.edu/atd/special/reading/

Zhoc, K. C. H., King, R. B., Chung, T. S. H., Chen, J., & Yang, M. (2023). Emotional intelligence promotes optimal learning, engagement, and achievement: A mixed-methods study. *Current Psychology (New Brunswick, N.J.)*, *42*(12), 10387–10402. https://doi.org/10.1007/s12144-021-02294-2

Zimmerman, C. B. (2009). *Word knowledge: A vocabulary teacher's handbook.* Oxford University Press.

Zolan, M., Strome, S., & Innes, R. (2004). Decoding genetics and molecular biology: Sharing the movies in our heads. In D. Pace (Series Ed.) & J. Middendorf (Vol. Ed.), Decoding the disciplines: Helping students learn disciplinary ways of thinking: Number 98. *New directions for teaching and learning* (1st ed., pp. 23–32). Jossey-Bass.

Zumbrunn, S., McKim, C., Buhs, E., & Hawley, L. R. (2014). Support, belonging, motivation, and engagement in the college classroom: A mixed method study. *Instructional Science*, *42*(5), 661–684. https://doi.org/10.1007/s11251-014-9310-0

Index

Page references for figures and tables are *italicized*.

Abbot, W. M., 4, 6, 138
academic discourse, 55–56, 147
ACRL. *See* Association of College and Research Libraries (ACRL) framework
Across the Disciplines (Horning, ed.), 4
active reflection, 162
Adams, B., 141
Adams, Marilyn Jager, 120
Adler-Kassner, L., 2, 9
affective domain, 42
Alexie, Sherman, 189
Allen-Handy, A., 124
American Association of School Librarians (AASL) Standards, 91
American Library Association (ALA), 90
Anderson, L. W., 85, 86
Anderson-Zavala, C., 194
antiracist reading, 5
Anzaldúa, Gloria, 57
Apigo, Mary-Jo, 187
Appeals in Modern Rhetoric (Killingsworth), 132, 133
apprenticeships: conscious, 51–57; expert-to-novice direction of, 68; facilitation, 21–23; reciprocal, 49, 140; tensions in academic, 10–11. *See also* Reading Apprenticeship (RA) framework
artificial intelligence (AI), 175–76
Association of College and Research Libraries (ACRL) framework, 9, 70, 88, 90–91, *91*
authentic learning, 119–24, 130–34

autism, 7
autonomy, 178–79

background knowledge, 98–100, 120
Bagwell, Lora, 141
Baron, N., 5
Barradell, S., 9
bias identification, 99
biochemistry classroom: problem-solving process in, 83–86
biology classroom, 157–63
Bloom, B. S., 85
Blummer, B., 70
Bootstraps (Villanueva), 133
Born a Crime (Noah), 37–41
Bourdieu, Pierre, 122
Braiding Sweetgrass (Kimmerer), 164
Bransford, J. D., 3
brave spaces, 53–54
Britt, M. A., 139
Broz, William, 100, 130
Butler, Octavia, 102

calculus classroom, 106–9
California Community Colleges' Success Network (3CSN), 18, 23, 42
California Learning Lab, 28
California State University, Long Beach, 45
California State University, Monterey Bay, 21, 58, 125, 193
California State University, Northridge, 45

Capturing the Reading Process routine, 24, 30, 68
Carillo, E. C., 6
CAST, 110
Center for Teaching, Learning, and Assessment (TLA), 21
Chaffey College, 46
Chávez, César, 133
chemistry classroom, 83–86
Chevalier, T. M., 7
Chronicle of Higher Education, 165
Citation Project, 6
classroom communities, 140
cognitive dimension of RA framework, 17, *17*; in the noncredit ESL classroom, 39–40; peer education in, 46; in Perusall, 127, 129; problem-solving strategies in, 68
cognitive psychology, 139
collaboration: courageous, 153–56; Perusall as a platform for, 126–29; reading groups as opportunities for, 183; semester-long groups, 157–63; social annotation, 101, 125–29, 141, 180–85; in the statistics classroom, 115; in the STEM classroom, 32–33
College of San Mateo, 27
college reading: digital reading, 4–5; disciplinary reading, 4; first-year snapshots, 130–34; implications for instruction, 8–9; learning differences and, 7–8; research on, 3; student struggles with, 6–7; teaching reading, 5–6
community agreements, 25, 188–89. *See also* norms
community of practice (CoP) approach, 23–24; in the STEM classroom, 27–35
community schemas, 54–55
complex instruction (CI) model, 158–63
Composition Studies, 8
conscious apprenticeship, 51–57
constructivism, 3
Cook, K., 7
CoP. *See* community of practice (CoP) approach
Covid-19 pandemic, 21, 24, 28, 125, 126, 128, 135, 164–65, 188
critical reading, 6–7
cultural circles, 164
culturally responsive teaching (CRT), 58–65, 141
Culturally Responsive Teaching and the Brain (Hammond), 50, 58, 64, 65
Curriculum Embedded Reading Assessment, 118
Curriculum for Accelerated Math (CAM), 149–50

Darder, Antonio, 57
Davies, L. J., 4, 70

Deacon, S., 7
decision trees, 162
Decoding the Disciplines Project, 1, 4, 70
deep reading, 5
Delphi method, 9
Delpit, Lisa, 55
dependent learners, 62
DiGiacomo, D. K., 141
digital reading, 4–5
Diigo, 184
directed learning activities (DLAs), 47
Disabled Students Programs and Services (DSPS), 110, 112–13
disciplinary reading, 4, 6
discourse: academic, 55–56, 147; bridges, 46; choices, 56; mismatches, 23; "rules," 55
"doing school," 8, 16, 119, 140
Donaldson, Jonan, 119, 124
double entry journals, 24, 104
Downs, D., 5
Dweck, Carol, 121, 123, 187
dyscalculia, 115
dyslexia, 7, 193

Elias, M., 147
emotional intelligence, 140
English, A. R., 120
equity and inclusion practices: conscious apprenticeship, 51–57; culturally responsive teaching (CRT), 58–65, 141; productive struggle and, 124; RA framework and, 49–50, 99, 193; in the STEM classroom, 33–34; Universal Design for Learning (UDL), 110–11, *111*
equity/excellence imperative, 140
Escalante, Aimee Beckstrom, 140, 141
ESL classroom: noncredit, 39–41; RA framework in, 102–5
evidence/interpretation notetaker routine, 24; in historical reading, 72, *72*; in the noncredit ESL classroom, 37–38; in the STEM classroom, 30
Expert Blind Spot, 68, 174–75

facilitation apprenticeships, 21–23
feel-the-text strategy: about, 142; evidence of learning, 146–47; evidence of struggle, 147; placement and sequencing, 143–44; steps, 144–46; teaching and learning outcomes, 143
Felton, P., 173
first-year college reading snapshots, 130–34
Fitchburg State University, 21
Folse, Keith, 40

Freire, Paulo, 57, 164, 165, 173

Gamberg, Julie, 101, 141
Garrison, R., 141
Garvey, Andréa Pantoja, 19, 141
Gay, Geneva, 54, 57
Gee, James, 3
Giroux, Henry, 57
Gogan, B., 8, 138
golden lines, 24, 62; in the ESL classroom, 104; in feel-the-text strategy, 143–44; in the noncredit ESL classroom, 37–38
Goldman, S. R., 4
Gonzales, Michelle, 177
Graff, Nelson, 9, 130, 139
Greenleaf, C., 7, 16
Grim, V., 70
groups, semester-long, 157–63
growth mindset, 83, 119, 123–24, 187
Growth Mindset Curriculum, 187
Gweon, G., 5

Hammond, Zaretta, 46, 50, 58, 59, 61, 62, 136, 194
Harvard University, 1
Hintz, A., 120
historical reading and thinking: about, 71; bias identification, 77–79, *78*; cognitive dimension in, 72–79; evidence/interpretation notetaker routine, 72, *72*, *78*; interpretation, 79–82, *80*, *82*; metacognitive logs, 72–79, *75*, *76*, *77*, *78*, *81*; talking to the text (TttT) routine, 72, *73*, *74*
history of reading difficulties (HRD), 7
Hogan, Nika, 87, 101
hooks, bell, 42, 57, 178
horizontal text sets, 120
Horning, A., 4
Horning, A. S., 6
Houtman, E., 70
Howard, G. R., 152
How People Learn II (National Academies of Sciences and Engineering), 1, 3
How We Read Now (Baron), 5
Hypothes.is, 101, 184

I-BEST courses, 151
idea tactic tutorial, 70
identities: insider, 189–90, 192–94, 196; outsider, 192, 194–96; practice-based, 141; reader, 136–37; social, 141
independent learners, 62

information literacy, 87–89, 90
information literacy instruction (ILI): ACRL framework, 91, *91*; collaborations and challenges, 90–91; metacognitive approaches, 92, *92*; RA framework in, 87–89; session examples, 92–95
information problem solving (IPS), 70
Inoue, A. B., 10
intelligent practice, 187–91
Intrator, Sam, 146

Jamieson, S., 6
Jeong, J. Y., 5

Kahlert, Shirley, 101
Kami, 184
Kenton, J. M., 70
Killingsworth, M. Jimmie, 133
Kimmerer, Robin Wall, 164, 172
Kindred (Butler), 102, 104, 105
Knight, V. F., 8
Knighton, Christie, 140
knowledge-building dimension of RA framework, 17–18, *17*; in the noncredit ESL classroom, 40–41; peer education in, 46–47; in Perusall, 127, 129
knowledge construction, 3
Kongshaug, Caren, 19, 140
Krathwohl, D. R., 85, 86
KWL routine, 44–45

labor-based grading, 56
Lambert, L. M., 173
Land, R., 2, 3, 9, 69, 197
large language models (LLMs), 175
Las Positas College, 177
Laziness Does Not Exist (Price), 167
Leadership Community of Practice in Reading Apprenticeship, 10
Leading for Literacy (Schoenbach et al.), 20, 28
Learning Assistance Project (LAP), 42
learning differences, 7–8
learning disabilities, 7, 101, 110, 112–13, 115
learning management systems (LMS), 184
Lee, Sue, 140
Lee, Yhashika, 50, 58–65
Leuzinger, Ryne, 70
Li, J., 101, 141
Li, M., 101, 141
Li, Wentao, 179
librarians, 87–89, 90–95
liminality, 3, 68, 98, 140

literacy: disciplinary, 139; as discourse-driven, 55; information, 87–89, 90; snapshots of first-year college reading, 130–34
Lochhead, J., 84
Lockhart, T., 6
Lombardi, A., 140
Lopez, Salina, 50, 58–65
Los Angeles Pierce College, 47
Lue, Sue, 19
Lynch, Alison, 101

making the invisible visible, 169
Manarin, K., 6, 8
Manasse, Mark, 42
Martinez, Michael, 121
math classroom: calculus, 106–9; RA framework in, 149–52; statistics, 112–18; use of Perusall in, 125–29
McLaren, Peter, 130
Megwalu, Anamika, 70
mental models, 139
Merced College, 119
metacognition: awareness of, 165–66; as central to reading process, 5; developing, 6; learning differences and, 7; as a problem-solving strategy, 120; student self-reports on, 175–76, *176*
metacognitive conversation, 1; apprenticeships through, 10–11; in classroom practice, 19; in peer education, 44–45; in Perusall, 126–27, *127*; in professional learning practice, 20; within RA framework, *17*, 18; restoring student agency through, 167–72; sharing problem-solving strategies in, 69; in the STEM classroom, 31–32; student knowledge and, 98–100; and TAPPS, 83–86
metacognitive logs, 24; in historical reading, 72–79, *75*, *76*, *77*, *78*, *81*; in the statistics classroom, 114–15; in the STEM classroom, 32
Meyer, J., 2, 9, 197
Miller, R. E., 5
Milton, John, 51–52
mindful reading, 5
Mitchell, Malcolm, 189
Moje, E. B., 139
Mount San Jacinto College, 45
Murdoch, D., 101, 119–20, 124

Naming What We Know (Adler-Kassner & Wardle), 8
Nantz, K., 4, 6, 138

National Academies of Sciences and Engineering, 1
networks of social relationships, 3
New Teacher Project, 7
Nilson, L. B., 101
Noah, Trevor, 37, 41
noncredit ESL classroom: cognitive dimension in, 39–40; knowledge-building dimension in, 40–41; personal dimension in, 38; RA framework in, 36–41; social dimension in, 39
norms, 25, 64, 141, 150; in the STEM classroom, 33. *See also* community agreements
"not reading" strategies, 100

Odom, M. L., 5, 139
online teaching and learning: cognitive presence, 141; RA framework in, 174–79; restorative pedagogy in, 165–72; social presence, 141; teaching presence, 141
Open Educational Resources (OER), 4

Pacansky-Brock, Michelle, 177
Padgett, Chris, 19, 70
Palmer, Parker, 57
Panadero, E., 101
Paradise Lost (Milton), 51–52
Parrila, R., 7
Pasadena City College, 21
Passeron, Jean-Claude, 122
Pearlman, S. J., 4, 139
peer education: in the cognitive dimension, 46; in the knowledge-building dimension, 46–47; learning spaces created by, 42–43; metacognitive conversation in, 44–45; in the personal dimension, 45–46; RA framework and, 43–44; in the social dimension, 45; training for, 43
peer-to-peer relationships, 140
Pei Songzhi, 180
Pellissippi State Community College (PSCC), 186
personal dimension of RA framework, 17, *17*, 18; developing, 186–91; in the noncredit ESL classroom, 38; peer education in, 45–46; in Perusall, 127, 129; in the statistics classroom, 113–14
personal reading history, 25, 63, 137, 189, 194; in feel-the-text strategy, 143; in the STEM classroom, 33
Perusall, 101, 125–29, *127*, *129*, 141, 184
Pierson, R., 194
Pittaway, Danny, 42

Polman, J., 141
Polya, George, 83, 85, 86
Porter, G. W., 101
Potter, C. R., 6
Powers, Miguel, 187
Price, Devon, 167, 168
problem-solving process, 8, 11, 67, 136; metacognition as, 120; modeling, 155; Polya's four-step method, 83; reading as, 138–40; in the science classroom, 83–86; in semester-long groups, 157–63; TAPPS strategy, 84–86
productive struggle: as an equity issue, 124; and growth mindset, 123–24; power of, 97–100, 101, 119–20; student feelings on text set challenges, 121–23; text sets and, 120–21
professional learning: community of practice (CoP) approach, 23–24; facilitation apprenticeships, 21–23; Reading Apprenticeship, 19–21
Project Zero, 1
Purdum, Kristen, 101

RA. *See* Reading Apprenticeship (RA) framework
reading a book by its cover activity, 41, 103
Reading Apprenticeship (RA) framework: about, 1–2, 16–18, *17*; apprenticeships within, 10–11; in the calculus classroom, 106–9; in classroom practice, 18–19; community of practice (CoP) approach, 23–24; as courageous collaboration, 153–56; in culturally responsive teaching, 58–65; as equity pedagogy, 99, 193; in the ESL classroom, 102–5; facilitation apprenticeships, 21–23; in information literacy instruction settings, 87–89, 90–95; in the math classroom, 106–9, 112–18, 125–29, 149–52; in the noncredit ESL classroom, 36–41; in online learning, 164–73, 174–79; in an online modality, 125–29; and peer education, 43–44; in Perusall, 126–29; in professional learning practice, 19–21; routines and terminology, 24–26; and Social Emotional Learning (SEL), 142, 143; in the STEM classroom, 27–35; threshold concept research within, 9–10; Universal Design for Learning (UDL) and, 110–18, *112*
Reading for Understanding (Schoenbach et al.), 16, 18, 19, 20, 26, 28, 67, 68, 120
reading in community, 135–37
reading instruction, 5–6
reading like a writer, 5
reading resilience, 162
reading response journals, 104–5

Reading Strategies List, 19, 20, 25–26; in feel-the-text strategy, 143; in the STEM classroom, 30
Ready for Rigor framework, 50
reciprocal apprenticeship, 49–50, 140
Reconsidering What We Know (Adler-Kassner & Wardle), 8
reification, 11
Relationship-Rich Education (Felton & Lambert), 173
relationships and restorative pedagogy, 165–73
RESOLV model, 139
restorative pedagogy: about, 164–65; how relationships support, 165–67; relationships central in, 172–73; student agency restored through metacognitive dialogues, 167–72
revision, self-regulated, 179
risk-taking, 102–5, 198
Ritchhart, R., 194
Rodrigue, T. K., 5
Roosevelt, Theodore, 85, 86
Rose, Mike, 132
Rose, Shelagh, 87, 100–101
Ruban, L. M., 7

safe spaces, 53–54, 103, 149–50
Saint-Martin, Monique de, 122
Sartini, E., 8
Schoenbach, R., 67, 69, 120, 121
science classroom, 83–86, 157–63
selective vulnerability, 168
self-regulation, 101, 179
semester-long groups, 157–63
Servais, Lauren, 50
Shelton, Ibrahim, 50, 58–65
Shereen, Peri, 101, 141
Slown, Corin, 70
Smagorinsky, P., 3
social annotation: applications for, 183–84; assignment prompts, 180–85; historically, 180; low-stakes "practice" sessions, 183; need for in cross-disciplinary settings, 181–82; social aspect of, 141; student perspectives on, 182–83, 184–85; using Perusall, 101, 125–29
social dimension of RA framework, 17, *17*, 18; developing, 186–91; in the noncredit ESL classroom, 39; peer education in, 45; in Perusall, 127, 129; in semester-long groups, 157–63; in the statistics classroom, 113–14
Social Emotional Learning (SEL), 140, 142, 143, 146, 147–48
social nature of reading, 135–38, 139

Soliday, M., 6, 139
Stanfield, Erin, 140
Stanford History Education Group, 70
Station, George, 58
statistics classroom, 112–18
STEM classroom: collaboration in, 32–33; equity and inclusion practices in, 33–34; incorporation of reading and texts in, 29–30; metacognitive conversation in, 31–32; professional learning for, 20–21; RA framework in, 27–35; routines supporting comprehension in, 32; semester-long groups in, 157–63; support for student efforts to comprehend texts in, 30–31. *See also* math classroom; science classroom
Stice, James E., 26
Strickland, Jonelle, 141
struggle as productive for learning, 97–100, 101, 102–5, 119–24
student agency, 167–72
student capability, 98–99
student retention, 153–56
Sullivan, P., 8
summarizing, 104
supplemental instruction leaders (SILs), 42, 43–44. *See also* peer education
Swanson, H., 8
SWBAT outcomes, 143

talking to the text (TttT) routine, 25, 60, 68, 162; in the ESL classroom, 103; in historical reading, 72, *73*, *74*; in information literacy instruction, 88, *92*
Talyn, Becky, 32
Tank, K.-S., 101
TAPPS (think-aloud paired problem solving) method, 26, 61, 70, 131; in the math classroom, 126; metacognitive conversation and, 83–86; in peer education, 46
teaching epiphanies, 146
teaching reading, 5–6; in the calculus classroom, 106–9; in information literacy instruction settings, 87–89; productive struggle, 97–100
TERC, 149
text features, 154
text sets, 120–23
think alouds, 25, 136; in the calculus classroom, 108; effectiveness of, 190–91; in information literacy instruction, 88, *92*; interactive video lesson, 177–78; in the math classroom, 126; metacognitive lesson, 178–79; in online learning, 169–70; in the STEM classroom, 30–31, 32
think-pair-share, 25
threshold concept theory: about, 2–3, 197; critiques of, 2; entrusting students with work of making sense of texts, 11–12, 97–101; methodology, 9–10; reading as transformation, 138; reading is a problem-solving process, 11, 67–70, 136; reading is social and personal, 12, 134–41
Thurgood Marshall Academic High School, 18
tracking concept development (TCD), 170–72
Trainin, G., 8
transactional model, 8
transformation, reading as, 138
transmission model, 8
Turner, Kisha Quesada, 177
tutors, 42, 43–44. *See also* peer education
TWBAT outcomes, 143
2030 Boyer Report, 140
Tyson, K., 120

Universal Design for Learning (UDL), 8, 101; action and expression recommendations, 117; engagement example, 113–14, *113–14*; framework, *111*; mastery-oriented feedback, 115–17, *116*; and RA framework, 110–11, *112*, 117–18; in the statistics classroom, 112–18
University of Colorado, 52
University of Hawai'i, 52
Urbanek, M. T., 101

Valencia, S. W., 7
vertical text sets, 120, 121
Villanueva, Victor, 133, 134
visualization, 70
vocabulary logs, 40
vulnerability, modeling, 137–38, 168
Vygotsky, Lev, 139

Wall, Erin, 30
Walls, Jeanette, 189
Wand, Jeffrey, 101, 141
Wang, N., 140
Wardle, E., 2, 9
Warren, Nanda, 19, 101
Wenger, Etienne, 11
WestEd, 18, 20, 21, 23
Whimbey, A., 84
Willingham, D. T., 120–21
Wilson, N., 141
Wineburg, S. S., 70

Wolf, M., 5
Wortham, S., 141
Writing in the Disciplines movement, 4
writing prompts, 139

Yancey, K. B., 5

Yeager, D. S., 134
Young, J. A., 6

Zhang, Fuhui, 179
Zimmerman, Cheryl Boyd, 40
Zolan, M., 70

About the Authors

EDITORS

A former high school English teacher, **Nelson Graff** taught English education from 2000 to 2015 and is now retired from teaching first-year composition and working with faculty across the disciplines in improving reading and writing instruction. He is a member of the steering committee for the CSU Expository Reading and Writing Curriculum (ERWC) and the CSU English Council. His research focuses on teaching for transfer of learning, reading and writing pedagogy, and assessment. He has a BA in English from San José State University as well as an MA in English and American literature and a PhD in Composition Studies from the University of Wisconsin, Madison.

Nika Hogan is a professor of English at Pasadena City College (PCC). She helped to develop the First Year Pathways program at PCC, which was awarded the California Community Colleges Chancellor's Office Award for a Student Success Initiative. Since an intensive period of learning and apprenticeship from 2007 to 2010, she has coordinated the college-level work on Reading Apprenticeship for WestEd. From 2011 to 2023, she supported the California Community Colleges' Success network (3CSN) to design and facilitate professional learning for educators across the 116 California community colleges. Her passion is building capacity and helping educators and students alike reach their full potential. She holds an MA and PhD in English with a focus on U.S. multiethnic literatures from the University of Massachusetts, Amherst.

Rebecca Kersnar supports faculty across disciplines as the teaching and learning specialist with the Center for Teaching, Learning, and Assessment (TLA) at California State University, Monterey Bay (CSUMB). Before joining TLA, she served for over 14 years as a science and environmental policy communications lecturer with the College of Science. Before then, she taught elementary through graduate students in San Francisco, Korea, Hungary, Thailand, and Mexico. Rebecca has a BS in biology with a concentration botany from San Francisco State University and an MA in Teaching English to Speakers of Other Languages (TESOL) and a certificate in language program administration from the Middlebury Institute of International Studies. She is also a campus Reading Apprenticeship lead, certified Koru Mindfulness teacher, and National Coalition Building Institute facilitator. At CSUMB, her work focuses primarily on reading and writing pedagogy, mindfulness and meditation, and equity.

CONTRIBUTORS

Lora Bagwell teaches the corequisite courses of reading and college success at Pellissippi State Community College (PSCC), where she also serves as assistant dean. Before returning to teaching at the community college level, Lora taught English in high school and middle school in Tennessee and Georgia. She chairs the General Education Strategy Team (GEST) at PSCC, which focuses on closing equity gaps through the implementation of reading support in general education courses. Lora also facilitates the Reading Apprenticeship professional development course RA 101 and chairs the Literacy Network for the National Organization for Student Success (NOSS).

Aimee Beckstrom Escalante started teaching while in middle school when she worked as a tutor to develop phonemic awareness and reading comprehension with students who had learning differences. Since that time, she has taught in multiple formats and institutions in Colorado, New Jersey, Florida, New Hampshire, and parts of California. In 2014, Aimee started teaching in the Liberal Studies Department at California State University in Monterey Bay. She specializes in topics related to education including Latine students, culturally diverse children's literature, technology in education, and reading and writing. In addition to drawing from her years of teaching experience, Aimee has a bachelor's degree in English literature from the University of Colorado in Boulder, completed the Live, Learn, and Teach program at the University of New Hampshire in Durham, and has a master of arts degree in writing in popular fiction from Seton Hill College. She continues her lifelong learning through professional development classes, community groups, webinars, and a Sisyphean TBR list.

Julie Gamberg teaches humanities, creative writing, and composition at Glendale College in California, with a focus on equitable, humanized pedagogy and online education. She loves collaborating with students and colleagues to continue to grow, as well as supporting fellow faculty in pedagogy and design. In 2022, she cofounded the annual Language Equity in Academia: Reimagining kNowledge (LEARN) Conference, which engages educators across disciplined in linguistic equity and justice practices. She also serves as a course facilitator, and occasional designer, for the California Virtual Campus—Online Education Initiative (CVC-OEI), which focuses on increasing student access and success in the California Community Colleges (CCCs) through excellence in online education.

Brazil-born, U.S.-naturalized, with pronouns she/her, **Andréa Pantoja Garvey** has been predominantly serving as a psychology professor at American River College since 2003—a community college located in the land of the Nisenan, Maidu, and Miwok tribal nations (settler name Sacramento, California). She earned her bachelor's degree in psychology from the Federal University of Pernambuco, located in the traditional coastal land of the Tabajara people (settler name Recife) in Brazil, with an emphasis in developmental psychology. Soon after graduating from college in 1994, she moved from South America to North America on a student visa to pursue her master's and PhD degrees in developmental psychology at the University of Utah, located in the traditional land of the Nuu-agha-tuvu-pu (Ute) people (settler name Salt Lake City). She has authored and coauthored numerous articles, book chapters, and a book as well as co-facilitating workshops on reading apprenticeship and equity-advancing practices. She is currently writing an Open Educational Resource (OER) developmental psychology textbook from a globally inclusive perspective geared toward undergraduate students, while also serving as department chair of the Psychology Department at American River College.

About the Authors

Tiffany Ingle loves inquiry into learning. In graduate school, she obtained an MA TESOL, learning specifically strategies for teaching students of other languages. In 2007, she started working in the California Community College system, where she started wondering how the learning environment that she created could best set up students for success in their future goals. At that time, her students were mostly international students and immigrants. After learning about Reading Apprenticeship, she began to apply the RA approach to her work with students, assessment, curriculum, and faculty professional learning.

Shirley Kahlert has taught in the California Community College system for many years. She holds a strong interest in pedagogies that contribute to student success: Reading Apprenticeship, Guided Pathways, the California Acceleration Project, Learning Communities, and On Course. She earned a master's degree in literature and the teaching of writing from San Francisco State University and a doctorate from UCLA in medieval literature and rhetoric. She has taught at the University of Hawaii, Manoa, several Bay Area colleges, including Evergreen Valley College; the University of California, Merced; and Merced College. Dr. Kahlert has been a college and university writing and literature professor since 1972. Her scholarly interests include Chaucer, Marie de France, and Celtic languages and literature.

Dr. Crystal Kiekel has been a full-time faculty member at Los Angeles Pierce College since 2011. There, she teaches tutor training courses and directs the Center for Academic Success, which provides course-embedded tutoring, general tutoring, workshops, and internships. Also, since 2011 she has been a coordinator for the California Community Colleges' Success Network (3CSN), an organization that facilitates professional learning opportunities by and for California Community College practitioners. There, she specializes in empowering the work and expertise of peer educators and learning assistance professionals. Crystal earned a Master's of Social Welfare (MSW) from UCLA with an emphasis on management and planning of nonprofit organizations, and a doctorate of education (EdD) at Cal State Northridge with an emphasis on community college leadership and policy development. You may contact her at kiekel@laccd.edu.

Christie Knighton has been teaching reading, basic skills, education, and I-BEST at Highline College in Washington since 1995. Her Master of Arts in Education (MAE) is in curriculum and instruction, developmental reading, and her PhD is in adult and higher education. The focus of her research is exploring how institutional systems support or hinder basic skills in students transitioning to postsecondary coursework, with a specific focus on surfacing how institutional racism impacts students. She currently teaches in I-BEST (Integrated Basic Education and Skills Training) cohorts for preservice teachers and supports students to and through college-level math and lab science. Ms. Knighton has been involved with Reading Apprenticeship since 2011 and has been leading her college in professional development opportunities with Reading Apprenticeship and I-BEST.

Caren Kongshaug, college readiness instructor, has been teaching reading, writing, math, and college success at Bellingham Technical College, in Bellingham, Washington, since 2002. She holds an MEd in adult and higher education from Western Washington University and a BA in history of ideas and a BA in literature from the University of Redlands, Redlands, California. She trains faculty in Reading Apprenticeship at BTC and is a consultant and facilitator for WestEd in California. Additionally, she develops curriculum for Washington State Board for Community and Technical Colleges for Integrated English and Civics Education. Caren is an experienced faculty mentor, and currently serves on BTC's accreditation committee, among others. Caren has earned both the Puget Sound Energy Award for Outstanding Faculty 2013 and the Recognition of Positive Contribution Award in 2017. Outside of the classroom, Caren is an artist; her paintings are shown locally in Bellingham.

Sue Lee teaches academic writing to adult basic education students and first-year university students at Kwantlen Polytechnic University in Canada. She enjoys applying inquiry-based learning methods, the Instructional Skills Workshop (ISW) model, and social emotional learning (SEL) strategies in her classrooms to help her students meet the learning objectives. Sue's interest in literature is creative nonfiction, especially the genre of the essay. She has a BA in English from Simon Fraser University and an MA in English literature from the University of Chicago. She is a certified CELTA instructor and an Instructional Skills Workshop facilitator.

Yhashika Lee is the codirector of the Helen Rucker Center for Black Excellence, an instructor, and a faculty associate in teaching and learning assessment at CSUMB. She has a BA from UC Berkeley and JD from UCLA Law with a concentration in critical race theory. Yhashika uses her background in critical race theory in her teaching and to reimagine solutions to the structural inequality that shapes our education system and continues to create barriers for students of color. Yhashika is also passionate about helping faculty create culturally inclusive classrooms through her work as part of CRE@TLA, a collective that focuses on culturally responsive teaching.

Ryne Leuzinger is the first year seminar director at CSU, Monterey Bay. At CSUMB, Ryne has also served as a research and instruction librarian and in this role has sought to bring best practices in reading instruction into the information literacy instruction that he provides for students in a range of departments. Additionally, he has served as a lecturer in sociology and global studies, teaching courses focused on social movements. Outside of his work at the university, Ryne has served as an elected member of the Executive Committee for the Instruction Section of the Association of College and Research Libraries and currently serves as president of the board of directors for the Community Association of Big Sur. He holds a BA in political science from the University of Wisconsin, Madison and an MLIS from the University of Illinois at Urbana–Champaign.

Salina Lopez is a seasoned academic leader and instructor with over a decade of experience in university-level teaching and educational administration. Holding a master's degree in general psychology and a doctorate in educational leadership, she fosters inclusive learning environments. She advances diversity, equity, and inclusion in all aspects of her work. Salina collaborates effectively with colleagues to optimize academic operations and student success strategies as a lecturer and faculty associate at CSU, Monterey Bay and its Center for Teaching, Learning, and Assessment. Known for her approachable demeanor and steadfast commitment to excellence, she is dedicated to nurturing individual student achievement while driving positive institutional change for students, faculty, and staff.

Alison Lynch is an associate professor of mathematics at California State University, Monterey Bay. She teaches across the mathematics curriculum, drawing on evidence-based pedagogies to support students in problem solving, collaborating, and communicating mathematical ideas. She is the course coordinator for Calculus I at CSUMB, and she serves on the leadership team for the high school course, Transition to College-Level Mathematics. She has a BS in mathematics from the University of Delaware and a PhD in mathematics from the University of Wisconsin, Madison.

Theresa Martin, a biology professor at College of San Mateo, has worked for over a decade to enhance education and support faculty development in scientific literacy. From 2012 to 2017, Theresa spearheaded CSM's Reading Apprenticeship initiatives, providing professional development for educators. Since 2013, she has provided leadership for Reading Apprenticeship professional development at WestEd and the California Community Colleges' Success Network (3CSN), leveraging her expertise to empower educators. Theresa holds a BA in physiology and cell biology from the University of California, Santa Barbara; an MS in exercise science from the University of California, Davis; and an MA in endocrinology from the University of California, Berkeley.

Anamika Megwalu is the Interim Associate Dean for Student and Faculty Engagement at San Jose State University's Dr. Martin Luther King Jr. Library. Previously, she served as the faculty director of Library Instruction and Assessment. She has a BA in mathematical science, a BS in computing and information science, an MS in information studies, and a PhD in information science. Megwalu has been a librarian for 18 years, conducting information literacy sessions for graduate and undergraduate students with diverse social, cultural, economic, and educational backgrounds. She also teaches graduate technical writing courses designed for students to develop advanced communication and documentation skills. She believes in creating a learning environment where students, regardless of their background, are equipped with transferable skills that will help them explore new and challenging information.

Chris Padgett is history professor at American River College in Sacramento, where he teaches courses in world and U.S. history. He has a BA in history from the University of the Pacific, and MA and PhD degrees in history from the University of California, Davis. His career-long interest has been working with colleagues and K–12 teachers to promote effective history education, and he served for several years as district and college lead for Reading Apprenticeship.

Kristen Purdum has been teaching mathematics full-time at Mission College since 2017. As a former high school math and physics teacher in Ohio, she worked closely with the school's special education teachers to teach students with 504 plans and Individualized Education Programs (IEPs). After moving to California, she was an adjunct math instructor for the Santa Clara University School of Engineering and for West Valley College. At Mission College, Kristen taught the MAPS (Math Achievement Pathway to Success) algebra program for Disabled Student Programs and Services (DSPS) students, and she is currently teaching elementary statistics (styled after the MAPS program) and liberal arts math. Kristen has a BS in mathematics from Mount Union College and an MS in applied mathematics from Santa Clara University.

Shelagh Rose is professor in the English and language studies department at Pasadena City College, California, where she has taught all levels of ESL and English over the last three decades. Starting in 2011, Shelagh collaborated with a group of interdisciplinary faculty to create a comprehensive first-year experience. This collaboration included developing a rigorous transfer-level first-year seminar that integrates college success behaviors, critical reading and information literacy, and a One Book, One College program dedicated to engaging students, faculty, and staff in a sustained text-based intellectual discussion. Shelagh is also active in professional development on her campus, having served as the new faculty and adjunct faculty Coordinator. In addition to teaching, she currently serves in a role helping to bridge instruction and student services.

Higher education transformed **Lauren Servais**'s life, and in her more than 20 years as an educator, Lauren has endeavored to pay the transformation forward. Her educational praxis centers equity, inquiry, community, culture, and aloha. As Dean of Arts and Humanities at the College of Marin, Lauren's newest inquiry is exploring what it means to be a culturally responsive dean. Lauren began her teaching career at Cascadia Community College, where she participated in accreditation, the scholarship of teaching and learning, college-wide learning outcome teams, and multiple learning communities. After moving to California, Lauren served in various roles at Santa Rosa Junior College, including English department chair; chair of department chairs; Basic Skills Initiative coordinator; equity coordinator; Puente co-coordinator; new faculty professional learning co-coordinator; Seeking Educational Equity and Diversity co-facilitator; Asian and Pacific Islander American Student Success co-coordinator; and Justice, Equity, Diversity, and Inclusion focused inquiry group co-facilitator. Lauren was born on Oahu, Hawaii, speaks Hawaiian Creole, enjoys talking story, is a working mom and wife, and weaves the fullness of her intersectional identity into her work as an educator.

Ibrahim Shelton is a lecturer of service learning (Social Justice/Civics) and liberal studies (teaching future educators) at California State University, Monterey Bay (CSUMB). In addition, Professor Shelton assists his colleagues in improving their art of teaching by implementing anti-racist, decolonial, culturally responsive educational practices in their art of teaching via his work as a member of CSUMB's CRE@TLA Educator Professional Development Squad. He describes himself as an educator, father, scholar, and lifelong learner, who is dedicated to the art of teaching. He realizes his time is short, and desires peace, critical learning, and social activism for justice and freedom for humans around the world. He sends greetings of peace to all, and a heartfelt Salaam Alaikum to those dedicated to the Oneness of Allah.

Peri Shereen is an associate professor of mathematics at CSU, Monterey Bay (CSUMB). She received her PhD in mathematics from UC Riverside. While at CSUMB, she has been engaged in actively developing her pedagogical approach to best meet the learning needs of her students. Her pedagogical practice has evolved to include Reading Apprenticeship, including leading Reading Apprenticeship workshops. Before joining CSUMB, Peri had taught across different institutions including Cal State Long Beach, UC Riverside, and Carleton College (in California and Minnesota). At CSUMB, she teaches a range of courses from calculus to upper-division courses for mathematics majors. She also practices her research in the areas of pure mathematics and math education.

A perpetual student, **Corin Slown** previously worked in industry as a chemist, taught high school science, and now teaches chemistry and biology at California State University, Monterey Bay (CSUMB). She works with faculty across the disciplines on Course Based Undergraduate Research Experiences (CUREs). She is the faculty associate for assessment in the College of Science. Her research focuses on preparation of future STEM teachers, active learning pedagogy and high-impact practices, and assessment. She has a BS in chemistry from Yale University and a PhD in organic synthesis from the Scripps Research Institute.

About the Authors

Erin Stanfield is a lecturer in the Department of Biology and Chemistry and Applied Environmental Science and vice coordinator for the supplemental instruction (SI) program for STEM with the Cooperative Learning Center (CLC) at California State University, Monterey Bay (CSUMB). She has been developing and implementing curriculum to increase equity in undergraduate STEM education since 2014. Recent projects include the creation of preparatory videos for introductory chemistry labs, a course-based undergraduate research experience (CURE) in field biology, and designing Reading Apprenticeship–centered classroom activities in large lower-division STEM classes. She also collaborates with interdisciplinary colleagues to design pedagogy and equity-driven training for peer-led learning at the CLC.

A former reading coach for AmeriCorps, **Jonelle Strickland** has taught as a paraprofessional, substitute, and academic director. Since 2018, Jonelle has served as interdisciplinary adjunct faculty at three Hispanic Serving Institutions in Southern California; she also teaches at an early college academy and remains committed to providing access to joyful reading and writing experiences for all of her students, including those impacted by the juvenile justice system. Jonelle has earned degrees from Occidental College and Chapman University and is a graduate of @One's Culturally Responsive and Equity Minded Teaching.

Jeffrey Wand has taught mathematics for over 13 years including at University of California, Riverside (as a graduate student) followed by Gonzaga University in Washington state (as a lecturer). He currently is an associate professor at California State University, Monterey Bay (CSUMB). While at CSUMB, he has taught a wide range of mathematics courses from lower-division precalculus to upper-division courses like Foundations of Modern Mathematics and Complex Analysis. His research spans three different areas: pure mathematics, statistics, and mathematics education. In this latter area, he has spent the last few years integrating more research-based pedagogies, such as Reading Apprenticeship, in his courses.

Nanda Warren teaches college writing at CSU, Monterey Bay and supports peer undergraduate and graduate student writing tutors in the campus learning center. Her professional background includes work in adult basic education, international teaching, and English language instruction for immigrants and refugees. She has a BA in English from the University of Minnesota and an MA in international educational development from Teachers College, Columbia University. She has lived and taught in various parts of the United States, as well as Costa Rica, Canada, and Spain.

www.ingramcontent.com/pod-product-compliance
Lightning Source LLC
Chambersburg PA
CBHW080537300426
44111CB00017B/2773